BEST
SELF

BEST SELF

BE YOU, ONLY
BETTER

MIKE BAYER

DEY ST.
An Imprint of WILLIAM MORROW

DEY ST.

A hardcover edition of this book was published in 2019 by Dey Street, an imprint of William Morrow.

FIRST DEY STREET PAPERBACK EDITION PUBLISHED 2021.

Library of Congress Cataloging-in-Publication Data has been applied for.

ISBN 978-0-06-291174-2

24 25 26 27 28 LBC 12 11 10 9 8

I dedicate this book to my mom, Aina Bayer, who taught me that no matter what kind of day you're having, you always show up for people in need, and to my dad, Ronald Bayer, who taught me that integrity is more important than opportunity, and to always do the right thing. I also dedicate it to those of you who are searching for your own best self. May your journey be exciting and rewarding.

Contents

Foreword

by Dr. Phil McGraw

Let's do some quick math: If you are twenty-five years old, you have lived 9,125 days. If you're forty, you've lived 14,600 days, and if you're fifty, you've lived 18,250 days. Out of those thousands of days, I'll bet only a handful *really* stand out. Positive or negative, there are only a few "red-letter days" that you'd define as life-changing.

Similarly, I'll also bet that out of the hundreds or even thousands of people you have encountered, only a handful have had an unforgettable impact on who you have become. Only a very few have written on the slate of who you are in an indelible way.

By acquiring, *and reading, Best Self: Be You, Only Better,* by Life Coach Mike Bayer, you are adding to your "core team" one of those people you will *not* forget.

Anyone with a business card and briefcase can call him—or herself a "life coach." But very few have accumulated the credentials, the experience, and the wisdom that can only come from helping complex people navigate the complex terrain of a fast-paced, demanding life in this current, ever-changing world.

Coach Mike is a true professional, and *Best Self* is his bible, his "how-to" manual on maximizing your potential by discovering the best person you can be in the most effective way you can. Mike Bayer is not a buzzword dispenser. He is a commonsense, action-oriented coach who will tell you how to get from where you are to where you want to be in every area of your life, whether it be personal, family, professional, spiritual, or all of the above. He is not a jack-of-all-trades; he just recognizes that the common denominator to all areas of your life is—*you*. Everything begins and ends with *you* being your *best self*.

Coach Mike is a legitimate change agent in peoples' lives. He is the real thing: smart, insightful, sincere, honest, straightforward, and committed. As I've come to know and work with him in helping me help people change their lives for the better, I have seen these traits in action. I am proud to call him a friend, proud to have him on the *Dr. Phil* team and proud to have him on our advisory board.

In *Best Self*, Mike Bayer has his say. It is the kind of book that leaves you significantly better than it found you. Within these pages, Mike will be *your* life coach, and along the journey he will be your leader through a series of thoughtful and provocative questions unlike any you've ever been asked before.

Mike meets people exactly where they are, with zero judgment, and gently and compassionately guides them toward their authenticity. Through the course of reading this book, you will feel that same care, and the thrill of meaningful breakthroughs as you examine every aspect of your life on your path to your best self.

As I often say, you cannot change what you don't acknowledge. Now is your time to start being truly honest. You might think that real change is an impossibility for you, that you've damaged your relationships beyond repair, wrecked your life, moved too far from your dreams. I'm here to tell you that none of that is true, if you're willing to do the work, and admit that there is work to do. But you must have the tools you need—a belief you can change, a desire to do so, and Mike Bayer's *Best Self*. The past is over; the future hasn't happened yet. The time is now. The book is *Best Self*.

Introduction

The airplane was on its final descent, and for the past half hour, I had really been feeling the effects of the flight. There's no direct way to get from Los Angeles to Erbil, Kurdistan—it's not exactly a common route—so I'd been traveling for a full day. But underneath the physical discomfort was an excitement that was propelling me forward every bit as much as the plane was.

Most everyone in my life thought I was crazy for making this trip and they weren't shy about telling me. But what did *they* know? They didn't understand the magnetic pull I felt to come here. I needed to help. These broken and lost people had endured so much. The closer the plane floated toward solid earth, the surer I felt of the reasons I had willingly plucked myself out of what was, by all accounts, my perfect American dream existence, and placed myself into what some would consider the heart of darkness.

Darkness; it is an interesting state. To be totally devoid of all light. Sometimes we must walk into the darkness in order to understand what light really is. I wasn't new to darkness. I had come face-to-face with it for the first time sixteen years prior, when I had glanced up at my gaunt, sickly reflection in the bathroom mirror after a weeklong bender and found that my inner light had been fully eclipsed by the darkness of my methamphetamine addiction. As any recovering meth addict will tell you, meth, more so than any other drug, steals your soul and robs you of your common sense. You're totally sleep deprived, not eating, drinking very little water, so your gas tank is on empty but you're running around thinking you're the smartest person in the room. At the time, I was twenty years old and I simply couldn't understand how I had gone from being a walk-on for the basketball team at Fordham University to a zombie who was completely out of touch with reality and existing in a state of pure paranoia. It actually got to the point that I was convinced I was possessed by the devil. It was bad; I was completely out of control. It would still be a while after I caught that terrifying reflection of myself before I would get sober, but everything else that has happened in my life has been a direct result of my own, personal journey out of the darkness of addiction.

Shaking the memory from my mind, I lurched forward as the airplane's brakes did their duty to slow the plane's velocity along the tarmac, the seat belt keeping me firmly in my now gently bouncing seat. *Back to reality,* I thought as I brought my mental focus back to the here and now. An alternate universe was a more apt description, I realized, as I exited the plane and was quickly ushered down the steps by a group of men wearing black suits— all packing heat—and escorted to a nondescript SUV with bulletproof windows. In a matter of seconds, we were flying down the airport road. It might have looked like something out of a movie, but it's a little more unnerving in person than on the big screen. We arrived at a nearby building where I went through customs. At my first opportunity, I asked for the restroom, and they pointed to a door. I headed over.

As I turned the doorknob, my mind wasn't on the facilities inside. Not at all. There was something far more urgent I needed to take care of first. I've lost count of how many times I'd engaged in this exact ritual (probably in the neighborhood of two thousand), but I'll never forget the first time. It'd been twelve years ago now—hard to imagine. If only I'd known then that it would become such a mainstay in my life, I would have thought twice about starting it in a bathroom, but really, it's the most logical place. Wherever you go in life—houses, grocery stores, airports, music venues, movie sets—there's most likely going to be a bathroom and it's most likely going to afford you at least a little privacy. (But not enough, apparently, because I've certainly had a few people look at me like I was crazy over the years and I still get a little embarrassed.)

This restroom was standard—there were several stalls, a bank of sinks, and a full-length mirror near the door. Perfect. I set down my bags, pulled two towels from the dispenser, gently wiped the floor, got down on my knees in front of a sink, and closed my eyes for a moment. This is the first part of my ritual I do before each new endeavor, and it's symbolic of humility. I was there in Kurdistan to serve others, not to celebrate myself. I approach all of my work that way. Getting down on our knees has, for centuries, been a physical reminder of connecting with our spiritual selves, with God, or whatever higher being in which we believe. I've found that to be true for me. It is a compelling way to silence my ego, dissolve any fears, and detach myself from the outcome, because as long as I'm acting within my own authenticity, the outcome does not matter.

I then stood back to my feet and looked at myself in the mirror—this is the second part of my routine. Being six feet, six inches tall and the only American around, I was pretty tough to miss, but if anyone who walked into the bathroom took notice of my odd behavior, it was unbeknownst to me. I was deep in it. There had been a time when this whole thing would have felt ridiculous to me. That was no longer the case, though, as it had become positively essential.

I continued to stare deeply into my own eyes in the mirror. Though it was tough to ignore the black bags under my eyes after the long flight, or the lines and creases that had formed along the edges, slowly the aesthetics became invisible to me. The point of this exercise is to look past all of the exterior distractions and straight into my soul. I was checking in with myself, making sure I was fully connected and acting out of authenticity before taking one more step on this journey.

It's a simple ritual—staring at one's self in the mirror as a mental check-in—but it's profound. That's one thing I've learned along the way; the simple acts can be the most powerful ones in our lives. I knew that as long as I took the time to enter into this meditative state, to center myself, and ensure I'm making decisions that are rooted in my spiritual truth, that I will be able to show up as the best version of myself and have complete focus on my client. In other words, it helps me approach each situation selflessly.

So, I stood there in that Kurdish public restroom, inches from the mirror, gazing into my own eyes when, just as it'd happened many times before, I could see a mental image of some of the people I'd worked with in the past, like a tapestry of faces unfolding before me. You see, as much as this ritual is about looking into my own soul, memories of other people come to mind because they help me connect with my own authenticity, my purpose, and my passion. These are people with whom I've been in the trenches, and I am deeply grateful for those experiences.

The image that came to the forefront of my mind's eye that day was that of Wyatt, a rotund, wealthy CEO, his cheeks flushed with rage, his eyes swollen and bloodshot. This was probably the fiftieth intervention I'd done in my career, and it was many years ago, but I'm still haunted by this particular case. Sarah, Wyatt's desperate wife, terrified of the husband she barely knew anymore, had asked me to come to their home and put an end to the violence. This once loving father had choked her out as their four children had watched in horror. His business was failing as employees grew weary of cowering in the corner while he seethed and spat in vicious tirades. His anger had become a runaway train, and no one knew how far off the rails he might go. But even in that first call with Sarah, I knew I was the right fit for this situation.

In preparation for the intervention, I had to go shopping. Sarah had warned me that I'd never have a shot if I didn't wear a suit and tie. An odd request, but I'd followed her instructions nonetheless, in the hopes it would earn me at least a little respect with this egotistical character. So, there I was, dressed to the nines in a borrowed suit (I couldn't afford one of my own back then), standing in the gilded foyer of the colonial mansion, waiting.

Then, suddenly, I could hear his loud footsteps coming down the hallway. The tension in the room immediately heightened and grew with each echoing footfall ringing through the house.

He appeared in the foyer and immediately furrowed his brow when he saw me but remained silent. Wyatt then began to slowly circle me like a hungry lion, watching me through squinted eyes. Finally, he asked through gritted teeth, "Who are you and why are you trespassing in my home?"

"I'm Mike, and your wife invited me, so I'm not trespassing. Nice to meet you, by the way."

"My wife, huh? Well, she isn't going to stop me from kicking your ass out that door," Wyatt spat back at me.

"If I go, she goes," I replied calmly. Sarah nodded in agreement, empowered by my presence—I was essentially acting as her protector.

Wyatt took two quick strides over to me, and in a flash, we were literally nose-to-nose. "Just who the hell do you think you are? Get out NOW!" he bellowed. I gave him a smirk and rather than continuing in this staredown, I sauntered over to the fancy sofa, kicked off my fresh-from-the-box, shiny, black leather shoes I'd bought just for this day, propped my feet up on the ottoman, and spread my arms wide on the pillows. I responded in that way because I'd learned that if something is not working, you don't force it, and with a guy like this, you have to be uncontrollable and just ridiculous enough to knock him off balance. Sort of meeting the madness where it is.

"Do you have any tea?" I was really trying to annoy him, and it worked. Wyatt looked at me like I had two heads.

Sarah, ever the hostess, replied, "Sure. We have black tea."

"Any herbal teas? Peppermint?" I could see Wyatt was starting to lose it. This was perfect. I wanted to provoke him because under that pissed-off façade is where the pain lives. The quicker we could get to the pain, the quicker we could make some progress.

"No, sorry, we only have black tea," she said.

"Really? Wow. You'd think, with a mansion like this, you'd have every kind of tea imaginable. All right, black tea is fine. Oh, and honey please." She turned toward the kitchen.

Boom. Wyatt went nuclear.

"Are you seriously going to allow this man, this *stranger*, to get involved in our private affairs?" Wyatt had rounded on his wife, but she stood her ground, unwavering.

"You're damned right I am. And you're going to sit down and listen to what he's got to say, or I'm taking the kids, walking out that door and that'll be the last you see of us." Surprising even herself, she caught my eye, and I winked. Just like when we'd practiced earlier, she'd nailed it. The words seemed to just flow out of her.

It had only been twenty-four hours since our initial meeting, and it was in that sit-down that she'd made some key realizations. She realized that her kids had seen their dad passed out on the floor too often. She realized that they were learning that women deserved to be demeaned and abused. She realized that she had allowed this vampire to suck the life out of her. She realized she and her kids deserved better. And most of all, she realized she no longer wanted to be a part of the problem.

Wyatt was reeling. He couldn't wrap his head around how he'd lost his manipulative power over his usually subservient wife. Red-faced, he stomped to the kitchen. The house fell silent as we awaited his next move. He returned with a highball in hand.

"Scotch. Is that your favorite?" I asked.

"Takes the edge off." Wyatt took a drink, sat down, loosened his tie. "Nice shoes," he quipped, with more than a hint of sarcasm in his tone.

"Thanks! I appreciate the compliment from someone who probably has a room devoted to his shoes," I said, but thinking to myself how I'd only bought this pair the day before, since I'd never needed a pair of decent shoes for an intervention before.

Looking around the room, I saw an elevator in the distance. "Nice elevator. Who has an elevator in their house?" I asked. Humor serves to break the ice, but it's also a risky move. Wyatt gave me a side eye.

"*I* do. And it's a pain in the ass. Been stuck in that damn thing one too many times."

The conversation went on and seemed to be productive for a while, but one scotch quickly turned into five and Wyatt's ego took the controls when I moved the discussion toward the game plan, which started with him going to rehab. He became belligerent, as I expected, and so Sarah took the kids and went to a hotel. She'd threatened to leave dozens of times before, but that night she'd followed through, having already packed her suitcases in case this very thing happened.

It wasn't so much the sight of his family walking out as just how easy it'd been for them to go that rattled Wyatt. Like any narcissist, he thrived on people being afraid of him. But they weren't afraid anymore. And that *terrified* him.

"I have some business deals I need to see through. I can't just up and disappear."

"I've got a place in mind where you can have access to phone and email. You'd be able to keep the business going."

Long pause.

"Okay. But not tonight. In the morning."

"Pick you up at eight."

Sure enough, the next morning, we'd sat shoulder to shoulder in the backseat of a car, on the way to a brand-new chapter in Wyatt's life.

I blinked the memory away, refocusing on the present moment, and said my mantra out loud: "You got this." This mantra has evolved over the years—it started as "believe in yourself," then it was "you're lovable," "be yourself," then "you're enough," "speak your truth," "you're exactly where you need to be," "I love you," and now it's "you got this." The ritual always stays the same, but the mantra changes. I started this whole ritual when, in my early twenties, I'd felt helplessly in over my head at my very first intervention. Everything had gone wrong that day—my printer was out of ink, and I hadn't memorized the speech the company I was then working for required I give to the family. It was one thing after another, and by the time it was over, the family called and asked for their money back, citing my inexperience. But I felt good regardless because I was connected with my best self.

That time, and every time since, my ritual has given me just what I needed—the feeling like I've already won, regardless of the outcome, because I was doing my work out of a true and deep desire to help others. I couldn't control or predict *their* actions, but I could be sure that *I* was always acting from that genuine place within myself, and that I am enough.

I took a deep breath, grabbed my belongings off the bathroom floor, met my security team outside the door, and we continued onward; we had a lot of ground to cover yet. Getting from point A to point B in Kurdistan wasn't exactly as straightforward as my usual commute back in Hollywood, even with the reality that is LA traffic. That said, I felt at home here. There's really no place that's more welcoming than Kurdistan—they accept and embrace all religions and all people. That is why so many people have sought refuge in this region. I'd spoken with my Kurdish guide a handful of times on the phone before arriving, so I had a sense of where I'd be going and who I'd be meeting, but still, it's difficult to prepare oneself for entering into a refugee camp on the other side of the world. What I knew for sure was that I needed a break from my usual clientele, at least for a little while, and to put my abilities to use in a new way.

I have always achieved balance in my life by seeking out the polar opposite of my current reality. The dichotomy keeps me grounded and grateful. For the most part, my recent clients had been celebrities who had every imaginable resource available to them, whereas the people here had seen their homes destroyed by missiles, had watched their families be murdered, and were stripped of everything except what they could carry on their backs. But this trip wasn't merely the result of picking a place in the world where people needed help and going there to act as some kind of savior. In fact, I knew it was highly unlikely I'd really be able to accomplish much of anything for these people over just the next week.

I'd visited this part of the world before; eight years prior, I'd felt drawn to Afghanistan because I just had a feeling that the way that region was being characterized in the American media—as overrun with terrorists, where everyone is a radical—couldn't be accurate. I just had to see for myself. Furthermore, that was the opium capital of the world, and I wanted to see firsthand what that looked like. I'm an experiential learner, and when I want to be educated on something, I need to be immersed in it. On that

Afghanistan trip, I visited rehabs and detox centers, and in some of them, barbaric methods were being used to get people off heroin. They'd just chain people down and leave them to shake, cry, and writhe in pain as their body detoxified of the harsh drugs to which they were severely addicted. It was harrowing. They desperately needed modern and medically sound detoxification and rehabilitation services. (I haven't been to that particular region again in a few years, so it could be that they now offer better treatment modalities, but at the time, that's what was going on in some facilities because they just didn't have the resources they needed.) What I gained from that trip and every other that has followed is a deeper understanding of the people's needs there, and that helping them is part of a larger purpose for my life.

When I sat down with government officials to gain a better understanding of the dire situation, I learned that Kurdistan, since the beginning of the war against ISIS, had been the most welcoming territory for refugees including the Yazidi Kurds, Christians, and Syrians. These folks left their homes after many of their families had been killed by terrorists. There were thousands of orphans. These were scenes we saw on the evening news, or on the front pages of newspapers, but it was finally time to witness for myself what exactly the refugee crisis looked like in real life.

As we pulled up to the dusty camp made up of rows and rows of rudimentary tents with tattered clothing hanging from lines between them, I was immediately struck by the number of children racing around, laughing and squealing with delight. They kicked a faded soccer ball that was splitting at the seams, and it was through that image that I was able to understand—against all odds, there was hope here. There was light.

When the car came to a stop near the camp, I got out and began walking around, and the children, with their dusty hair and threadbare clothes, immediately flocked to me. I knew many of them were orphans, and though their reality appeared bleak,

I could see just a clear sense of happiness. That innocent wonder in their eyes had not been lost. Those with the least in terms of worldly possessions seemed to possess the most hope. I'd come here to help them, and already, just hours into my journey, I knew I was on the receiving end of this gift. My heart was filled and brimming over.

I share this story with you because it was the physical manifestation of a mental and emotional connection with my authentic self. Years prior, if you'd told me I'd be going to Kurdistan, I wouldn't have any more believed you than if you'd said I'd be colonizing the moon. But that's the kind of incredible and unexpected thing that happens when you're living a life that is congruent with who you really are.

Sometimes following your authenticity means taking a leap of faith and not fully understanding where it's going to take you. When I got on that plane, I was not at all sure of my goal. I knew I wanted to help a vast community of people who had been victimized by war, though the steps toward achieving that were hazy at best. But once I was standing there in that camp, surrounded by orphaned children, I wanted to do whatever I could to create and contribute to programs that would prevent those kids from being brainwashed into becoming the next generation of terrorists. They were so vulnerable, so defenseless, like tiny minnows surrounded by bloodthirsty sharks. If I could just give them access to counseling and help them build up their self-worth, they might be less likely to fall prey to the terrorist groups. The pieces of the puzzle became clearer to me on that trip, and it's a continuing journey fueled by my desire to help change the course of their lives.

What does all this mean for you? I want you to realize that *the journey is the destination*. We, all of us, are constantly evolving and transforming, and we have no idea what, who, or where we'll be at the end of our transformation. And along the way, should you uncover any darkness—which I define as an area where you are living out of sync with your best self—then our job is to shine the light and get you realigned.

Part of the reason I know I can help you accomplish this is that I've done it in my own life. As I shared with you earlier, there was a time that I was living *anything* but an authentic life, as I was in the grip of a bad drug addiction. Though I'd sincerely tried to get clean many times before with outpatient programs, I hadn't understood why I kept relapsing on drugs. I would buy crystal meth, do a line, then flush the rest down the toilet and swear to myself that was the last time—it was over and done. Then, just three days later, I'd be buying another bag of drugs. I had zero understanding of chemical dependencies and could not wrap my mind around why I kept returning to the drugs. I painted my apartment red, convinced I was possessed by the devil. I believed there was a camera embedded in the peephole of my door, watching me at all times. I thought that if I just stopped using meth, that meant I was sober. My life was in shambles, and I was utterly powerless. This happened again and again, until finally I knew without a doubt that I had to check myself into rehab. That's what I did, and I followed every recommendation down to the letter that time, because I wanted to give myself the best possible shot at recovery. In recovery, I finally got a road map for doing that. It was grueling, and it took months, but I did crawl out of that darkness of addiction.

As a sober man, I was finally able to connect with my authenticity. And boy, did things ever turn around after that! Despite having never done well in school before, I suddenly discovered a passion for learning everything I could about drug and alcohol rehabilitation. And out of that newfound passion, I found the confidence to build a thriving business on my own and help lots of people along the way.

I've spent about half of my career in the trenches with people who are at their lowest points, helping them dig their way out. For the other half of my career, I've helped people who weren't necessarily at low points but who knew they could be happier in life and just didn't know where to start. Many of those clients came to me in unexpected ways, and I believe opportunities have arisen in my life because I stay open to them. I like that balance of working with people who are facing different types of problems; I seek balance in all areas of my life. It gives me a broad perspective, and it also means that no matter where you're starting from, I can meet you there and help take you to where you want to go because I believe there are some universal laws of living that apply to all of us.

I'm willing to bet most of the people I've worked with were *way* worse off than you are right now. I started out as an alcohol and drug abuse counselor, and I worked at some of the most prestigious rehabilitation facilities in the country. I then shifted and became an interventionist. That means people would call me when someone in their life was completely unwilling to change. These interventions were often very volatile situations. No one expects to come home to see their family, friends, and some stranger sitting in the living room, poised and ready to intervene on them. It's usually very tense and can be quite dramatic, but in the end, I've been able to help people change who had no interest in changing. If you're reading this book, you have a desire to change, so you have taken a big first step. Change is well within your grasp.

When I opened the CAST Centers in 2006, it was out of a desire to create a humanistic strategy for tackling any struggle in your life. From the get-go, when we were just operating out of my tiny apartment in Venice Beach, California, we offered various evidence-based approaches to help people improve their lives. It's so much more than just a simple diagnosis. The real problem is that people are living lives that are incongruent with their authentic selves either because they're following in their family's footsteps instead of carving their own path, or they're doing what worked for them ten years ago but simply doesn't anymore, they've closed themselves off to what life has to offer because of fear or any number of other reasons. Every situation is unique. Some people require medication. Others might need specific treatment for depression or post-traumatic stress disorder (PTSD). Cognitive behavioral therapy might be called for in some cases. Maybe someone is experiencing grief from a loss and they just haven't been able to move forward. It just seemed to me that there was such a need for a clear, individualized plan people could follow to get back on track, or to embrace their new normal after a life-altering occurrence.

Imagine if someone's house was on fire. First, you get them safe, you remove them from the burning structure. But there are many more steps after that, right? You don't just stop once the person is out of harm's way, and then let the sucker burn to the ground. The fire department comes, puts out the fire, then you've got to deal with the insurance claim, clean up the aftermath, rebuild or move, get new furniture, and so on. But when someone's experienced a significant emotional event in their life, they often don't take all the necessary steps to deal with it in a healthy way. It'd be like moving them back into that burned-out house and telling them to just ignore the ashes.

Working in the capacity of an interventionist for all those years, I helped gambling addicts who'd lost their family's college and retirement funds, agoraphobics who hadn't left the house in months after the death of a spouse, rageaholics and victims of domestic violence, pop stars who needed to get cleaned up in the middle of a global music tour, you name it. I then parlayed that experience into becoming a crisis manager. Sometimes it isn't necessary to send someone to treatment, but they need help navigating their way through a crisis in a way that sticks. That ultimately led me to work with celebrities, who have to manage crises on a seemingly regular basis.

Think of me as a change agent. I know what makes people

change. There's this pervasive belief in society that people can't change. That's 100 percent untrue. If people couldn't change, I'd still be penniless and addicted to drugs. If people couldn't change, no one would ever lose weight. If people couldn't change, no one would ever quit smoking. If people couldn't change, everyone would basically be *doomed*. I've seen people overcome all odds—trauma, loss, mental illness, physical disabilities—to change their lives. People change. They did. I did. You can.

Maybe part of you feels like you're beyond help and you've just come to accept your circumstances. Well, to you I say this—if you're living and breathing, there's hope.

Remember Sarah, the wife who'd called me out of desperation when Wyatt, her once loving husband had turned into a savage monster? Well, she got her kind, gentle man back and she once again found her voice. Wyatt went to alcohol rehabilitation and participated in anger management, but just as important, he realized that the business he'd inherited had been chipping away at his soul. He'd been spending seventy-plus hours a week on something he didn't care about in the least. So, he sold the family company and bought a horse farm. He hadn't ridden since he was a teenager, but it's what had been missing for him. Before he knew it, he not only had several champion Thoroughbreds in his stables, but he was running a successful equine therapy camp. He greets each day with a renewed purpose. I often receive heartfelt emails from Sarah with photos of their kids, all of whom are thriving and reaping the benefits of his decision to face his problems. The ripple effects when someone chooses to change and live in their authenticity can be astounding.

Last year, as I looked back on all the people who had turned their lives around through the CAST Centers, I started to yearn for a way to share these strategies with the rest of the world. I wanted so desperately to reach people who had been too ashamed to talk about how they'd been feeling, or who were just going through the motions of life without any real direction, or who simply weren't living the life they deserved. So, I created CAST on Tour, a seventy-city event with motivational speakers and celebrities who had stepped out of their own darkness into the light.

Over thirty thousand people attended the events, which sold out almost as soon as we announced them. People are thirsty for knowledge about how to live a better life. I had dozens of people approach me after these events and tell me they'd never talked about the emotional struggles they'd been enduring, but now they're ready to make a change and get aligned with their best selves. It fuels me onward to witness that moment of connection, that powerful breakthrough, where suddenly someone gets into sync with their life's purpose. Everyone can be their Best Self! They just have to be very clear what their Best Self looks like and find the way to embrace that version of the person they are.

I recently conducted a survey that has netted thousands of responses, and one of the questions I asked was, "Do you believe you are currently living your best life?" It might shock you to learn that 81 percent of people answered "no," but it didn't surprise me in the least. How would *you* answer that question? Here's the key: there is always room for improvement.

If you're having trouble admitting to yourself that the life you're currently living is nowhere near the one that you really desire or deserve, I want you to know that you're not alone. But as my friend Dr. Phil always says, "You can't change what you don't acknowledge." Let's acknowledge that something needs to change. I'm here to help you do it. That is the purpose of this, my first book. I am so excited to share with you my insights, the lessons I've developed through years of working with clients over many years, and the exercises that have helped so many people uncover their own best selves.

We can agree that you only get one shot at this life, but there's no rule saying you're stuck with the life you've got. Within the pages of this book, I'm going to give you a personalized plan for reinventing your life by discovering and becoming your best self. I've reinvented myself several times—in fact, as I write these very words, I'm in the midst of yet another reinvention. It's up to you to bring about the change but once you've begun, I think you'll be surprised at how quickly it will happen. You got this. So let's go!

Discovering Your Best Self

You are unique.

Maybe you've heard that before, but this time I want you to let the idea wash over you in a new way. No one could truly know what it has meant to walk in your shoes because only *you* have walked in them. Your sum experiences, thoughts, feelings, genetics, and spirit are yours alone. There has never been another you, nor will there ever be. You are no better or worse than anyone else, and even when you don't feel like you are anywhere near good enough, you are *enough* because of one simple truth . . . you are you. The only one.

When you were born, you arrived with some innate traits that distinguish you from others. You carry specific genes that you received from your parents. You probably appreciate your parents for some of those genetic qualities they handed down; others, well, you may wish you could give them back! But your DNA is only part of the story of you, and a small part at that.

Our stories begin at a very young age, despite the powerlessness we have to control what and who is around us in that stage of our lives. Children are blank slates, and in the early years, our parents and others write on those slates for us. But it is important to know our origin stories nonetheless, so that we can be aware of whether we are expressing ourselves as adults in a way that aligns with who we truly are and, more important, to understand if any negative aspects of our origin story might be affecting our current behavior in some fashion.

You might be wondering how it's possible to get out of alignment with our truth, so let's investigate and take an objective look at a typical upbringing. This may not exactly represent your experience but based on my years of coaching, I'm willing to bet it's not too far off.

We have no choice in how we are raised. We're all born into a family system of some kind. The core family dynamics vary widely, and there are fundamental values within family systems that may or may not match up with our own, individual values. We'll have an in-depth discussion about values in the Relationships chapter, but the bottom line is that much of the early shaping of our personality occurs as a result of the family dynamic in which we are raised. Most of us attend school or group activities that begin to teach us how to socialize. We develop hobbies. At some point in our early lives, we start to develop a gut feeling about right and wrong. Eventually, as we physically mature, we become responsible for our own self-care and our physical health.

We learn in school the importance of a general education, but then later in life, many of us seem to disconnect from the idea of learning and just settle for what knowledge we've already attained. I believe many of us cease yearning for new information because we may have felt forced to learn things we found to be useless later in life, and as a result experience a level of disenchantment.

Our very first relationship actually begins in the womb—our relationship with our mother. Then, we form relationships with those in our immediate family as we evolve from helpless infant to young adult. Puberty sets in, along with a flood of confusing emotions due to hormones, and many of us experience our first romantic love.

As we prepare for independence, we learn about financial responsibility. We may start out with jobs that don't exactly reflect our life's purpose; instead, they are a solid training ground on which we transition into adulthood.

Depending upon our upbringing, we may embrace religion or spirituality. Later, we make a conscious decision as to whether we continue those practices, make shifts within them, or choose a new spiritual course.

The above is all very broad strokes, a big picture view of the most common paths from child to adult. But I ask you this—at what point in that journey do we learn how to connect with our best self?

Schools don't teach us this skill, our parents likely do not, as they themselves may not be in touch with their Best Self, and even if they are, then it may not be on a consistent basis. Our friends certainly don't have the tools. Therefore, later on, most of us end up with aspects of our life that just feel off. It's not something we can fully articulate, but we know something isn't quite right. The problem? We aren't being authentically ourselves in one area of life or another.

Life happens around us and through our experiences, we define who we are or who we *believe* we are. Some events help us solidify our authenticity, and others push us further away. For example, we may discover a passion for volunteering in some specific realm, which is an intrinsically rewarding activity that serves to solidify some of our Best Self attributes like generosity and altruism. On the other hand, if we experience some type of abuse or neglect, and form negative beliefs about ourselves as a result, that can push us further away from our Best Self. We can even begin to form false truths about ourselves and the world around us. Our minds are like cameras, watching our lives unfold, and we snap pictures of significant moments. These moments create different thoughts and feelings which we then attach to the memories. Some are important; they stand out. Others we wish never existed, though they sometimes pop back into our brains at the most unexpected times.

As you embark upon this odyssey of self-discovery, I want you to keep in mind that no matter what you hope to achieve in your life, you can use the tools within this book to do it. Though we are all unique, our journeys are all unique, and our goals are all unique, I believe there are some universal tools and concepts that will help us get to where we want to go. These days especially, we operate within a world that loves to tell us who we should be— from what to wear to what to eat, what to believe in politically, how to present ourselves to the world, and even what we should desire out of life—but that's so bogus! Those are all decisions you should be making for yourself, based on what resonates with who you truly are. Many of society's "rules" simply don't apply to us as individuals, and if we spend all our energy on trying to be, do, say, and act like society wants us to, we are simply wasting time we could be spending on discovering and connecting with our Best Self.

The magic of this book is that it'll help you uncover which areas you need to improve upon in your life and how to do that if you choose to do so. In my own life journey, I've discovered that I am passionate about helping people become their Best Self. It's what drives me each and every day. I have found that the biggest challenges in people's lives occur when their life is not in alignment with who they truly are. That may sound overly simplistic, but I have found it to be true time and time again. I recently came to a point in my career that I knew I wanted to take everything I've learned over the years about living consistently as our Best Self and mold all of it into book form. My goal is simply to give you a guide to help you problem solve and grow in your life from that Best Self place within you.

No matter where you're starting from, this book can help you improve your life in powerful, even unexpected ways. You could be starting from your lowest point—maybe you're in the midst of facing some of your biggest challenges to date—this book can help you find your way and come out on the other side feeling more empowered than ever before. Or you might feel like you're "coasting" right now, like life is just okay, but you know deep down that you want and deserve more. This book can help you discover or rediscover your purpose and invigorate you in un-imaginable ways. It could even be that your life feels pretty darn good overall, but you've got just one problem area that you know needs your attention, but you just haven't found the right way to approach it yet. This book can give you that clarity, so you can both face and resolve those problems effectively. Whether you're hoping to . . .

- have better friends,
- improve your relationship with yourself in terms of your inner dialogue or compassion for yourself,
- prioritize your health in a meaningful way,
- evolve more in your life by expanding your knowledge or understanding of the world,
- improve your relationships,
- have a fulfilling career,
- develop a stronger sense of spirituality

. . . you *can* reach your goals. And even if you're not yet sure what it is you want to change, but just know you aren't currently living your ideal life, together, we can find your goal and get you there.

We all know life is unpredictable. Since I won't physically be there to function as your thinking partner when problems arise or when new seasons in your life shift your purpose, I want to make sure you have a clearly defined inner voice that can guide you. You need to be able to summon a levelheaded, critically thinking, logical, and objective opinion when the going gets tough. To do so, we will be using the **Best Self Model**, which is made up of exercises that I have done with my clients over the years. Whether it's one of the biggest executives, or someone struggling just to make rent, the Best Self Model works.

The Model helps you evaluate yourself and the people in your life. We look at what is truly working in your life and what's not, within your seven life SPHERES, an acronym that stands for the following segments of your full life—Social life, Personal life, Health, Education, Relationships, Employment, and Spiritual development. And because I also believe the team of people you choose to have in your life is very important, we will take a realistic and objective look at those folks. We'll determine who you may need more of, and who you may need to dial back. Your inner circle can help make or break you, so this is a key step in the process.

The reason why the Best Self Model works for so many different folks is that I will not be telling you who to be, other than your own definition of your Best Self. There is, however, a handful of characteristics I have found to be universal in all of our best versions of ourselves, and one is a kind inner voice. At our core, we are not meant to be critical of ourselves or others. For example, I reject the notion that people who bully others are "just being honest." I believe that generally, those individuals are expressing their own pain outwardly, in the form of aggression. Also, I believe someone with low self-esteem is not being their Best Self. The thinking little of themselves story is simply one they've crafted out of some kind of pain. I also believe that, at our core, we are universally fearless, shameless, honest, empowered, grateful, and free.

We'll find your authentic inner voice by first taking a close look at the characteristics that you like the most about yourself. Then, in chapter 2, we'll look at what I'll refer to as your character defects. We all have them, and we usually don't address them until forced to, or we meet someone else with the same issue. We like to keep these "defects" in the shadows, but we're going to do something really cool with them by bringing them into the light—we're going to use them to your benefit. In other words, they are hardly defects at all; they're just part of you we're going to start using differently.

Once we've identified these parts of ourselves, we're going to get a little creative. Together, we're going to create two (or more in some cases—I actually have several) very well-defined characters that both exist within you. You can think of them as the classic "angel and devil," "hero or nemesis," whatever you like—but we'll get specific and give yours names, and I'll even ask you to draw them! I'm very serious about this—the more detailed you can make your characters, the better, because then you'll know which one is in charge when you behave certain ways or have certain thoughts or feelings.

This will be a powerful and highly effective exercise, so I want to be sure you're giving it your complete attention. Plus . . . it's fun!

THE POWER OF A JOURNAL

I often hear people say they wish they had more time to journal. Well, now is the time to start! Because this book is going to ask you to do a lot of soul-searching through writing, I highly recommend you either purchase a journal that you will enjoy writing in or put a journaling app on your phone if that's your preferred method. The material you're going to be writing down will be useful to you both now and in the future! You can refer back to it anytime you find yourself drifting, you're facing a big life decision, or you just want to maintain your newfound connection to the best version of yourself.

A story that always comes to mind when I think of this process is about a superstar musician I worked with years ago. This person is one of the most generous, kind, funny, and clever humans I've have had the pleasure of working with. And on top of that, he's an incredibly talented singer and entertainer. One day, I got a call from his manager asking me to come see him in New York. I had not seen him in a while, but as soon as we got together, I noticed that he was quite a different person from when I saw him last.

He had been the frontman and lead singer in the band. Ladies loved him, guys wanted to be like him, and at one time he had been the quintessential superstar. But the man I saw that day was not the fiery, upbeat dude that I had known. His team explained that he had essentially been "treading water" since the band ended. He would get offers for various projects, start to pursue one, but suddenly decide not to do it. He was really struggling with his new identity now that he was a solo artist. He needed to do his own reinvention because his identity had been completely tied up in the band.

We got right to work and started making a list of all the things he currently felt. He used words such as *depressed, unsure, untrusting, dark.* When I asked him to name his antihero, it didn't take long for him to come up with "Minus." He explained to me that Minus just sucked the life right out of the room. I asked him how often Minus was calling the shots in his life, and he said it was about 80 percent of the time.

We then began discussing his Best Self, whom he'd named "Ralph." As soon as we started fleshing out the details around Ralph, he became visibly more confident. He explained that Ralph was a squirrel. This is the picture he drew of Ralph:

Cute, right? The more that Ralph started to take shape, the more my client realized he could let Ralph run the show instead of Minus. Of course, this wasn't an instantaneous switch—we had to go into quite some depth with who Ralph really was within him. But my client learned quickly that he could consult with Ralph, whom he began to think of as his very best friend, at any time for empowerment and encouragement. If Minus tried to get a foot in the door, he could call upon Ralph to take over and shut Minus out again. What a powerful tool!

Soon after we worked together, my client went on to write a smash record for which he won multiple awards. As you can see, the work we do in this internal world of someone's mind has tangible effects in the real world. That's because thoughts lead to actions, or behavior. If you take control of your thoughts, the resulting behavior follows suit. When he put Ralph in charge, he sidelined the negative thoughts, feelings, and limiting beliefs that Minus had been creating and amplifying. He turned down the noise of Minus and focused on the confidence Ralph gave him. The resulting behavior was to write meaningful and powerful music, which resonates with listeners because it came from a place of authenticity within him.

Of course, I'm not suggesting that by the end of this exercise you'll make the Billboard Top 100. But I am saying that this powerful exercise can help you reinvent yourself or make your way back home to the authentic part of you that you've lost along the way.

YOUR UNIQUE EXPERIENCE

There is no right way to do the work in this book. You're on a journey of discovery, and what matters is that you remain curious, honest, open, willing, and focused along the way. This book only works if you work it, so work it; you're worth it! If you just read this book as a passive consumer, you will not get from it everything you deserve. Answer the questions, do the exercises, dig deep, and it will pay off.

This is also the type of book that you can refer to again in the future, depending on what's going on in your life, and I guarantee you will have different results. Since your journey is always evolving, you can apply the Best Self Model at any time in your life.

Write Your Traits

Now it's your turn to write down all the best traits, or characteristics, of yourself that feel authentic to you. As you think about these traits, put yourself into different scenarios and ask how you shine in those moments. These should all be positive attributes. Later you'll see and understand all of these qualities are coming from your Best Self, which I'll also refer to as your authenticity, your truth, your authentic self—they all mean the same thing, which is the core of who you are. I've had a lot of clients and friends who experience an "aha! moment" when they realize that their negative traits are not really part of them—they are just fleeting feelings. At our core, we are all good.

Here are some examples of questions you could ask yourself to get this process started, but if these don't necessarily resonate with you, that's okay. I'm just throwing out ideas to get your juices flowing.

- Are you compassionate toward yourself and others?
- Are you optimistic, always looking on the bright side or for the silver lining?
- Are you forgiving toward those who have tried to hurt you?
- Are you brave in that you speak up for yourself or someone else?
- Are you imaginative, often thinking out of the box?
- Do you act kindly toward others, even when no one is looking?
- Do you demonstrate efficiency at work?
- Do people consider you to be a loyal friend and/or trusted confidant?
- Are you loving toward your children?
- Are you creative and often express your creativity?
- Do you pick up litter when you see it on the street?
- Do you try to resolve conflicts as they arise?

Here is a list of positive traits to consider. You can circle ones that apply to you or add them to your own list.

able	charming	disciplined	functional
abundant	cheerful	discreet	gallant
accomplished	cheery	directed	generous
achiever	clean	dutiful	gentle
active	clear-headed	demonstrative	genuine
adept	clever	dynamic	good-natured
admirable	colorful	ecstatic	giving
affectionate	comfortable	efficient	gracious
affluent	companionable	elegant	gorgeous
agreeable	compassionate	eloquent	graceful
alert	complete	empathetic	grateful
altruistic	conciliatory	energetic	great
amiable	confident	enthusiastic	hardworking
approachable	constructive	ethical	happy
appreciative	content	exciting	healthy
articulate	conventional	expert	hearty
attractive	cool	empowered	heroic
amicable	cooperative	fair	helpful
at ease	considerate	faithful	honest
attentive	contemplative	fearless	honorable
autonomous	courageous	firm	humble
beneficial	courteous	flexible	hospitable
blissful	cordial	free	humane
brilliant	creative	forgiving	humorous
benevolent	daring	friendly	idealistic
balanced	decent	focused	imaginative
calm	decisive	forthright	incorruptible
capable	dedicated	fun-loving	independent
captivating	deep	fruitful	innovative
careful	dignified	full	inoffensive

intuitive	perceptive	responsible	sweet
ingenious	personable	responsive	sympathetic
inspired	persuasive	reverential	teacherly
inspiring	playful	romantic	tender
intelligent	philanthropic	sage	thorough
inventive	perceptive	sane	thoughtful
kind to others	polished	satisfied	tidy
kind inner voice	positive	scholarly	tolerant
knowledgeable	powerful	secure	trusting
leader	practical	selfless	trustworthy
liberated	precise	self-sufficient	unassuming
lively	popular	sensible	understanding
logical	principled	sensitive	uncomplaining
lovable	profound	shameless	undogmatic
loyal	protective	serious	urbane
loving	prudent	skillful	undivided
magnanimous	punctual	smart	useful
mature	purposeful	sober	valuable
methodical	private	sociable	venturesome
meticulous	productive	sophisticated	vigorous
modest	proficient	spontaneous	warm
moral	prolific	sporting	warmhearted
neat	prosperous	spiritual	watchful
nurturing	proud	stable	welcoming
open	quick	steadfast	whole
optimistic	rational	steady	wise
orderly	realistic	stoic	worthwhile
organized	reflective	strong	zany
objective	reasonable	studious	zealous
passionate	relaxed	suave	
patient	reliable	subtle	
patriotic	resourceful	stylish	
peaceful	respectful	supportive	

Anything about yourself that you find to be a positive attribute, that you don't see above, write down below:

My Best Self Traits _____

_____

_____

_____

_____

It can be tough to write down our best traits because we don't exactly sit around thinking about how great we are constantly. That's not human nature. We're far more prone to pick ourselves apart. But hopefully by the end of this book, you will be truly embracing and acknowledging all your best traits—it is a far more productive and proactive activity!

Soon you're going to be looking at yourself objectively, as if you're on the outside looking in, and really *seeing* yourself, maybe even for the first time. This requires a heightened self-awareness, so it might take some time. You may even want to ask a trusted confidant, if you have one, for some help in getting started. If you do, just make sure that person has no agenda, and only wants you to be at your best.

Exercise: Create Your Best Self

Refer back to the list of traits you just wrote down, the ones you like most about yourself. These will help you give shape to your Best Self character. I want to take a moment here to remind you that this should be fun; you can infuse this exercise with humor or you can be serious. Whatever you feel.

These questions can help you get started:

Is your Best Self:
* A particular gender?
* An animal?
* A mystical creature? Or a wise voice inside yourself?
* A character inspired by a book or movie?

Does your Best Self have a motto or tagline?

Does your Best Self behave in a particular way when someone is being kind to you?

Does your Best Self behave in a particular way when you're feeling threatened?

What does your Best Self believe about you?

Does your Best Self move/walk/dance in a specific way?

What is your Best Self's #1 superpower?

Now, write a full description of your Best Self here:

_____

_____

_____

_____

_____

I'll share with you now a little bit about my Best Self, a wizard named Merlin. I have always been a bit of a nerd when it comes to fantasy games. For years, I've played a role-playing card game called Magic: The Gathering. In the game, everyone is a wizard, and in order to win you must cast spells. (I know, so nerdy. But so fun!) My friends and I have always given each other names while playing. One friend of mine was the Beast, another was Gozar the Gatekeeper. To me, wizards of the fictional world represented wisdom, faith, and good prevailing over evil.

Inspired by my love of this game, my Best Self, Merlin, is wise, kind, clever, loving, smart, has total faith in how the universe works, thinks anything is possible, and never acts in ego. He is a cool dude because he marches to his own beat and never misses a step. He never feels insecure or fears he is missing out. He is patient and compassionate, he accepts himself as he is, and he believes in himself always. He holds no resentment. He offers complete forgiveness to others, even when they were in the wrong.

Now, what better way to have a good visual of your Best Self than to draw it? You can use a pen, crayons, markers, colored pencils, whatever you like. I drew an image of Merlin when I first did this exercise many years ago and unlike my Anti-Self (we'll get to that next), Merlin has pretty much stayed the same.

No matter what you draw, I am very proud of you for making the effort. We aren't all visual artists, so if it's not much more than a stick figure, that's okay! The image you have in your mind is likely more detailed than your drawing, and that's what's important. You can imagine the kind of looks I get when I sit down with major corporate executives to do this exercise! But the results are always worth it.

Draw your Best Self here:

Now, look at your drawing. Give your Best Self a name, and then write it across the top of the picture you drew.

I'll bet that when you bought this book, you did not imagine you would be doing an art project! I was so inspired when I created Merlin, I created a daily exercise to remind myself of his strength (and thus, my own!) that I had an original piece commissioned by an artist named Ryan Pratt. He created his version of the Tree of Life, and in the tree, Merlin is chilling in the branches. I have it in the entryway of my house and I love looking at it every day. Here is a close-up:

How Are You Coaching Yourself?

Folks typically hire me as a life coach because they want to improve an area of their life; they're usually stuck in place and need help getting unstuck or finding a new perspective. The role of a life coach varies—but any good one will not only help you identify your goals, but also coach you on how to get them. They should also hold you accountable to what you want to create in their life.

As you will see throughout this book, I will also coach you toward identifying your blind spots and booby traps because they can be problematic. I like to ask folks if they have clear goggles. What I mean by that is if they are looking out with clear focus, or their vision is being blurred by their ego. We all have behaviors or thought patterns that are negatively impacting our lives and preventing us from evolving and growing. Some examples are when we lack humility or have an insatiable need to be right. Now is the time to confront them and, if they are not serving you in a positive way, release them and replace them with positive ones. Or, if you have a tendency to set yourself up for failure in certain areas of your life, we'll also put a stop to that. Since I won't be by your side to talk through every decision you need to make, make sure you give some "life coach" qualities to your Best Self character so that he or she can step up in my place for the rest of your life.

Here are some questions to get you thinking like a Life Coach:

- How will your Best Self help you remain fearless?
- How will your Best Self help you to feel no shame about who you are in this life?
- How will your Best Self help you remain honest with yourself and others?
- How will your Best Self help you maintain that kind, compassionate inner voice at all times?

- How will your Best Self help you feel empowered in all situations?
- How will your Best Self help you remain grateful?
- How will your Best Self help you feel free to be who you truly are?

Write out the "life coach" characteristics of your Best Self here:

_____

_____

_____

_____

_____

As we proceed with the plan in this book, you can begin to "train" your Best Self to ask you the same questions I'm asking you so that you can effectively guide yourself through your life, always with your sights set on staying fully aligned with your authenticity. Notice the key questions I'm asking you in relation to your thoughts, feelings, behavior, and patterns so that you can ask yourself the same questions in the future.

I wanted to start the book off by asking you to create your Best Self because you will get more out of everything we are doing in the rest of the book if you maintain a clear vision of your Best Self along the way.

Gratitude

Expressing gratitude is always an excellent way of connecting with your Best Self. I can guarantee you that your mood will shift upward when you are thinking about what aspects of your life for which you are grateful. I do daily gratitude lists with my morning coffee because for me, it's a great way to start a day. Other folks may do gratitude lists when going through a tough time to reframe their perspective. Gratitude lists take very little time. In fact, I'll share with you a few examples of gratitude lists that my friends have created.

Eddy's Gratitude List:

I am grateful for . . .

1. family
2. job
3. health
4. friends
5. education
6. Hispanic culture
7. speaking two languages
8. physical abilities
9. religion
10. for having a great childhood

Jon's Gratitude List:

I am grateful for . . .

1. My health and physical abilities
2. My home
3. My safety and well-being
4. My partner
5. My mom and dad
6. Lucy, Kashi, Vida (dogs)
7. My friends
8. Steady flow of income
9. All my clients
10. My spiritual connection

Casey's Gratitude List:

I am grateful for . . .

1. My faith
2. My family
3. A job that is fulfilling to me
4. My ability to learn and absorb new information
5. My body that allows me to exercise and live pain-free
6. My house that is safe and cozy
7. The ability to buy healthy food
8. All of the beautiful art in the world
9. The loving community of people around me
10. Every breath of air I draw into my lungs

What is on your gratitude list?

Right now, think of ten things for which you are grateful and write them down. Remember—nothing is too insignificant to add to your list. If you're feeling grateful for the comfortable chair you're sitting in, write it down! Or if you've been watching a TV show that leaves you feeling good, write that down. Sometimes you might even feel grateful for unexpected things like traffic, because it allowed you more time to listen to an audio book, or to be alone with your thoughts as you drove home. Finding new things to be grateful for is a wonderful exercise and a fun way of being even more connected to our Best Self in the present moment. As you think about each item on the list, really embrace how it makes you feel and let that feeling radiate through your body.

After you write down these ten things, check in with yourself. Do you feel better than when you started? Happier? If so, then realize that you've just found a very simple exercise that could help you create an awesome day or that can help you pull yourself out of a funk. I always find it to be a powerful way of getting back into balance.

_____'s Gratitude List

I am grateful for . . .

1. _____
2. _____
3. _____
4. _____
5. _____
6. _____
7. _____
8. _____
9. _____
10. _____

Now that you've completed chapter 1, know that by the end of the book, your Best Self may morph. He or She is going to likely have some new characteristics, become more fine-tuned, or change into something new altogether. You may look at what you create and say, "Holy moly, I am so much more than I ever knew!"

In the next chapter, you're going to do a similar exercise, but for your Anti-Self. This is equally as important and, for many folks, even more empowering because that can be what's holding you back from having a more empowered life. Our Anti-Self runs contrary to our Best Self, and the first step in taking their power away is to recognize them.

Understanding Your Anti-Self

She was sitting in traffic. Total gridlock is a more accurate description—you know, the kind of traffic when the freeway looks more like a parking lot. It was a blistering hot, still day in the San Fernando Valley of Los Angeles. "Rush hour," she thought, "ought to be called standstill hour." The cars looked like they might spontaneously combust at any moment. She tightly gripped her steering wheel, the air conditioner blasting warmish air at her face, and she could feel a steady stream of sweat down her chest and back. Her phone rang.

"Hello?" she said with a not-so-subtle twinge of anxiety.

"Hey, Suzanne! You have a sec?" She heard my voice, and a big smile spread across her face. Even if she was totally miserable in this epic traffic jam, at least she could spend a moment talking to a good friend.

"Hi, Mike! Sure, what's up? Just driving home from work."

"I wanted to see if you can go to dinner on Thursday night. We need to catch up!"

"I'd love that! Let's do it."

"Sounds good. I'll text you details. Is eight p.m. good for you?"

"Yep, that's perfect. Looking forward to it!"

"Cool. Talk to you later! Drive safe!"

"Bye!"

As soon as the conversation ended, her face fell, she sighed loudly, and she looked around. Everyone's speed was finally picking up a little bit. Maybe she would make it home this century after all. Then, without any warning, a car zoomed right in front of her, cutting her off with only inches to spare.

She lost . . . her . . . mind.

"Are you frigging kidding me? You asshole! What in the hell do you think you're doing?" Suzanne continued screaming with a string of colorful language, practically growling as she threw her arms around in outrage, her car gently swaying back and forth with her wild movements. Suzanne was unhinged.

After a full minute of expletives spewing from her mouth like molten lava and honking so much that other people started honking back at her, she finally took a breath. She worked her way through traffic and pulled up next to the person who'd cut her off, but before she could flip her the bird, she saw that the driver was actually a lovely elderly woman who was simply on her way from point A to point B. Just like Suzanne.

Now, fast-forward to later that week, when Suzanne and I were meeting up for dinner. We sat across from each other at our favorite steakhouse, digging into our salads.

"So, when I called you the other day on your drive home, were you feeling pretty stressed?"

"I mean, no more than usual. Work is kind of crazy right now, but I'm managing. Why do you ask?"

"Well, because when we said good-bye, you didn't actually hang up. I heard your little fit of road rage."

She froze and went slack-jawed. "Oh my God. That's so embarrassing." And then she giggled. "Bet you didn't know I could curse like that!"

"I did not! You definitely had some choice words. Is that a regular thing for you?"

"What, yelling at jerks cutting me off? I mean, sure. This is LA. It kind of comes with the territory. You can't tell me you've never screamed at someone for driving like a maniac, as most of the people in this town do."

"Traffic just doesn't trigger me that way. Road rage fascinates me, actually. The person in the other car can't hear you. Everyone's windows are rolled up. What purpose does it serve?"

"It's not about the other person hearing me. It's just to release the tension I feel."

"And does it make you feel better afterward?"

That one gave her pause. "I'd like to think so, but the truth is, sometimes I get so worked up that I feel like my heart is going to beat out of my chest. So I guess the answer is no."

"Grab a couple napkins. I want to do an exercise with you."

"Oh, here we go! Another one of your exercises."

"Come on, you know you love them. This one will be fun. I want you to write down all the traits you don't like about yourself, or that hold you back in some way. Just anything that makes you feel less than your best self."

Suzanne kind of rolled her eyes but smiled and agreed to indulge me. All of my friends are used to this kind of thing when they hang out with me, and Suzanne is no exception. At the time, we'd known each other about five years, and had even worked together on a project. We had a lot of mutual respect for one another. It didn't take her long to come up with her list, and when she was done, she handed it to me, somewhat indignantly.

"Okay, great. Now, we're going to create your Anti-Self character."

"My what?"

"Your Anti-Self. We all have one, or even several of them. These are the sides of us that get triggered by negative things, like our fears and our anxieties. The point of the exercise is to get to know your Anti-Self characters and what makes them surface so you can keep them in check. You don't want to end up with your Anti-Self running the show."

"So, like, the side of me that has over-the-top, potty-mouthed vengeance when behind the wheel is Road Rage Regina or something?"

"Exactly! And now, to make her even more tangible to you, I want you to draw what she looks like on this napkin."

"Hmmm. Okay. Regina, I think you'd have big, mean-looking, bushy eyebrows, bulging biceps, and a lovely pair of horns on top of your head." She doodled on the napkin and then showed me her handiwork.

"Perfect! Now, next question. Other than sitting in bumper-to-bumper traffic, what else brings Regina out of you?"

Suzanne thought for a moment. "It's sort of anytime that I'm feeling completely fed up. Like I've just taken it and taken it but I can't take one more second of whatever is frustrating me. Then I turn into Regina and everybody better watch out. Just ask my husband."

"Have you ever made that link before? That this aspect of your personality rears its head anytime you're feeling fed up?"

"Not really, no. But now that I'm seeing it, I realize that I could probably do things to prevent it from happening."

"Like what?" I asked.

"Well, I could probably have a discussion with my husband or whoever is driving me nuts sooner, rather than trying to ignore or stuff down the feelings until I blow up. I could just tell him that I need him to dry out the shower so it doesn't grow mildew, instead of waiting until the mildew is taking over our bathroom and then scream at him."

"Right. So, while we're at it, from that list of traits you don't love about yourself, is there another Anti-Self character you can create?"

"For sure. But she's very different from Regina. She goes inward, gets self-conscious, and just clams up. Whenever I'm in new territory or I'm feeling inexperienced, I sort of shut down."

"Draw her, too." Suzanne was already on it. She knew this side of herself all too well. She was drawing a small person at a big conference table, and her head was down, her hair hanging all around her face like a shield. She had her knees up and her arms wrapped around them.

"That image says a lot. What's her name?" I asked.

"She's Nell."

"So, Nell comes out when you feel in over your head at work?"

"Yes, or in any situation when I just don't feel like I'm prepared. I can literally remember when I was a kid and I had been out of school a lot because I was sick, and I had to take a test that I hadn't studied for. I was such a perfectionist in my classes, but I froze up and couldn't fill in one answer. I relive that moment every time I find myself in a conversation or situation that I don't know much about."

"So, you feel like you can't fall back on your instincts or wisdom in those instances?"

"Right. I'm paralyzed. Well, *Nell* is paralyzed."

"Exactly. So, now that you know what triggers her, do you feel like you can keep her at bay?" Suzanne's facial expression went from disheartened to enlightened in a matter of seconds. By being able to identify Nell and give her a face and a name, suddenly Suzanne gained power over her.

"You know what? I do. I feel like I've been holding on to the past in some weird way and letting it rule me. Is that crazy?"

"Nope. Not at all. That's very normal. But now you're back in control and you never have to let her take over again."

"I always learn something when we get together, Mike, but this is big. I'm glad you overheard my road rage."

"Me, too, and now I can ride in the car with you. Because for a minute there, I was going to refuse to let you drive ever again."

"Oh, now. It's not like Regina would've hit someone on purpose." At that, I raised my eyebrows a bit. "Okay, you're right—who knows what that crazy lady would do! I'm glad she's gone now."

We had a good laugh and enjoyed the rest of our dinner. Over the next few weeks, I checked in with my friend to see if Nell or Regina had shown up at all, and I'm happy to report that Suzanne hadn't heard from either.

Identifying your Anti-Self characters is a profound exercise and it's no exaggeration to say that it can change your life. Time and time again, I've seen people go to unimaginable new heights in all areas of their life because they've stopped allowing their Anti-Self to stand in their way.

I'll give you another example of an Anti-Self that one of my superstar clients identified within herself. She was having recurring issues in her relationships and couldn't figure out why she wasn't able to maintain a healthy, solid relationship with a man. She continuously entered into relationships that started great but quickly devolved into unhealthy. Everyone around her would tell her she was with the wrong person, but she turned a blind eye and allowed her boyfriend's insults, condescension, cheating, and even his emotional and sometimes physical abuse . . . time and time again.

When I asked my client about her definition of a good relationship, she went off on a tangent that sounded like every romance novel or romantic comedy ever written. It was pure fantasy! I helped her test her theories around a perfect relationship by taking her out in public on a search for what she believed was the perfect couple, who had everything she wanted. The funny thing was that most of the people around us were either on their cell phones ignoring each other or appeared to be just flatlined—you know, couples that may be sitting together at the same table, but it's evident from their body language and lack of eye contact that they are both actually thousands of miles away from each other. Sure, there were some who were engaged in lively conversation and were even flirting, but no one was staring deeply into each other's eyes, holding hands across the table, and playing footsie. The more we looked around, the more she realized that her expectations for a fairy-tale romance do not exist in reality. She understood that she was acting like a hopeless romantic with unrealistic ideals. So she named her Anti-Self "Rapunzel."

That's not to say that wonderful relationships don't exist in the real world. Of course they do! Plenty of people are in deeply fulfilling, emotionally satisfying, passionate, and loving relationships. But they're not floating around on a cloud, wearing ball gowns and tuxedos, sweeping each other off their feet with grand, romantic gestures every day of their lives. Life isn't a movie! Once this client embraced that fact and became more grounded in her beliefs around intimate relationships, her expectations became reasonable.

In her next relationship, she was able to ask herself if her thoughts and feelings were coming from the Rapunzel version of herself, or her Best Self. She could then easily identify anything that resembled "fairy-tale thinking," and sideline it. I'm happy to report that she's been in a perfectly healthy, romantic, and stable relationship for years now. She was able to choose a much more suitable partner since she wasn't focused on finding that prince who would sweep her off her feet or rescue her from a tower—instead, she looked for a stable, decent man. Birds may not chirp overhead every time they kiss, but thankfully, that's no longer cause for her to head out the door.

Rapunzel still lives in her a bit, but she is much less of an influence because my client knows what to watch for. I have found that identifying this character is far more powerful than just labeling our issues. If I had approached her relationship issues by saying, "Wow, you really keep making bad decisions," or "You're really out of touch with reality and borderline delusional," or "You're a love addict," all of that would've fallen on deaf ears. She had to come to her own conclusions, and then create a character within herself that she fully understood, so that she could keep her from interfering with her life.

Here is another example. This is just how my client shared her Anti-Self story with me:

"My boyfriend and I had the best time ever at the Arcade Fire concert, and it was something we had been looking forward to and planning for ages. We danced together, sang along to our favorite songs, and connected with each other. It was so much fun that we didn't want the night to end!

"I asked Johnny, 'Should we grab a nightcap before we go home and stay out just a *litttttle* longer? I don't wanna go home just yet.'

"'Yeah, let's, that sounds fun,' he said.

"We went to this cute neighborhood bar; one of Johnny's friend's girlfriend was a bartender there. She was very warm and friendly, and greeted us with big hugs. I observed her as she spoke to Johnny; she was pretty and had an edgy look. She had tattoos and an attractive, uninhibited nature. Little triggers started popping up in my mind and 'Jealousa'—my alter ego, the devil to my angel, my Anti-Self—came out.

"Jealousa is passionate, fiery, dramatic, possessive, and jealous, just like her name implies. She is insecure and feels unattractive and inferior to others. She thinks her current boyfriend, and every boyfriend she has had, is always checking out other women.

"While I watched Johnny and this girl interact, I started asking myself questions. 'Is Johnny attracted to her? Wow, he seems very interested in their conversation. He's being overly attentive.' All these thoughts were racing through my mind, and my emotions were boiling up.

"First, blame and anger projected all my negative energy toward his behavior, and then it turned into insecurity and comparison. 'Does he think she's prettier than me? Is he physically attracted to that kind of girl? She's skinny and tall, I'm curvy and short, I'll never be skinny or tall. He loves me and tells me I'm beautiful all the time, but does he mean it?' The tone of the night immediately shifted and my mood got sour. The seed had been planted in my mind and there was no amount of reassurance or communication that would help because the worst of me had taken over and I had made up my mind about how I felt.

"Johnny had no idea what happened; he was just having a conversation and being engaging; it's in his nature to be friendly! When I confronted him about it, he didn't know what I was talking about. The best night ever turned into an argument. As I was falling asleep, I wondered, *Was what I felt real, or did I make it up?*

"Jealousa sneakily comes in and creates these situations to fuel her fire, to keep her possessive and jealous ways alive; she likes to create drama that is not real. There is no need for her to be paranoid or suspicious of her boyfriend. Johnny is with her because he is attracted to her and in love with her."

Exercise: Identify Your Anti-Self Traits

Since life is constantly evolving, it's unrealistic to think that you can act from within your Best Self 100 percent of the time. Instead, the idea is simply to reduce the amount of time you spend in your Anti-Self.

As an example, I have some insecurities in certain areas of my life, so my ongoing goal is to feel secure in myself with any new ventures and to focus on enjoying the journey. For instance, even in writing this book I've experienced some insecurities. As you'll find out in a later chapter, I didn't do very well in school, particularly in my English classes. Essays were definitely not my thing, so you can imagine how the notion of writing an entire book might have made me feel at first! I started worrying what others would think of the way that I wrote, and I wondered a lot if I was good enough. The same goes for television appearances—which is also a relatively new endeavor for me. I thought so much about how producers and viewers perceived me that it began to affect my confidence. But all of that is driven by fear, and I've noticed my insecurities really come out when I'm thinking too much about whether people like me or my work. But when Merlin (my Best Self) gets in the mix, I'm not insecure at all. I imagine the Anti-Self as trying to sabotage us, doing anything it can to keep us from being ourselves—thus, it keeps you from enjoying the journey of life.

First, as Suzanne did, write down traits that you consider to be your character flaws. Some questions to help get you thinking about these types of traits include:

- Do you harbor unforgiveness toward yourself or others?
- Are you quick to anger?
- Do you often knowingly make unhealthy choices?
- Are you impatient much of the time?
- Do you act like a know-it-all?
- Do you often give up before accomplishing a goal?
- Do you believe you are not good enough?
- Do you let people walk all over you?
- Do you often act selfishly?

I want you to think about the last time you acted in a negative way, when afterward you thought, *Man, I really wasn't myself in that moment. I didn't handle that well.* Perhaps it's not as obvious as that—maybe it's more like a bad feeling that lingers. It could even be that you don't like the person you become when you speak to certain family members. Something happens, you get triggered, and all of a sudden, you hang up the phone.

Another example is when people in a relationship begin to create a false narrative due to their partner's behavior. Like if a husband comes home from work and wants to unwind in front of the television for an hour. His wife might see that pattern and begin to believe that he doesn't like spending time with her, or that she's become unattractive to him. She can go deeper and deeper into the story she's created, and then begin to believe that she's unworthy of love. That's the Anti-Self in action.

Anything you dislike about yourself should go on this list. Interestingly, I find that my clients often find this list much easier to create than their Best Self list. But that's why I'm so excited for your journey through this book—because eventually, we are going to flip the script and improve your life.

This is only for you to see, so set aside any feelings of guilt or shame. Burying our head in the sand and remaining in denial about certain aspects of ourselves actually gives those aspects power over us. Remember, things appear scarier when shrouded in darkness. So, let's shed some light!

Here is a list of common Anti-Self traits to consider. You can circle ones that apply to you or add them to your own list.

abrasive	bland	colorless	cynical
abrupt	bitter	complacent	cheater
agonizing	boring	complaintive	clingy
aimless	brutal	compulsive	conceited
anxious	calculating	condemnatory	confusing
angry	callous	conformist	deceitful
apathetic	cantankerous	confused	demanding
arbitrary	careless	contemptible	destructive
argumentative	charmless	cowardly	depressed
arrogant	childish	crass	disagreeable
artificial	clumsy	criminal	devious
asocial	coarse	critical	dishonest
awkward	cold	crude	dirty

discouraging

disloyal

disobedient

disorderly

disrespectful

disruptive

dissonant

distractible

dogmatic

domineering

dull

egotistical

egocentric

erratic

escapist

faithless

false

fatalistic

fickle

fixed

foolish

follower

gloomy

greedy

graceless

gullible

grim

hateful

haughty

hostile

ignorant

impatient

inconsiderate

indiscreet

inferior

insecure

insensitive

intolerant

indulgent

incurious

impulsive

inert

inhibited

insincere

insulting

irrational

irresponsible

irritable

jealous

lazy

lethargic

loud

malicious

mannerless

mean

miserable

misguided

money-minded

monstrous

moody

messy

narcissistic

needy

narrow

neglectful

negative

obnoxious

obsessive

one-dimensional

one-sided

overly
opinionated

oppressive

passive

paranoid

pedantic

perverse

petty

perfectionist

pessimistic

pompous

possessive

questionable

rude

regretful

repressed

resentful

ritualistic

rigid

reactionary

scheming

self-centered

sedentary

secretive

shortsighted

self-indulgent

selfish

sly

small-thinking

stiff

stingy

stoic

tactless

treacherous

thoughtless

tense

troubled

unappreciative

uncaring

undisciplined

unhealthy

ungrateful

unreliable

unlovable

unfriendly

unable

unaffectionate

unethical

unexciting

unintelligent

unpleasant

unpolished

unrealistic

unsupportive

unwelcoming

uptight

unstable

unreliable

vacuous

vague

venomous

vindictive

vulnerable

vain

weak

Anything about yourself that you find to be a negative attribute, and that you don't see above, write down below:

Anti-Self Traits _____

_____

_____

_____

_____

Create Your Anti-Self

Referring to the negative traits you wrote about above, let's now begin to give shape to your Anti-Self. As you dip into your imagination for this exercise, remember that this is meant to be an exaggeration of this version of yourself. I believe it's healthy to be able to laugh at ourselves, if only a little. If we're so tightly wound that we can't poke fun at ourselves at times, then we're just taking ourselves too seriously. Also, the overexaggeration of our traits helps us remember them. Thus, when we think or behave in a certain way, we can stop and assess: "Am I acting out of my Best Self, or my Anti-Self?" And we have powerful imagery attached to both.

One of my Anti-Self characters is "Angelos." He loves to provoke people, he's impatient, and he really rears his ugly head whenever he feels like people are being dishonest. He lacks compassion and refuses to accept that some folks will tell white lies out of their own fear. He's impulsive. He can't stand news, weather, and sports conversations. He is untrusting. My friends know about this character and they have pointed him out to me in the past, but I can honestly say that Angelos's volume is low to non-existent these days.

As you work on fleshing out your Anti-Self, keep in mind that it's perfectly fine if you need to create several different characters that are various versions of your Anti-Self. You can give each of them their own set of qualities and appearances.

In the same way that a screenwriter fully fleshes out his or her characters before writing a word of dialogue in a movie script, I want you to have a full, complete picture and understanding of who your Anti-Self character is. The clearer the image is in your mind, the easier it will be for you to predict what might trigger him or her to react or influence your behavior. And it will also help your Best Self in keeping him or her at bay.

Here are some questions to get you started on creating your Anti-Self:

Is your Anti-Self:
- A particular gender?
- An animal?
- A mystical creature?
- A character inspired by a book or movie?

Does your Anti-Self have a tagline?

Does your Anti-Self move/walk/dance in a specific way?

Does your Anti-Self behave in a particular way when someone is being kind to you?

Does your Anti-Self behave in a particular way when you're feeling threatened?

What does your Anti-Self believe about you?

What does your Anti-Self wear?

Write a full description of your Anti-Self here: _____

_____

_____

Name five recent events or situations when you know your Anti-Self was taking charge of the situation.

1. _____

2. _____

3. _____

4. _____

5. _____

Now, grab a pen or pencil, marker, or paintbrush; it's time to sketch out your Anti-Self. Get as detailed as you can!

Draw your Anti-Self character here:

Before we go on, take a moment to assign a name to your Anti-Self and write it at the top of the image you created.

Now ask yourself how you would handle those five situations if you were acting as your Best Self. In other words, what would your Best Self tell you differently if he or she were in charge instead?

1. _____

2. _____

3. _____

4. _____

5. _____

Look at that! I'll bet you're seeing a pattern here! I'm pushing you to dig deep and really look at yourself. Even if you have rolled your eyes once or twice so far, I get it. This is probably a bit out of your comfort zone, but it's certainly work worth doing.

I'll share with you a scenario in which I often find myself, and that used to easily trigger Angelos. As the CEO of a company, I manage a lot of different employees. When one of those employees isn't performing well in his or her position, I would confront them about it with no regard for who else might be present in the room at the time. I wasn't thinking about how that might feel humiliating to the person—of course, I was not *purposely* trying to humiliate them, but I just was thoughtless as to their feelings. That was all Angelos. I would act impulsively rather than putting thought into how to empower that employee to excel. When I would get into the Angelos mind-set, I just did not care who I was talking to, I would confront him or her right then and there. I realized, though, that this kind of behavior did not create more peace in my life—quite the contrary! It would just create more unresolved tension, and the employee often would not improve their performance, either. It was a lose-lose situation all around when Angelos stepped in.

The Anti-Self Evolution

Now that you have a very clear understanding of the various versions of your Anti-Self, the next time you're faced with a situation that would usually bring him or her to the surface, you can actually choose to let your Best Self handle it instead. It can be a split-second decision, and over time, it will become automatic. You will start to subconsciously summon your Best Self instead of your Anti-Self to rise to every challenge or obstacle put in your way.

Life isn't static—it's constantly moving and changing—and neither is your Anti-Self. Our experiences shape our mental and emotional landscape, so it's possible that a new version of your Anti-Self might pop up. I encourage you to check in with yourself from time to time and do this exercise from the beginning again. You may be surprised by what you discover.

Anytime you experience some kind of shift in your life—a new job or career change, moving, the loss of a loved one, and so on—those are good times to have some additional awareness around your Anti-Self. Doing so can help you maintain equilibrium across the board.

As you can see, the simple process that we have done in the last two chapters can be incredibly empowering and insightful on your journey to being your best self. In the next chapter, we'll be packing all the right items in your bag as you continue on the exciting road ahead.

Your Unique Journey:
The Best Self Tenets of Change

We are all artists. I define an artist as someone who expresses their self through their own authenticity. We all have an ability to do something that is beautiful, that others can benefit from, and that is unique to us. I'm not talking about the kind of art that requires a paintbrush and canvas; there are as many different and unique forms of art in the world as there are people.

I accidentally discovered my own art form, as I think many of us do. My life journey has been filled with twists and turns, ups and downs, and even some moments of moving nowhere at all, and it's been through those experiences that I have connected with myself and others. Within those connections, I stumbled upon my art, which is helping people find the freedom to be the best version of themselves. I suppose you could say that *my* art is helping you discover *your* art. And that is the essence of the journey that you are on right now, as you apply the Best Self Model to your life.

Everyone I have worked with will tell you that, at one time or another, I have asked them, "What is your art?" They usually just look at me, puzzled. What I'm really asking is how they are expressing who they are at their core in their everyday life, whether it be through their chosen profession, how they interact with their family, their hobbies, and so on.

As an example, the therapists I employ at CAST Centers express their unique art each and every day that they work with clients, always with the greater purpose of freeing people from what is trapping them. The staff at our transitional living home have honed their art of helping folks feel cared for and loved. The woman who cleans the offices before everyone arrives has an art of making a space feel orderly and well-kept. The HR manager has an art of keeping the peace and crossing all the *t*'s and dotting all the *i*'s. It's truly a wonder to be among a group of people who are actively expressing their unique art forms on a daily basis, with a common goal that inspires and motivates them all.

People often say to me, "You must feel so good about yourself because your life's work is about helping others improve themselves." But I always balk at that because if you're living as your Best Self in every area of your life, it doesn't matter if your art is making plumbing fixtures, writing computer programs, designing clothes, waiting tables, building furniture, writing songs, growing vegetables, decorating homes, or anything else—you can and will feel great about yourself. That's what I want for you!

Five Tenets for Change

I think at this stage you realize that I completely believe that your journey of life is different than anyone else's. There are, however, some fundamental tools that have proven time and again to be essential to a successful experience with the Best Self Model. These tools, which I have come to call the five tenets for change, help us prepare ourselves mentally for the process we'll be undergoing.

To get you into the right mind-set for change, I want to make sure you are committed to approaching everything with:

- Curiosity
- Openness
- Focus
- Honesty
- Willingness

Curiosity

I'm naturally a very curious person, and because of that, I ask a lot of questions, especially when I meet someone for the first time. I don't even realize I'm doing it anymore. But I'm grateful for my innate curiosity about myself and others, because it contributes so much to my ability to help others. Very often, it's through a series of simple yet powerful questions that I'm able to help people connect their own dots in their life and experience breakthroughs. I just follow my curiosity.

I've realized, though, that not everyone has that same innate curiosity, and specifically, I've found that many struggle with being curious at all. They are going through the motions of life until a crisis occurs that forces them to reevaluate. But when we become curious about ourselves, we get inspired to change.

Curiosity simply means "a strong desire to know or learn something." If you've stopped being curious, you can't explore yourself. I know it's sometimes scary digging deep, peeling back those layers, brushing the dust off something that's been sitting there, planted in your psyche for decades, insidiously growing roots. But by shining light on the dark corners of your mind and heart, you'll see that whatever is there isn't nearly as scary as it seemed, and you'll start to take your power back in ways you never thought possible.

When we think of the curiosity of children, it conjures images of kids running their hands through sand and gazing as it falls through their fingers or watching with wonder as a flock of birds takes off in flight or squealing in delight as they splash in a bubble bath. This is experiential learning; they are understanding the world around them using all of their senses, and this is the type of curiosity I want you to engage in, as specifically applied to *yourself.* I want you to become acutely aware of your thought patterns, your behavior, and the way in which you move through the world.

Walt Disney once said, "We keep moving forward, opening new doors, and doing new things, because we're curious and curiosity keeps leading us down new paths." I think that speaks to the

---

CAUTION FLAG

I want to put something on your radar. Sometimes when people become deeply curious about themselves, they fall down a rabbit hole of self-deprecation. The deep dive takes them only toward negative thoughts and behaviors. If you feel yourself going in that direction, stop immediately, and redirect.

The point of being curious isn't to beat yourself up. It's simply to start to see connections between your thoughts and behaviors, and to see, and I mean really *see*, yourself for who you are right now so that you can understand where you want to go.

profound nature of curiosity and what it can do for us if we just embrace and nurture it. And while the primary realm in which I'm asking you to remain curious is that of your own inner landscape, it also projects outward to include the world around you, new ideas, perspectives, and beliefs. Curiosity is the means by which you can absorb knowledge. Without curiosity, you cannot truly learn.

Honesty

Since the fundamental goal we're working to accomplish is alignment with your Best Self, you can see why honesty is going to be imperative. If you're lying (which is something your Best Self wouldn't do) to yourself about anything, including any fears that have built up along the way, you're only putting up roadblocks to your own progress. Thomas Jefferson said, "Honesty is the first chapter in the book of wisdom." And isn't wisdom what we're really pursuing? In all things, let us make the wise choice. Honesty is where wisdom begins.

Honesty and integrity are one and the same—it's all about doing the right thing. I want you to do right by yourself throughout this process. Without total honesty, you won't be able to really connect with your Best Self. You may think you will align if you keep secrets, but let me tell you, you will fail. If you've been trying to avoid something, it's time to face it—and I promise that the confession, and fallout, isn't as bad as you might think it is. We are only as sick as our secrets. Secrets and shame can keep you from achieving positive outcomes in your life by tripping you up on the journey. I am excited to help you make peace with all of your "stuff," so let's agree the best way to move forward is by operating from a place of truth.

Openness

Choosing to be open is like opening our mind's eye so that we can see answers that have been there all along but were hidden to us because we were blind to them.

Because our brains are hardwired for survival, we aren't naturally open-minded when it comes to new things or ideas. Our brains recognize that what we're doing right now is working well enough, so we avoid change. We're not in any grave danger, so we just maintain the status quo. Basically, our brain's baseline is "if it ain't broke, don't fix it." But we aren't talking about escaping an immediate danger; instead we're talking about upgrading our operating system to go from surviving to *thriving*.

Openness is fundamental as we tinker and adjust how you live your life. Let's put it all out on the table and work together to discover where even small changes can have huge positive outcomes. The more open you are to new concepts, the higher your likelihood of success. Being open essentially means being teachable. One of the greatest realizations I've had in my own life is how freeing it is to always be in that teachable mode. I can guarantee that your life will improve if you remain open to the idea that you don't always have the answer, that new information can be added to the answers that you do have, and that you can do things better than you are right now. Remember that Greek philosopher Socrates said, "The only true wisdom is knowing you know nothing." Embrace that belief. Wrap your arms around it and give it a great, big hug because once you accept the notion that you really know nothing at all, you suddenly become like a sponge, always soaking in new ideas and points of view.

Imagine if you'd lived your entire life standing behind a wall. You never dared to even consider stepping out from behind it until, finally, one day, a friend came and took you by the hand and dragged you to the other side. There, you witnessed the majesty of a sunrise for the very first time. Let this book be that friend taking you by the hand, and let that sunrise be the beauty of your Best Self. Be open to everything put in your pathway.

Willingness

When I finally got sober more than sixteen years ago, I learned through the recovery process that I had to go to whatever lengths necessary to remain clean. I knew I didn't want to relapse, so I did anything and everything that was suggested to me by my mentors, sponsors, and therapists. That included going to twelve-step meetings every day, calling a mentor every day, volunteering to give back to the community, praying every morning, and reviewing my day each evening. I was desperate for a solution because I no longer had an answer for my addiction, therefore, I asked anyone who had what I was missing (which was peace of mind) for suggestions. You can rest assured that anyone who has made a radical change in their life, from getting sober to losing a lot of weight or making a big career change, has maintained their willingness. Willingness is the action step; being willing to stay in action, not just in thought.

You, too, need to be willing to go to whatever length is necessary in order to better yourself. Yes, it's possible this may require you to step far out of your comfort zone, so you need to be willing to do that, too. Like I said before, this doesn't need to be hard! I think you'll be shocked to find that once you've properly visualized your goal, it won't be such a stretch to do the work that's necessary to reach it. I believe if you're willing to do something, that's when you actually will do it. Sir Richard Branson, the British magnate who founded the Virgin Group, said "Life is a hell of a lot more fun if you say yes rather than no." That's exactly what I'm talking about. Be willing to say yes and then follow through with action, and you will not be disappointed.

Focus

The final tenet for change is focus, which you can also think of as staying on track. Ask any leader for the main reason they've reached their extreme level of success, and they will answer with one word: *focus*.

Oprah Winfrey once said, "Feel the power that comes from **focusing** on what excites you." Oprah certainly seems very happy doing what she loves, doesn't she? Warren Buffett: "Games are won by players who **focus** on the playing field, not by those whose eyes are glued to the scoreboard." LL Cool J said, "Stay **focused**; go after your dreams and keep moving toward your goals." He's obviously managed to do both, and I'd say it's paid off! Well-known businessman and investor Mark Cuban has said, "What I've learned is you've just got to stay **focused** and believe in your-self and trust your own ability and judgment." Focus is key.

A real-life scenario that can demonstrate to you the power of focus is to look at the flip side—thinking of what can happen when we are *not* fully focused on an important task. Texting and driving is really the ultimate (and most pervasive) example of people trying to split their focus between tasks, and it has deadly results. According to the National Safety Council, 1.6 million crashes each year are a direct result of cell phone use while driving. That's one out of every four car accidents. At least nine people are killed every day because of a distracted driver. We are not capable of being in two places at once, physically or mentally. In order to do the work required to improve our lives we need to minimize distractions and create a setting that is supportive of the focus required.

Now we need to determine what focus actually looks like for you. What is your unique way of staying the course? I say "unique" because everyone has different ways of focusing. For example, while reading this book you may find that you are better able to focus by reading alone in your quiet bedroom with a cup of tea and a pen. Alternatively, maybe you thrive on energy around you, so it would be better for you to do your reading in a coffee shop with your laptop. If you're not sure, do a little experiment, try a couple of different environments, and determine which one allows you to stay the most tuned in. From minute one, we need to make sure you are present and fully focused on the work at hand.

I stay focused by first getting myself into the right environment. Coffee shops work for many folks to do their work, but for me I need a comfortable chair and as few distractions as possible. I also prioritize what I am trying to focus on and I tune out everything else on my to do list.

What Charges Your Authenticity Battery?

What were you doing the last time that you felt truly alive, like you were firing on all cylinders? When you felt like you were fully plugged in to your life?

The answers to those questions may pop right into your mind, allowing you to relive those moments. Alternatively, you might still be scratching your head and wondering if you've ever *really* felt that way. But having those moments of ultimate rejuvenation, feeling fully charged, is what I like to call charging your authenticity battery. These moments are key in your life, and necessary.

Let's explore together and discover what it is that charges your authenticity battery.

- Right now, take a moment to think about what makes you feel truly alive and write it here: _____

  _____

  _____

- When was the last time you did that activity? _____

  _____

  _____

- Based on the type of activity that you've identified as charging your authenticity battery, what does this tell you about your Best Self? _____

  _____

  _____

- What areas of your life match up with your Best Self? _____

  _____

  _____

- What areas of your life do not match up with your Best Self?

  _____

  _____

When you look at the information you wrote down above, does it seem as though what you do in your life mostly matches up with who you are authentically? If so, that's exciting because it means our work together will be focused on fine-tuning and/or working problems in specific areas.

On the other hand, does it seem more like you've buried your core self under piles of the messy stuff in life? That's okay too, because we're about to start digging!

Now, Rate Your Readiness for Change

It's time to start your journey. Are you really ready? I'd like for you to rate yourself, on a scale of 1–10, on the five factors we've been discussing: curiosity, honesty, openness, willingness, and focus.

1=Not at all   5=Getting there   10=100%, I'm all in!

1. How curious are you to learn about who you really are, even if you might find that person to be different from who you are right now?

CIRCLE ONE: 1   2   3   4   5   6   7   8   9   10

2. How honest are you going to be with yourself as you do the exercises in this book? Will you shine a bright light on every corner of your life and mind?

CIRCLE ONE: 1   2   3   4   5   6   7   8   9   10

3. How open are you to making changes necessary in order to improve your life?

CIRCLE ONE: 1   2   3   4   5   6   7   8   9   10

4. How willing are you to go to whatever lengths are necessary to improve your life and create a consistent connection with your Best Self?

CIRCLE ONE: 1   2   3   4   5   6   7   8   9   10

5. How focused are you on the tasks at hand within the pages and exercises in this book?

CIRCLE ONE: 1   2   3   4   5   6   7   8   9   10

If you did not circle 10 on all of these questions, ask yourself this: what do you need to do right now in order to reach a 10? Write it down here: _____

_____

_____

_____

If you're not altogether sure what you need to do in order to feel ready, read on. And don't worry, everything is a process. We'll get there, together.

Stages of Change

Now that you've committed to remaining curious, honest, open-minded, willing, and focused, I want to talk to you for a minute about the stages of change/improvement. Here they are:

The Stages of Change/Improvement*

- **Pre-contemplation:** You have no intention of changing any of your existing behavior. You're likely unaware a problem even exists.
- **Contemplation:** You've become aware that you need to take action in some area of your life, but you have no intention to change just yet.
- **Preparation:** You're intent on taking action to correct the problem. You're convinced that you need to change something in order to improve some or all areas of your life,

---

* *The Transtheoretical Model* (Prochaska and DiClemente, 1983).

and you believe you are capable of doing what is required of you.

- **Action:** You are actively modifying your behavior in order to improve your life.
- **Maintenance:** You're sustaining your changed behavior and new behaviors have replaced the old ones.

I spent many years doing interventions where I helped people who lived in absolute resistance because they were afraid of the consequences of change. Many ended up doing a 180 in their lives and some of those people even work for me today.

We all have warning signs when we need to make a change, and if you're like most people, you've probably overlooked or ignored them. But I'm here to help you identify warning bells that are going off in different parts of your life, so that you can tweak your behavior and thus prevent even bigger issues from appearing. Let's not wait until you're at a crisis point before recognizing the need for change.

When I was an interventionist, I very often got calls from parents of grown children who were desperate for them to change. One such set of parents was Cindy and John, and they called me about their nineteen-year-old son, Marty, who had dropped out of college and moved into their basement. He spent most of his time playing video games (which he did all night long, then slept until noon), eating meals prepared by Cindy, and loafing around the house. He, of course, had zero motivation to change. Why would he? To him, life was sweet. School hadn't been his cup of tea, so he just flew back home to the coop for some R&R for an unspecified period of time.

John figured the best way to get Marty motivated to participate in life was to hire him at his company—a local chain of restaurants. Marty was supposed to work at headquarters (so John could keep an eye on him) from 9 a.m. to 5 p.m. every day. But despite being paid as a full-time employee, he was showing up for just a few hours *maybe* three days a week. And even when he was on the clock, he didn't do much of anything at the office, and his coworkers reported that he was not a team player and didn't adhere to the same code of ethics they all had—he was late, constantly texting on his cell phone, and so on.

I sat down with John and Cindy to talk through the situation, and I could hear Marty playing his video games downstairs on full volume the whole time. First things first—I needed to get John and Cindy on the same page. They needed to be aligned and understand that Marty was only going to be motivated to change if: 1) there were real-life consequences if he did not choose to change, or 2) he was in such emotional, physical, or spiritual pain that he just couldn't handle one more day of it. We all knew he was living a pretty pain-free existence, so he needed consequences. Stat.

John said, "Okay, so do we need to kick him out? Let him see what life's like out on the streets?"

A horrified Cindy jumped in: "John, that's our baby you're talking about! We couldn't possibly! I'm just as tired of waiting on him hand and foot, but we've got to help him! He's so lost."

I simply said, "This is a choice Marty has to make for himself. If he's going to live here, there are certain rules he must adhere to. John, if he doesn't show up to work on time every day, there have to be consequences. Otherwise you're just rewarding bad behavior. Would you do that for any of your other employees?"

John shook his head vehemently. "No way."

I posed a question to both of them. "So, in your minds, what is the ideal scenario here?"

Cindy dived in: "If Marty is going to live here, he has got to pull his weight around the house. And that includes him grocery shopping, cooking, and fending for himself, as well as helping us out with household chores. He is an adult and we really need him to act like one."

John nodded in agreement and added, "We have tried every which way to get him to be responsible, but I think we both realize we haven't been consistent and that ultimately, we're enabling his behavior."

In almost every case like this, parents are completely aware that they are enabling their kids. They really just need someone else to essentially give them permission to take a different approach and to take their power back. That's where I came in. The next step was to sit down with all three of them. So, we went down the basement stairs into Marty's room. His parents entered first, and I went in behind them. The room was pretty much what I had expected and seen dozens of times before—messy, dark, food wrappers and soda cans strewn about, and a lanky kid in sweats comfortably ensconced in his easy chair. It had the look and feel of a college dorm room. He gave a halfhearted eye roll when he saw his parents, but the moment his eyes registered me, he sat up a little straighter and his pupils dilated a bit—classic deer-in-the-headlights style. My size has a tendency to strike just a bit of fear in guys, and in this instance, that was useful.

"Marty," his dad started, "your mother and I have talked to you before about your living arrangements, but today is the day things are going to change. This is Coach Mike, and we've asked him to be here today."

"Hey, Marty. Nice to meet you," I said.

"Um. Yeah. So, what exactly is going on?" He stood up, a look of bewilderment spreading across his face.

"We love you very much, as you know, but we've been enabling you and not helping you with your life, so moving forward, things are going to be different," Cindy said, with a calm strength that surprised Marty. From there we sat down and talked about a specific plan that Marty had to follow in order to remain living at the house, with a clear out-by date. They informed him that we'd be handling this in phases—I'd be coming to meet with the family once a week for a period of time to make sure everyone was living up to their expectations (him following the rules, them not enabling), and then once every two weeks as we developed and progressed through the steps of the strategy. There was no room for Marty to interject or disagree. He had one choice to make. He could agree to this new regime and follow through on his part, or he could move out right away.

You see, sometimes a person isn't going to go through the precontemplation, contemplation, and preparation stages on their own. In this case, with that particular set of circumstances, Marty had no impetus for going through those stages of change. He did not *want* to change! But his parents, once they became a united front and had a clear strategy, helped push him right into Action. The consequences of Marty choosing not to follow their new rules were tangible, so that served as motivation for him.

Once he was in Action—and remember it was his *choice* to be in Action ultimately, because his parents made him choose between shaping up or moving out—he started to feel good about himself. There was a transition period, and of course he had his moments of backsliding, but overall, he was becoming a participant in his life instead of a spectator. Eventually, we all agreed it would be best for him to branch out and find a job outside of the family business, so he interviewed and got an entry-level position selling insurance. We continued to have our meetings and evaluate where they were in the process and strategize moving forward. The more independence Marty achieved, the higher his self-esteem got, and the less defensive he became toward his parents. He was morphing from a recalcitrant teen into a team player and active member of the family and of society.

About a year after that initial meeting, Cindy called me with an update: "Mike, I just can't believe the transformation I've seen in Marty. He moved into his own little apartment, and on the day he moved out, I went to look around the basement to see if he left anything behind, and I saw the video game console still by the TV. I mentioned it to him and he said he was done with video games—because they wasted too much time! Imagine that! And you know what else? He's got a girlfriend! And she's lovely! Thank you so much!"

"Of course! Be proud of yourself, too. I know you and John had to work hard to stick to the plan, but you persevered."

Getting ourselves into Action as quickly as possible pays off because we begin to see ourselves in a new light. We witness first-hand that we are capable of what's required of us, because we're actually starting to *do* it! We have absolutely nothing to lose by just diving in and initiating change in our lives—but we have a lot to lose if we choose to put it off. That's when days can turn into weeks, and weeks into months—and then suddenly, we realize we've just wasted years doing things the same old way when we could've been using that time to evolve and improve our life in different and amazing ways.

Preparing Your Way . . .

Lady Gaga once said, "Don't ever let a soul in the world tell you that you can't be exactly who you are." She's exactly right, and sometimes it's *you* who's in your way of being exactly who you are. That's why in the next chapter, you're going to learn how to identify and handle any obstacles that could threaten your progress toward living each day as your Best Self. We don't want anything holding you back!

4

Identifying Your Obstacles

On any journey, roadblocks are to be expected. They can take various shapes, and they differ slightly for each of us. As you work toward your Best Self, I want you to keep your eyes open and be aware of anything that's blocking you from success. If you can see a potential roadblock coming, you can figure out a detour.

There are some universal themes when it comes to these roadblocks, and we'll go over those in this chapter so that you can identify any potential areas you need to focus on or walls you need to tear down. If you can really understand what's blocking you from connecting with your core, you can discover just how to remove it and continue on.

Fear Inventory Quiz

All too often in our lives, we succumb to fears. We may not realize that fear is at the heart of something that we're allowing to stand in our way, so an imperative step is to examine what's holding us back and find out whether fear is at the heart of it. Franklin D. Roosevelt famously said in his inaugural address, "The only thing we have to fear is fear itself." Why is that? Fear is a liar. It would have you believe that you are not good enough, that you are not capable enough, that everyone is judging you, and then you act accordingly. Most of the time, the things we are afraid of never even occur. Imagine that—we are spending time and energy worrying about something that never plays out. What if we were able to use that brainpower on positive action, on something that helps us move forward in our life, instead of making us stand still, stuck right where we are? We can. It's possible. It begins by getting honest with ourselves about our fears so that they can't become entrenched in our minds.

I don't want any fears standing between you and your Best Self, so let's take the time to identify them and then tackle them, one by one.

Part 1: What are you afraid of?

We're going to start this process off with a little free association. I'm going to ask you a question, and I want you to start writing down all the words that come to mind immediately after you read it. Don't hesitate for even a moment—just start writing. And don't stop until you run out of words or start repeating them.

Looking at what we are afraid of is a vital step in this process, though it's a very powerful and often emotional exercise. It's tough shining a light on your fears, but it's so worth it in the end. All of us, at some point in our lives, have allowed fear to have power over us in some way. Once you've mastered the ability to recognize what triggers your fear as well as, crucially, when it starts, you can keep fear from taking root and actually shaping your life. *You* call the shots in your life, not fear. So, let's clear out the fear!

Ready? Good. Now, here's the question:

What are some of the fears that have held you back from making changes in your life?

_____

_____

_____

_____

_____

Part 2: Fear Pattern

You may not have realized that some of those fears were prowling around in your mind, or maybe you've just been avoiding them. What I want you to know right now is that you are not alone. Other people have overcome these same fears. You can, too. By being bold and brave enough to bring those fears to the forefront, you've just taken the first step in facing them down. Now, let's take the next step.

Looking at your list, do you notice any patterns? Can you easily group several of your fears into broader categories such as humiliation, worthlessness, or lack of approval? Maybe most of your fears boil down to the notion of you not being lovable or valuable to others? When you look at the list, does one overall theme seem to be present? For instance, does the through-line seem to be that you're afraid you can't stick with the plan required for your life to change? Or are you petrified of failure? Of what other people think? That you don't deserve better? Take a close look and then write down what you see.

The overarching reason I've been afraid to change is:

_____

_____

_____

_____

_____

Part 3: Put Your Fear to the Test

You're doing great—look how much you've just learned about yourself in a matter of minutes! When we really start asking these questions, we begin to understand ourselves and our motivations on a whole new level. Now, let's build on the great work you've done so far.

Think of your brain as a muscle. In the same way you can go to the gym and strengthen your biceps through training, you can train your brain. In fact, whether you're doing it purposely or not, you're constantly training your brain to think in certain ways. Taking that concept a step further, it could be that you've inadvertently trained your brain to be afraid of things that you don't need to fear. That's right; you might be operating every single day and making decisions around a fear of something that isn't *real*.

For the sake of clarity, I'll give you a simple example. Let's say you are preparing for a presentation at work. You've prepared your talking points, you've done your research, and you know just what you want to say. But every time you go to practice the talk, you freeze up, paralyzed with fear. You're imagining all of your coworkers laughing out loud as you stand at the head of the conference table. You see yourself showing up to the meeting naked. You fixate on a certain point you want to make and get tongue-tied every time you try to utter it. The reality is—it's a two-minute presentation that is well within your abilities and experience, but your mind is caught up in a sticky spiderweb of fears run amok. If you believe the lies that your fear is telling you, it can have real-life consequences.

In your everyday life, are you spending valuable time and energy being afraid of something that isn't real and poses no actual threat to you? Are you letting it drive your decision making on a big scale? Has your imagination gotten the best of you?

Refer to your answer in Part 2—the reason you've been afraid to change. Now, let's test that fear:

1. Is it factually true?
2. Does it serve your best interests?
3. Does it generate progress toward healthy goals?

These questions can help you determine if your fear is rational or not.

For example, if you're miserable in your job and you want to start your own business, have you been afraid that you won't be able to make ends meet or you'll lose everything? That could be a very rational fear, but there is a way to address it. What is going to help you overcome that fear and start that business? The answer is a financial safety net. In this case, you've identified a fear of financial ruin, so the way to prevent that fear from becoming a reality is to save up enough money that you can survive for _____ number of months (you fill in the blank with what makes you comfortable) before you quit your current job. In so doing, you've mitigated the risk and effectively abolished that fear. Now that you've moved that fear obstacle out of the way, you can confidently continue on your journey toward being your own boss.

So, now I want you to write down your rational, legitimate fear, what it's stopping you from doing in your life, and then create a plan that you can put into place to prevent the fear from becoming a reality.

My fear is: _____

_____

_____

_____

It is keeping me from: _____

_____

_____

_____

My plan for preventing my fear from becoming a reality is:

_____

_____

_____

Here's an example:

My fear is: *Being rejected*

It is keeping me from: *Trying new things, meeting new people, and allowing life to work itself out. It causes anxiety when I have to meet new people, it makes me feel like I'm not myself when I'm around coworkers because I'm wanting them to like me, and I feel the need to try to control everything.*

My plan for preventing my fear from becoming a reality is: *To remind myself when I feel rejected that life is trying to deliver something new and better, and to find happiness in that belief.*

Do this as many times as you need for as many fears as are standing in your way. Once you've got a plan in place for each one, you have taken the power away from the fear and therefore rendered it powerless.

Part 4: Faith Beats Fear Every Time

I believe the opposite of fear is faith. There's an old English proverb that I had inscribed on a key chain years ago. It says, "Fear knocked at the door. Faith answered. No one was there." If you have faith that things are going to work out and faith in yourself that you are capable of doing what's required, then you take all power away from your fears, and in fact, your fears cease to exist. For many people, getting past our fears is a matter of letting go of them and replacing them with faith.

The next time you recognize that fear has crept in and is keeping you from positive change, try this visualization technique:

1. Close your eyes and imagine the fear. Gather up all the visual images in your mind that accompany the fear, as well as the negative feelings it produces within you.
2. Now put all of those items inside a big, cardboard box in your mind.
3. Then, make the box smaller, and smaller, and smaller until it fits right into the palm of your hand.
4. Now imagine yourself standing at the edge of a giant canyon, so deep that you can't see the bottom.
5. Throw the box in and watch it fall until it's out of sight.
6. Imagine yourself turning around, and when you do, there's an outdoor shower.
7. Turn on the water, and let a warm, loving sensation wash over your entire body.
8. Open your eyes and embrace the feeling of being refreshed and renewed by your faith.

You can return to this visualization anytime you need to, as it can strengthen you and help you have freedom over your fears.

Ego vs. Your Best Self: It's Your Choice

I consider ego to be the single biggest threat to your ability to operate as your Best Self. To be clear, I'm not a psychoanalyst, so I'm not looking at ego from a Freudian perspective. When I talk about ego, I'm defining it as a deep-seated level of fear, not an obvious fear like one of spiders or dogs, but one that is related to how we feel about ourselves and how we think the world perceives us. When we let fears really take root inside of us, they can become part of us—sort of like they've been written into the DNA of our personality. It sounds insidious, I know, but it can happen so easily.

If you occasionally find yourself thinking, doing, or saying things that aren't really "you," that's ego. Anytime that you snap or lash out at someone, or you get into a heated argument where it feels like you're not in control anymore, that's ego. Or if you claim to be better at something than you really are in order to avoid embarrassment, or if you overpromise and underdeliver, even if you tell a little, white lie—those are all manifestations of ego. You can probably think of more examples, too—we all get caught up in ego from time to time. But I don't want you to let your ego stand in your way of being your Best Self!

Here's the really exciting news—if you're worried that ego is blocking you, there's hope! You will be able to wrangle your ego much more easily than you might think, and I'm going to help you. Let's get busy discovering first how to recognize ego and then how to silence it.

Step 1: Recognizing Ego

In order to really understand whether our ego is sitting in the driver's seat in some aspect of our lives, we need to understand the types of thoughts, feelings, and resulting actions we might have when under its spell. And keep in mind, ego doesn't always manifest in the form of extremes. We can all probably point to someone in popular culture, professional sports, or politics that we'd deem as an "egomaniac," or at minimum an "egoist." I'm not here to point fingers, so I'll refrain from naming names. But the point is, there's never any shortage of extreme examples of ego gone wild in our world. Yours, however, might show up in subtler ways. Our reactions can be unpleasant when we're steeped in our ego, and that's no fun for us or for those around us. I want to save you a lot of time and heartache by helping you tune in and become acutely aware of when you're acting in your ego rather than in your Best Self.

Here are some common ways in which ego can show its ugly head in our lives. There are the more obvious big-headed egos, and then there are the quieter, harder-to-recognize fears driven by ego, so I'm separating these examples into those two categories. This is not an exhaustive list, but it gives you the general impression of what ego can look like in your life.

Big-headed Ego/Obvious examples

Defensiveness

- Have you ever talked to someone and found them overly reactive? If you respond with "You're being defensive" and they can't own it or they deny it that's defensiveness; it's a lack of ability to take constructive criticism.

Right fighting/Need to win

- This is when someone goes above and beyond to prove that something they said was true. They may even spend a few hours investing in the fight just to prove they were right.

Pride/Boasting

- This is a form of selfishness/self-obsession, a constant need to remind everyone around them how awesome they are. For example, think about the former football star who still talks about his glory days twenty years ago whenever the opportunity presents itself.

Revenge

- When someone purposely hurts others who they feel have wronged them. They use faulty logic to justify their actions.
- They believe it helps them to take other people down.

Possessiveness

- These are people who refuse to share. They shield anything they view as their "possession" (including people!) from others.

Talking poorly about others

- Online or in real life, these people believe they will feel better about themselves by speaking ill of others. They often take pleasure in landing the perfect insult or crafting a nasty narrative about someone else.

The "gym flexors"

- People who are so driven by insecurity that they are constantly looking at themselves in the mirror . . . at the gym, in window reflections, their rearview mirror, their phone camera (selfies!), and so on and so on . . .

Dishonesty

- People who are afraid to get real and honest for fear of judgment, rejection, etc., will indulge in lies about themselves or others in order to create a false reality they like better than the real one.
- Those who lie by omission, leaving out important details from their lives or narratives in order to protect their façade.

Bullying

- I think one of the ultimate expressions of ego run amok is when someone resorts to threatening or intimidating others. This is a serious problem in society today, and it's a direct result of ego.

Victim mentality

- This is when someone refuses to accept their part in a problem. (We're going to explore this one in more depth in an upcoming portion of this chapter, as I believe this issue is currently rampant, and a behavior I don't want you to fall in to!) *Important: There are real victims of terrible circumstances, but those are not the folks I'm talking about here. A victim of a crime is different than someone with a victim mentality. Just being offended by something does not make you an actual victim and is disrespectful and hurtful to real victims.*

Less Obvious Examples of Ego

Seeking outside approval/reward

- Those who build their self-esteem solely through others' opinions of them.

Not being able to be alone

- People who are afraid of loneliness are generally this way because it doesn't give them the rush/validation they need.

False Advocates

- These are the folks who bully others because they do not subscribe to their same worldview. This is a prevalent issue today on college campuses. I've also seen people online who claim they are mental health advocates, but who also bully other people for their beliefs.

Offended by criticism

- These people don't believe they have character flaws or any need to grow. Instead of accepting criticism, sitting with it, considering if/how they could apply it to their life, it only hurts their pride and often causes them to lash out.

Stuck in the past

- Those who cling to their past life when their present life isn't giving them the feelings of importance or positive experiences that they once had.
- Another version of this manifestation of ego is people who remind others of negative experiences from the past, as a way to inflict guilt or pain.

Insecurity/self-doubt

- Those crippled by feelings of inadequacy, who are constantly seeking out something to compensate for their feeling of insignificance, either by making others feel insecure or through self-isolation.

Constant apologizing (to the point of coming across as false)

- People who say "I'm sorry" on repeat do so because they have a deep desire to be liked and approved by others because they haven't accepted themselves.

Worrying about what others think

- Someone plagued with a constant anxiety about themselves (their looks, performance, status, intelligence, etc.), and who looks to other people to define their significance and worth.

Sometimes it's tough to recognize these kinds of behavior in ourselves, so a good way to get to the truth is to ask a trusted friend or loved one whether they've ever witnessed you behaving out of ego. It's not always easy to hear the answers, but I encourage you to remain open to their constructive feedback.

Another great way to test your thoughts or behaviors to discover whether their origins are in ego is to ask your Best Self what he or she thinks. You can literally stage a conversation between yourself and your Best Self character and discuss it. Ask, "Am I behaving in this way because of some type of deep-seated fear, or am I acting on behalf of my Best Self?" or "Is this behavior indicative of my Best Self, or does it appear to be coming from a place of ego?" Prompts like those can easily help you get to your own answers about thought patterns or behaviors in which you are currently engaging. Think of the last time that you were very frustrated, anxious, or just overall didn't like the way a moment played out. What would your Best Self have done in that moment, or how would your Best Self have reacted to that moment? That can help you get really specific about it.

Now, if any of the qualities/manifestations of ego we've talked about so far remind you of things you've said or done, or if they are similar to some of the Anti-Self traits you wrote down in chapter 2, I don't want you to pathologize. Nothing is wrong with you. As I mentioned earlier, we all get caught up in ego from time to time. The goal is simply to begin to recognize ego at work in your life so that you can take control over it, instead of letting it take control of you.

Refuse to Play the Blame Game

If I had to choose one pervasive mentality in today's culture that I would deem the most dangerous, I would select the *victim* mentality.

Playing the role of the victim means pointing the finger at someone or something outside yourself for things that are going wrong in your own life. This has to do with something called your "locus of control."

Someone who has an internal locus of control believes that he or she can influence events and their outcomes, but someone with an external locus of control blames outside forces (other people, circumstances, or even fate) for everything. Everywhere I look in today's society, it seems that more and more people have an external locus of control. For example, if someone is having trouble getting a job and they blame it on the current political or economic landscape, they are demonstrating an external locus of control. Or if they often catch colds and blame them on their coworkers or germ-riddled work environment, that's an external locus of control mind-set. Another one is when someone is constantly in debt, and they blame inflation or the high cost of living rather than taking responsibility for their own financial planning and budgeting. If someone goes through a divorce or bad breakup and is still in pain five years later and blaming it on the ex, that's an external locus of control. Essentially, we are choosing to have an external locus of control anytime that we are pointing the finger away from ourselves for anything going on in our life.

Here's the problem with this kind of thinking: it takes away your power. By playing the blame game, you're effectively throwing up your hands and saying, "Well, I'm a victim, and there's not a damn thing I can do about it." The moment you blame someone else for something you're feeling or experiencing is the moment that you give up your power. By giving your power away, you are making a decision to effectively let life happen to you. You are refusing to take responsibility for your own life. As you might imagine, that can be a very destructive pattern to set. In order to stay connected with our Best Self, we need to always take responsibility for what happens in our life. We need to find a way to have control, even in moments where it just seems like the world is out to get us.

Sure, bad things happen that are outside of our control. But here's the key—we are 100 percent in control of our reactions to those things. We can choose to spiral into depression, anxiety, anger, resentment, or frustration and just pull the covers back over our head. Or we can choose to react in a way that benefits us and those around us. If we fail a test, we can analyze what went wrong, and study in a more effective way before taking it again. If we keep catching a cold, we can learn about how to boost our immunity and overall health. The list goes on and on—but the bottom line is that we have a choice: blame someone or something else that we can't control, or find a way we can take responsibility and change what we're doing so we can change the outcome.

Here are some questions to help you determine if you're playing the blame game in certain areas of your life:

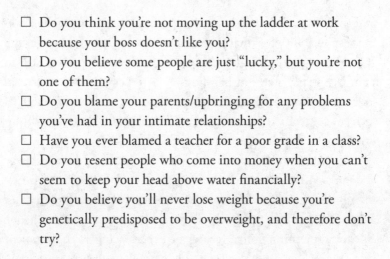

☐ Do you think you're not moving up the ladder at work because your boss doesn't like you?

☐ Do you believe some people are just "lucky," but you're not one of them?

☐ Do you blame your parents/upbringing for any problems you've had in your intimate relationships?

☐ Have you ever blamed a teacher for a poor grade in a class?

☐ Do you resent people who come into money when you can't seem to keep your head above water financially?

☐ Do you believe you'll never lose weight because you're genetically predisposed to be overweight, and therefore don't try?

These specific questions may or may not apply to you, but they should give you an idea of what victim mentality looks like. I want to put you on high alert for any area of your life where you might be passing the blame for your own unhappiness, lack of success, or tough situations onto someone or something else.

Something else to keep in mind is that your locus of control applies to both good and bad things in your life. So, if we accomplish something positive like winning an award, saving up a certain amount of money, or even just having a good day, saying that it was because of someone or something else rather than acknowledging our part in the accomplishment is also an example of external locus of control. It's not about hogging all the credit for yourself, but it's definitely important for us to recognize the role we play in *all* aspects of our own lives.

Remember, other people may do or say something that is intended to harm you, but ultimately *you* decide how those things will affect you. All of the outside interference is just noise. You're in control of the volume, so turn it off! Your feelings are your own—don't let others influence them.

Step 2: Turn Off the Noise of Ego

Anytime we think to ourselves, "I'm not smart enough for this," or "I need to prove myself in this area," or "I'm terrified of _____ (getting fired, not being noticed, being rejected, failing, etc.)," those are all "noise," or ego-based thoughts. And they're all fear-related. Lack of confidence is fear. A need for approval by others is fear. And any time we are outright saying to ourselves that we're afraid of something, and thus we need to do something to avoid that fear coming true, we are acting purely out of fear.

Luckily, there is a powerful antidote to these fear-based thoughts. They are called self-affirmations, and they are the essential truths about ourselves. If you look back to your Best Self characteristics in chapter 1, those are affirmations that you have already created. They are ready for you to use. As you know, these traits make up the true essence of *you*. By naming them and by knowing them, they become an energy that pushes fear out of focus.

I once worked with a woman who I believed attracted incredible greatness in her life because every day she would say the most kind and loving self-affirmations to herself. She was an incredible actress, who was divorced and raising several children, and when we worked together it became clear that her self-affirmations were what she needed to stay grounded.

Affirmations are like food for the soul. They can regenerate us energetically. I'm constantly amazed at how many people I talk to who have never actually done a self-affirmation. I don't know how they get through life without them! Granted, they aren't always easy to do, but they're powerful.

Remember, there is no "right" or perfect way to do this exercise, or any exercise in this book, for that matter. Find what feels comfortable for you or use these instructions more as inspiration for creating your own version.

Exercise: Self-Affirmations

- Look in a mirror or your phone. Typically, when we look in the mirror, we are purely looking at our aesthetics: the outfit we're wearing, our hair, or maybe we even zero in on a mole we should have checked. But for our purposes, you're looking beyond aesthetics. When was the last time you looked, and I mean really looked, into your own eyes?

- What do you see? Who are you? What are some things that you truly love about yourself? Do you see someone who is strong? Kind? Generous? Loyal? Loving? Funny? Outgoing? Quiet? Think about words that describe not how the world sees you, but how you see yourself, **positive** words that are *true* about you, on every level.

- The ego inside of you may make this difficult in that it might make you drift away from your positive attributes and toward negative aspects. You might even think something **positive** like "I'm a loving person," but then that ego voice pops up and says, "Yeah, but if people really got to know you, they'd discover you're not *that* lovable." Be aware of that voice.

- Write down 5–10 truths about yourself, starting with the phrase "I am _____ ..." Fill them in here:

    1. I am _____

    2. I am _____

    3. I am _____

    4. I am _____

    5. I am _____

    6. I am _____

7. I am _____

8. I am _____

9. I am _____

10. I am _____

Now, say these sentences out loud to yourself, while looking in the mirror.

The first time people try out self-affirmations, they can be a little intimidating or even make you feel foolish, but I promise it gets easier with time. They are a cornerstone of the work we'll be doing together because they get to the heart of who you are inside, and they help you stay connected to your Best Self.

Turn Down the Noise

These days, there is more information coming at us than we could possibly process, and it's very easy to let all that "noise" keep us from getting what we want and from staying clear in our minds. This is why I have gotten very careful about what type of content I allow into my own life. Just as we must be careful about the types of foods we eat to make sure our bodies are properly nourished, I believe we must also be choosy about the information we consume. We need to nourish our mind, not inundate it with junk content that doesn't serve us or feed our passions.

We're constantly being bombarded with information we don't choose, and it can feel like we're being forced to listen to a type of music we don't want to hear. Think about billboards, commercials, ads on social media, pop-ups on websites, the list is endless!

Add it all up and suddenly the noise overtakes everything else. The result can be that we become reactive or irritable and not even really know why. It used to be that we had more control over the information stream we consumed. Now it is just pouring in from all angles, at all times.

You might find yourself having an emotional reaction to something you saw in the news. I think that's due in part to this concept of a panel of "experts" debating each other about the news of the day. They often discuss, in great detail, the lives of people they don't know personally. Imagine if that panel were talking about *you*, as if they knew what was going on in your life? It's bizarre. I do believe you should be informed about world affairs, but I encourage you to receive that information from sources that you trust to deliver it in a factual, nonbiased way so that you don't get caught up in the ego of it all. When you turn off the news, you should feel more educated, not more inflamed.

Here's a question—are you turning up the volume on your Best Self, or are you creating more noise? There are ways to cut through the noise, and even make your noise more beneficial. For example, on your social media platforms, you can choose to only follow thought leaders that you're interested in, thereby turning up the volume on the information that is useful to you on your journey. On the flip side, I've learned to unfollow people on social media if they fill me with negative thoughts. I can love who someone is but just not like the noise they're making online. It doesn't mean I can't be friends with them; it just means I don't want to hear the noise.

I once worked with a country music artist who had all the makings of a superstar. He had such talent and good looks, yet he allowed the noise of life to interfere and keep him from his own potential. In this case, the noise came in the form of Internet trolls who relentlessly harassed him on social media. Anyone with even one ounce of fame can tell you this type of harassment is par for the course these days, but this particular artist made a fatal mistake—he engaged the trolls. Never engage the trolls! Once he got too far down the road of communicating with these people, he reached a point of no return, and when he looked up, his career was a smoldering pile of ashes all around him. He just could not turn down the noise and he paid a price. When Dr. Phil and I talk about this topic, he says, "If you roll with the pigs, you're going to get muddy, and the pigs like it!"

Over the past few years, my own career has become more public, and more people comment about me online now. Being in the public eye is a new thing for me—up until very recently, I've worked strictly behind the scenes. Even in that, there was a lot of noise. Now that my work and life are far more public, the noise is louder. And, when noise is directed at you by people who don't know you, remember that you don't owe them a thing—you don't need to read what they're saying, and you most certainly don't need to respond. Stay focused on your own goals.

Could Your Routine Be Blocking Your Progress?

Your routine, and especially your morning routine, can either help or hinder your mission to be aligned with your Best Self. With just some simple adjustments, you can create a routine and daily rhythm that helps make this alignment much easier to achieve.

I always say that it's important to greet the day rather than let the day greet you. By this I mean, set your clock at night and determine that you are going to wake up with a positive intention

ENJOY YOUR UNIQUE JOURNEY

From time to time, we've all fallen into the trap of comparing ourselves to someone else. In today's social media–obsessed society, it seems there are more ways than ever for us to compare our lives to the lives of others. For example, I could go online and compare myself to other life coaches out there—ones who have far more followers than I and speak all over the country—but my intention in doing so would be to measure where I'm better or worse than them. No thanks, as that would just be an ego-driven intention, and one that wouldn't be coming from my Best Self. Sure, I could trick myself into believing that I'm just looking to learn or to do research. But the bottom line is that if I'm on the road to enhance, and do good work to help others, I need to focus on the people who inspire me, not people to whom I'm comparing myself.

Everyone experiences feelings of inadequacy. At times, we've all felt unlovable, we've all felt like we're not enough. That's part of our journey and we all have to go through those patches. I've worked with families from all across the world—rich, poor, and everything in between—and I can tell you that the struggle is all internal. Have some solutions in place for the next time those feelings sneak in—now that you have some awareness, it's time to create some solutions that you can easily implement when you need to.

for the day. I also encourage you to begin the day by spending just a few minutes focusing on all the things in your life for which you are grateful. Try to think about the intangibles when you make this gratitude list; it's less about material objects and more about the gifts in our lives that mean the most to us. Creating this inner gratitude list can set your day on the right path. You can do this at any time that makes sense in your morning. When I'm at home in the morning, I sit in my favorite chair with my feet up, and I put one of my pillows on the back so it's very comfortable.

Remember to keep your routine authentic to you. Ask yourself, is this realistic for me, and will it make it easier for me to tap into who I really am? For example, if every morning you wake up only when your child cries out for you, and you never have a moment thereafter to catch your breath, your routine could certainly be blocking your progress. It's tough to connect with your Best Self if your roller-coaster lifestyle kicks in before you've taken a moment to check in with yourself. You can think about your gratitude list when you're commuting to work, or when you roll out of bed, you go straight outside for a walk, and that's when you focus on what you're grateful for—however you need to arrange it.

Some other morning rituals to consider are writing out your goals for the day, doing yoga or stretching, listening to meditative music, starting off your day with a healthy meal that gives you energy, and doing affirmations in the mirror after you shower.

Whatever your current situation might be, I encourage you to experiment with some new routines and see what works best for you.

Plug into the Power of Rituals

In order to combat any number of things that may be blocking your ability to be your Best Self, I want to share with you something more that has worked for me in amazing ways—plugging into the power of rituals.

Do you recall the ritual that I shared with you in the introduction? It powerfully aligns me for my day, every day. I do this ritual before important meetings, I've done it before every writing session for this book. I do this ritual all the time! Now it's your turn.

Exercise: What's Your Mantra?

- Think about what phrase, when said while you look yourself in the mirror, is going to pump you up, energize you, connect yourself with your core, and make you feel humble, so that you're not acting out of ego or trying to prove yourself.
- Remember: your mantra doesn't have to be the same for the rest of your life—I've changed mine multiple times. It should evolve as you do. Some of my mantras have been: "You are enough." "You got this." "Be yourself." "It's God's plan." "You're better than you think you are."

Once you've discovered your mantra, I suggest you create some kind of ritual around how you say it to yourself. As you read earlier, I like to look at myself in the eyes, kneel down as a symbolic gesture, and then say my mantra. This works for me, but you need to find what works well for you. You might need to try a few different methods to determine what feels right. Some people I've worked with liked to clear out their dressing room a few minutes before they had to walk out on a stage, and they'd do breathing exercises. Or another client liked to write out twenty-five things they were grateful for each day and that was their daily mantra. It could even be playing with your pet first thing when you wake up in the morning.

Once you have created your own, specific mantra, now it's time to put it into use. I suggest doing your mantra before you give a work presentation, before a date, before a difficult conversation, before a family event, and anything else you do that is important to you and for which you want to be aligned with your truth. People around you will feel that positive energy you've created within yourself.

Moving Forward

I know we covered a lot of ground in this chapter. Remember, you can refer back to the information and exercises here anytime that you're feeling blocked in some way, if you're worrying about something or feeling afraid. And remember that you can always ask your Best Self what you need to do!

We're now going to get very specific in helping you truly align with your Best Self so that you can embrace your ideal life. We're going to accomplish this by entering into the seven SPHERES of your life. You're now ready and prepared for this journey, and if you take it seriously, then you can rest assured that your life is about to change for the better.

5

Your Social Life

There are assessment and screening tools in almost all industries. A doctor or therapist has clinical assessments, but I wanted to create a screening tool that would be appropriate for life coaching work. That's why I created the SPHERES, which look at every area of a person's life to help him or her to identify their strengths and weaknesses. SPHERES stands for Social life, Personal life, Health, Education, Relationships, Employment, and Spiritual life.

In this chapter, we are focusing on the first "S" in the SPHERES acronym, which stands for Social life. For our purposes, we are going to be looking at your social life in terms of your communication skills, but we're also going to really dive into how you feel in your own skin when you are interacting with others. Are you able to be your Best Self in any social situation?

You might wonder why we're spending time looking at your social life, as you may not really think of it as a priority. Well, as you know, the main objective I want to help you achieve in this book is to find the freedom to be your Best Self *at all times*—which means when you're alone, when you're with loved ones, and when you're out living in the world. You've already begun to make this shift *internally*, so now we need to focus on how you can shift into your Best Self *externally*.

At the end of this and every SPHERES chapter, you will find a quiz that will help see in very clear terms what is working in this area of your life, what's not working, and what types of actions will help you move past any roadblocks in this area. First, let's work through the chapter and do some thinking about your social life.

The Benefits of Socializing

There's been quite a bit of research around the positive power of socializing. You might be surprised to learn that spending time engaging with other people can induce feelings of happiness, combat depression, and even increase your brainpower.

Researchers at the University of Michigan found that "social interaction helps to exercise people's minds. People reap cognitive benefits from socializing. It is possible that as people engage socially and mentally with others, they receive relatively immediate cognitive boosts."* So you can think of socializing as a form of exercise for your brain—it can help make you smarter in the same way that exercising your body makes you stronger.

In a Gallup-Healthways survey of more than 140,000 Americans, researchers discovered that we are happiest on days when

---

* The article, "Mental Exercising Through Simple Socializing: Social Interaction Promotes General Cognitive Functioning," written by Oscar Ybarra, Eugene Burnstein, Piotr Winkielman, Matthew C. Keller, Melvin Manis, Emily Chan, and Joel Rodriguez of the University of Michigan, and published by SAGE in the February issue of *Personality and Social Psychology Bulletin*.

we spend 6–7 hours socializing with friends or family.* That says a lot right there! How much time we spend socializing directly correlates to our happiness. Building time into your schedule for interacting with friends or family is important, and I would even argue that it will enrich your life when you make new friends along the way.

As you continue on your unique journey, think about ways you can tap into the energy and ideas of people around you. You never know when inspiration or a true connection might strike—it could be in a meditation group or the line at the grocery store! But it won't be found if you're sitting home alone on your couch!

Social Skills Inventory

The following inventory exercise can help you take a step back and look at how you interact with others in an objective manner. As you go through, make sure you fully understand each statement before you answer, and then answer as honestly as you can.

* James Harter and Raksha Arora, "Social Time Crucial to Daily Emotional Well-Being in U.S.," www.gallup.com, June 5, 2008.

PART 1: Sending Clear Messages

	USUALLY	SOMETIMES	SELDOM
1. Is it difficult for you to talk to other people?			
2. When you are trying to explain something, do others tend to put words in your mouth, or finish your sentences for you?			
3. In conversation, do your words usually come out the way you would like?			
4. Do you find it difficult to express your ideas when they differ from the ideas of people around you?			
5. Do you assume that the other person knows what you are trying to say, and leave it to him/her to ask you questions?			
6. Do others seem interested and attentive when you are talking to them?			
7. When speaking, is it easy for you to recognize how others are reacting to what you are saying?			
8. Do you ask the other person to tell you how she/he feels about the point you are trying to make?			
9. Are you aware of how your tone of voice may affect others?			
10. In conversation, do you look to talk about things of interest to both you and the other person?			

PART 2: Listening

	USUALLY	SOMETIMES	SELDOM
11. In conversation, do you tend to do more talking than the other person does?			
12. In conversation, do you ask the other person questions when you don't understand what they've said?			
13. In conversation, do you often try to figure out what the other person is going to say before they've finished talking?			
14. Do you find yourself not paying attention while in conversation with others?			
15. In conversation, can you easily tell the difference between what the person is saying and how he/she may be feeling?			
16. After the other person is done speaking, do you clarify what you heard them say before you offer a response?			
17. In conversation, do you tend to finish sentences or supply words for the other person?			
18. In conversation, do you find yourself paying the most attention to facts and details, and frequently missing the emotional tone of the speakers' voice?			
19. In conversation, do you let the other person finish talking before reacting to what she/he says?			
20. Is it difficult for you to see things from the other person's point of view?			

PART 3: Giving and Receiving Feedback

	USUALLY	SOMETIMES	SELDOM
21. Is it difficult to hear or accept constructive criticism from the other person?			
22. Do you refrain from saying something that you think will upset someone or make matters worse?			
23. When someone hurts your feelings, do you discuss this with him/her?			
24. In conversation, do you try to put yourself in the other person's shoes?			
25. Do you become uneasy when someone pays you a compliment?			
26. Do you find it difficult to disagree with others because you are afraid they will get angry?			
27. Do you find it difficult to compliment or praise others?			
28. Do others remark that you always seem to think you are right?			
29. Do you find that others seem to get defensive when you disagree with their point of view?			
30. Do you help others to understand you by saying how you feel?			

PART 4: Handling Emotional Interactions

	USUALLY	SOMETIMES	SELDOM
31. Do you have a tendency to change the subject when the other person's feelings enter into the discussion?			
32. Does it upset you a great deal when someone disagrees with you?			
33. Do you find it difficult to think clearly when you are angry with someone?			
34. When a problem arises between you and another person, can you discuss it without getting angry?			
35. Are you satisfied with the way you handle differences with others?			
36. Do you sulk for a long time when someone upsets you?			
37. Do you apologize to someone whose feelings you may have hurt?			
38. Do you admit when you're wrong?			
39. Do you avoid or change the topic if someone is expressing his or her feelings in a conversation?			
40. When someone becomes upset, do you find it difficult to continue the conversation?			

* Adapted from *Learning Resources*, 2002.

Scoring Key

Good work completing the inventory! I hope you can already see how it is useful to look at how clearly you currently communicate with others. Now go back and look over all of your answers and in front of each question, write the appropriate score using this table.

For example, if you answered "usually" for Question 1, you would write down 0 in front of Question 1 on the inventory. If you answered "seldom" for Question 2, write down a 3 in front of Question 2.

Each part of the inventory has ten total questions. After you've scored them all, add them up and then write them below. Repeat the process for all four parts.

Part 1 (Sending Clear Messages)   Total Score: _____

Part 2 (Listening)   Total Score: _____

Part 3 (Giving and Receiving Feedback)   Total Score: _____

Part 4 (Handling Emotional Interactions) Total Score: _____

SCORING KEY

QUESTION	USUALLY	SOMETIMES	SELDOM	QUESTION	USUALLY	SOMETIMES	SELDOM
1	0	1	3	21	0	1	3
2	0	1	3	22	3	1	0
3	3	1	0	23	3	1	0
4	0	1	3	24	3	1	0
5	0	1	3	25	0	1	3
6	3	1	0	26	0	1	3
7	3	1	0	27	0	1	3
8	3	1	0	28	0	1	3
9	3	1	0	29	0	1	3
10	3	1	0	30	3	1	0
11	0	1	3	31	0	1	3

QUESTION	USUALLY	SOMETIMES	SELDOM	QUESTION	USUALLY	SOMETIMES	SELDOM
12	3	1	0	32	0	1	3
13	0	1	3	33	0	1	3
14	0	1	3	34	3	1	0
15	3	1	0	35	3	1	0
16	3	1	0	36	0	1	3
17	0	1	3	37	3	1	0
18	0	1	3	38	3	1	0
19	3	1	0	39	0	1	3
20	0	1	3	40	0	1	3

Your Social Skills Profile

Now let's interpret your scores for each part.

- Scores in the 1–15 range indicate areas that need improvement.
- Scores in the 16–21 range indicate areas that need more consistent attention.
- Scores in the 22–30 range indicate areas of strength.

Write down your areas of strength and areas that could use some more attention or improvement.

Area(s) of Strength: _____

_____

Area(s) that need more consistent attention: _____

_____

Area(s) that need improvement: _____

_____

What to Do Next

Sending Clear Messages:

If it's indicated within your scores that you need to give more attention, or you have room to improve in the area of sending clear messages, ask yourself why this might be a challenge for you. Could it be coming from a self-limiting belief you have developed around your ability to communicate with people? Is it possible that you are allowing something from your past to inform how you talk to people today? Are you acting out of fear or ego in some way? Sometimes people are so afraid that they won't be heard, they create a self-fulfilling prophecy. It's easy to fall into the trap of coming across as a know-it-all if you have fear around not being taken seriously. If you're so focused on the message you want to convey that you forget to genuinely listen to someone else's ideas, then your message is likely to be lost because you are offering no reciprocity.

CRIPPLING SOCIAL ANXIETY

If you're dealing with extreme social anxiety, the good news for you is that it is fixable. You may need to seek the advice of a professional therapist or life coach so that you can find freedom from it. As we know from creating our Best Self, we know that social anxiety is not coming from our Best Self. It is completely within your grasp to overcome it.

I often find that people who struggle with effectively talking to others usually have built up some fears or anxieties that are standing in their way. On the other hand, it could just be a lack of awareness about how they communicate with others, and if that's the case, refer back to the questions in Part 1 and really study them. Think about how you can set specific goals toward improving your ability to communicate clearly with others.

Listening:

If your scores indicate that you need to work on your listening skills, ask yourself why that might be the case. Being a good listener means being willing to stop focusing on what you want to say and really open yourself up to the ideas of the other person. Are you afraid of what they might say? Are you desperate to be the only person in the room with good ideas? Have you allowed your ego to cloud your ability to listen? Here's the good news: listening is a skill that you can vastly improve with just a little practice. The next time you talk to someone, try hearing what they have to say, and then saying to them, "So, what I'm hearing is . . ." and then repeat back what they said. That way, you can ensure that you heard and really understood their point. You can act as a mirror to them, too, so that they can see how their tone is coming across to you, and whether that was the intent. This creates a benefit for both people. When you are being a good listener, you are most likely acting from your Best Self rather than from your ego because you are not acting selfishly—rather, you are giving of yourself to someone else. You are focusing your attention on another person and their thoughts, needs, ideas, or desires. Communication is a two-way street, so let's make sure you're sharpening your listening skills as well as your speaking skills.

Giving and Receiving Feedback:

If your total scores are showing that you need to be more open to giving and receiving feedback, ask yourself when you first noticed yourself struggling with accepting feedback from others—either negative or positive. Were you bullied by someone in the past, and are you allowing that experience to inform your present? Do you believe you aren't worthy of praise? On the other hand, have you given feedback to someone and gotten a negative response from them in the past? In order to socialize from a place of authenticity, you have to be willing to put all of those experiences behind you and be in the moment with others.

Giving and receiving feedback is key because it's how we help one another improve ourselves and continue on our path of growth with forward momentum. If someone is willing to be honest with you, it's important that you're willing to accept their honesty. For example, when someone pays you a compliment, look at that as a gift of the sincerest kind, and accept it graciously. Presentation is everything, so if you're giving feedback to someone else, make sure you're doing so in a way that they can hear you. In other words, barraging someone with negativity and telling them they're doing something all wrong will probably fall on deaf ears. No one wants to be attacked. But if you can present the information in a way that is gentle, caring, and solution oriented, and only *after* you've made sure they are open to hearing it, then your feedback can be helpful to them.

Handling Emotional Interactions:

If your scores show that you need to focus on how you handle emotional interactions, think about how you currently deal with those moments. We've all experienced highly charged situations before, and they can make us uncomfortable. But being outside of your comfort zone is really just an opportunity to connect more deeply with your authenticity and with another person. Rather than shutting down and letting ego take the reins when emotions run high, think about ways you can meet the other person where they are, and act with compassion for that person and for yourself. For example, if someone is expressing emotion to you, it's important for you to know that you do not have to rescue them in some way. When someone is crying, for instance, you might feel like you need to do something in order to get them to quit crying. But if you just let them express their emotions and you don't respond, eventually they empty their emotions and stop crying. I actually find that the kind thing to do is to give someone a tissue if they are crying. Let them ask for anything else they might need—they will tell you if there's something you can do. But it's important to realize that you are not responsible for other people's emotions. You are only responsible for your own. If someone is upset at you for some reason, also realize that you are not responsible for making them not be upset toward you. If someone is yelling at you, and you do not believe you've done anything to warrant it, then it's not your problem to fix—it is theirs. Of course, if you owe amends to someone, then make amends, and then it will be up to them whether or not they choose to accept that.

Sometimes the energy in a room or a conversation can get really chaotic when there is heightened emotions, and in those times, I will often just hold on to a pillow next to me so that I don't feel the need to engage. If you don't engage in the drama, you are not in the drama. In some families, get-togethers are like a Whac-A-Mole of emotions. This is especially true over the holidays. You may need to show up more guarded in your family environment because it may be more toxic than your home life, and that's okay, and you don't need to fix your family because you can't fix your family. You are responsible for your own emotions and no one else's.

Life is bumpy. It's messy, and it's often emotional. In fact, sometimes it can feel like a roller coaster. Emotions are an important part of our lives and one of the ways in which we grow and connect with others. Don't run from your emotions or from the feelings of others; instead, embrace them and use them to deepen your relationship with yourself and the people within your orbit.

We, each of us, represent a different thread on the collective quilt that is society, and we are all woven together in interesting and beautiful ways. Allow your social life to flourish by embracing the human emotions that we all experience.

Simple Tools for Socializing Authentically

Few of us are born with fantastic social skills; it's something we have to learn and continue to practice to make better. Here are some tips for having a positive experience socializing the next time you are in a group.

- *Have something in mind you want to share:*
    Prepare for the gathering by thinking of one or two pieces of information that you've learned or an experience you've recently had, so that you can contribute to the conversation without having to search your mind for something to say. Just make sure it's appropriate for the group you'll be with.

- *Remain present:*
    When you're socializing, take steps to remain in the present moment. Try to keep your mind focused. Soak in your surroundings, the conversation you're having, the people around you. You will increase your own

enjoyment of your social time and others will enjoy
your company even more. I often meditate an hour or
so before I attend an event, and I always do my ritual
and mantra right beforehand, so that I can remain
connected with my authentic self and thus project that
authenticity to the people around me.

- *Ask questions*:
  For the most part, people enjoy talking about themselves,
  so ask them about their interests, their work, hobbies, or
  family. Don't just *act* as if you genuinely care about their
  answers—make sure you actually *do* care about them.

- *Be a good listener*:
  The best conversationalists are the best listeners. Stay
  engaged in conversation by listening carefully and
  relating to the responses you hear. Also, make sure you
  aren't interrupting someone when they're talking.*
  You might have formed a habit of jumping in if you're
  anxious to say what you have on your mind, but I
  encourage you to hold your tongue and wait until those
  you are with have finished talking, and then share your
  thoughts.

- *Maintain open body language:*
  The messages you send with your body are very powerful.
  In fact, some say that nonverbal cues account for up
  to 70 percent of your communication. Maintain a
  confident posture by standing up straight, with your
  shoulders back. Avoid crossing your arms in front of
  you so that you don't appear defensive or insecure.
  And remember to smile, but make sure your smile is

---

* "'Is Service with a Smile' Enough?" *Organizational Behavior and Human Decision Processes* (January 2005).

authentic. As one study at Penn State showed, people can detect if your smile is fake, but a real smile can result in people perceiving you as likable, courteous, and competent. Think about smiling with your whole face, not just your mouth.

When I first started being on camera, I realized that when I was listening to someone, my face looked like a mixture of concern, anger, boredom, and tiredness. I'd watch myself playing back on camera and I'd yell at the screen and say, "What are you doing, Mike? You look so flat!" But in reality, I was simply observing the person, looking at nonverbals, listening to their words and tone, and trying to connect with them. This just goes to show that you can't always assume what someone is thinking by the look on their face! I've learned by doing this on camera that it can intimidate people when I get that particular look on my face. So I've practiced and learned to smile more, which actually has given me better results and I feel better. I'm still being authentic, but I'm lighter, more comfortable and aware.

- *Be aware of your tone:*
  The tone and volume of your voice communicates a lot of meaning to the other person. Different situations call for different tones, certainly, so the key is to understand your audience and the setting. There are times for a formal rather than informal tone, a funny rather than serious tone, respectful or irreverent and enthusiastic or matter-of-fact. Choose wisely, because the tone you convey is just as important as the words you say!

- *Chat, don't preach*:
  Everyone has an opinion, but unless someone asks for yours, don't walk around shouting it out. Don't assume

that someone shares your opinion on any given topic—
especially a hot-button topic. You risk alienating or
offending someone in the group by climbing up on
your soapbox. I'm not suggesting that you hide how you
really feel about a certain subject matter—rather, focus
on the right time to discuss your feelings and opinions.

- *Maintain eye contact:*

    There's nothing worse than talking to someone with a
    wandering eye. You have the ability to make the other
    person feel heard by keeping your eyes on theirs. No
    matter what, don't look down at your phone or your
    hands while you're talking to someone. I see that
    happening a lot these days, and I know it is a pet peeve
    for many. Also, try to avoid placing your phone on the
    table when you are having a meal with someone and
    glancing down every time it dings. Remember to smile
    and keep your eyes on the other person while they're
    talking so that they know you're engaged in what they're
    saying.

- *Give positive feedback:*

    When you go into a social setting, take note of details that
    you can comment on in a positive, truthful way. Give
    compliments! There's no better way to make someone
    feel comfortable and open around you than to pay them
    a genuine compliment.

- *Acknowledge strangers:*

    Just because you haven't met someone before doesn't mean
    you should ignore them in a social setting. Walk over to
    a stranger, shake their hand, and introduce yourself. You
    never know; that person might become a lifelong friend!

Social Media

Now more than ever, it seems so much of our social life is inter-twined with our social media life. There's no doubt that social media has become an essential tool in the modern age—a tool for engaging with friends and family around the world, as well as a tool for building one's brand and business. Like anything, we can choose to use social media in healthy, helpful ways, or we can choose to use it in destructive ways. Your social media profile has become your "first impression" that you make on the world. It's part of our identity.

The question is—are you being your Best Self on social media? Or are you actually putting your Anti-Self out there? Ask yourself that question when you look at your various social media profiles and your comments on other people's pages.

Here are some more questions to ask about your social media life:

- Do you keep your online conversations positive and uplifting? In other words, do your friends and acquaintances see your posts and laugh or smile, or do they wince?
- Does your social media profile identity match up with your identity in real life? Think beyond just the filters or editing tools you may use on photos—are the words you say online (to friends and strangers alike) reflective of your Best Self?
- How much time are you spending perusing your various newsfeeds? Did you know that spending two hours a day on social media equates to an entire month out of every year? Are you sure that's how you want to be using your time?
- Do you engage in negative social media posts that leave you feeling sad, depressed, angry, or outraged? Is that serving you?

- Do you find yourself commenting or posting about social issues that upset you, but not following through with any action in real life?
- Have you used social media to deal with problems you are afraid to face in real life?
- Have you attacked someone you know on social media instead of discussing your issue with them in person?

Based on your answers to the above questions, do you feel you need to make any adjustments to how you engage with social media? Keep that in mind as you work on the overall social life quiz coming up next.

Your Social Life SPHERE Quiz

PART 1: **Rate your social life on a scale of 1–10. A "1" would mean that you feel your social life is in dire straits and in need of your immediate attention. A "10" would mean you feel that your social life is in fantastic shape and requires little or no improvement.** Aspects of your social life to consider when assigning your rating include:

- Your communication skills, such as how you listen to others and how you accept and give feedback
- The quality and quantity of your social interactions
- Your social media life
- And most important, if your Best Self is who shows up in all of your social settings

Social Life Rating: _____ as of _____(date)

PART 2: Now, list out some behaviors that are working in your social life and why they're working.

Examples:
- I feel confident and authentic when I'm socializing.
- I make time for a robust social life.

Behaviors that are working in my social life are:

_____Why? _____
_____Why? _____
_____Why? _____

PART 3: What are some behaviors that you know are keeping you from what you want in your social life?

Examples:
- I don't believe I'm good in social situations, so I make every effort to avoid them.
- I am not authentic in my interactions with others in social settings and/or on my social media.

Behaviors that are not working for me in the area of my personal life are:

_____Why? _____
_____Why? _____
_____Why? _____

PART 4: Based on everything you just wrote down, I want you to think about what you need to do in order to go from your current rating to a rating of 10 in this SPHERE of your life.

The way you'll do this is to look at behaviors you need to *continue* doing because they're working for you, behaviors you need to *stop* doing because they're keeping you from what you want, and behaviors you need to *start* doing.

In order for my social life to feel like it's at a 10,

I need to continue: _____

I need to stop: _____

I need to start: _____

At the end of the seven SPHERES chapters, you will find a chapter devoted to how to create and acquire new goals for each area of your life. You'll refer back to the exciting exploration you've done within your social life and use the valuable information you've uncovered to further your journey and improve your life on a whole.

Next, we'll venture together into your personal life, and discover new information about your most important relationship—the one with yourself.

6

Your SPHERES ersonal Life

In the previous chapter, we talked about how you outwardly project your authenticity to the world in social situations. Now, in this chapter, we're going to turn our focus inward and investigate the most significant relationship in your life—the one you have with *yourself*.

The main goal in the pages that follow is to make sure you have an abundance of respect and compassion for yourself. Sounds obvious, right? You'd be surprised how hard this is to accomplish for some people. Or, maybe you wouldn't be surprised at all, because you are someone plagued by a feeling that you just don't like who you are. But know this—time you spend taking care of yourself and nurturing an authentic, positive self-image is time well spent and the benefits will spiral out into all the other SPHERES of your life.

In this chapter, we are going to evaluate and improve how you currently exist in these key areas: internal dialogue, self-care, and your passions as expressed in hobbies and play. I've found with many of my clients and friends that the personal life sphere easily gets lost in the fray of daily life. Other SPHERES can cast their big shadows, and a rich inner life can disappear altogether if we allow it. That's why I'm so drawn to a quote from Robin Mc-Graw, Dr. Phil's wife. I think it is brilliant; it's such a meaningful and important message to remember. "*It's not selfish to take care of yourself first.*" This is so basic, but it's so easy to forget to take care of yourself first. Robin is such an inspiration to me, and she has really figured out some things in life. She knows that parents especially struggle with this concept because they so deeply want the best for their kids, so they often end up taking themselves off the list of priorities altogether.

Robin witnessed this firsthand in her own mother. In *What's Age Got to Do with It?: Living Your Happiest and Healthiest Life*, she wrote,

> *Many of my memories of my mother are of her doing for others: cooking for our family of seven, baking our favorite cakes for our birthdays, ironing my father's shirts, leaning over her sewing machine making all of our clothes, and many years later, babysitting and doting on her grandchildren. Even her final moments on this earth were spent focusing on someone other than herself—a true symbol of exactly how she lived. I was thirty-two years old at the time, and Phillip and I had just moved into a new home. The move didn't go as smoothly as planned—a delay meant that the movers arrived after midnight and a downpour turned our houseful of boxes into a soggy, stinky mess of cardboard. Wanting to comfort me while I dug through my waterlogged belongings, my mother baked me a pumpkin pie. And that was the last thing she did before she died. Imagine, she was dy-*

ing from a heart attack and there she was rolling out pie dough! More than two decades later, the thought of that still gives me a lump in my throat and brings tears to my eyes. I admire and try to emulate an endless number of my mother's qualities, like her Christian faith, her fierce love for her family, and her strength during difficult times, but her decision to neglect herself is not one of them. From the day she died, I vowed not to continue the legacy of self-neglect.

In order to show up as your Best Self as a parent, a role model, an employee/employer, a friend, son, daughter, sibling, and so on, you must show up for yourself first. If you're not taking care of yourself, you won't have the emotional or physical energy to take care of your loved ones in the way you really want to anyway. So, I suggest that you remind yourself of this truth numerous times a day until it becomes engrained.

With that in mind, let's get to it!

Internal Dialogue

Have you ever listened to the messages you tell yourself? Some remarkable research shows that we are actually able to change the structure of our brain when we change the way we talk to ourselves.[*] This is an exciting idea to me. I think a lot of folks believe that their brain is hardwired in one way or another, and we are powerless to change it. But as neurologists have discovered, our brains are malleable. It's a concept known as neuroplasticity,

---

[*] *Translational Psychiatry* (2016): e727.

which scientists define as "the ability of the nervous system to respond to intrinsic or extrinsic stimuli by reorganizing its structure, function and connections."* That essentially means that the brain and nervous system change throughout our lives in response to occurrences within our body as well as external occurrences. You can also think of plasticity of the brain as "the ability to make adaptive changes related to the structure and function of the nervous system."† The thing that really excites me about the latest discoveries in neuroplasticity is this—you are not stuck with your brain as it is right now. You have the ability to change it—and you can do so in one of many ways. Right now, I want to discuss how you can change the structure and function of your brain through your internal dialogue—the messages your mind is sending to your brain. If we tell ourselves that we are capable, strong, and smart, our brains will act accordingly. Alternatively, if we tell ourselves that we are ineffectual, weak, and unintelligent, our brains will take those marching orders quite literally. You will live up to the truth you are telling yourself. In a study conducted by researchers at the Institute of Psychiatry, Psychology and Neuroscience at King's College London, they found that repetitive negative thinking may increase a person's risk for developing Alzheimer's disease.‡ In another study, researchers have found that when we practice self-control, we can improve our brain's ability to exercise self-control.§ We've all heard it anecdotally, but now there is scientific evidence that proves that our mind has the power to alter our brain.

You are in the driver's seat on this journey. You tell your brain

---

* https://academic.oup.com/brain/article/134/6/1591/369496.

† *Neural Plasticity*, Volume 2014, Article ID 541870.

‡ https://psychcentral.com/news/2014/11/18/prolonged-negative-thinking-may-increase
-alzheimers-risk/77448.html.

§ Mark Muraven, "Building Self-Control Strength: Practicing Self-Control Leads to Improved Self-Control Performance," *Journal of Experimental Social Psychology* 46, no. 2 (2010): 465–68. PMC. Web. 10 Oct. 2018.

what to do, and it will follow—not the other way around. So, let's tune in and listen to your internal dialogue, and then shift it into a new gear. You'll now be telling your brain about the kind of person you are, and the kind of life you desire, and as a result, those things will unfold in reality.

The following exercises can help to focus your habits and patterns and set you free of some of your negative internal dialogue.

Exercise 1: What do you say to yourself on a normal day?

How often do you really stop and listen to what you are saying to yourself? Most people rarely or never analyze their internal dialogue, but there's real value in this and here's why: our thoughts create our emotions. These emotions then dictate more thoughts, and depending upon the circumstances, they can turn into negative ones unless we are able to recognize that it's happening, hit the brakes, and redirect ourselves.

Your harshest critic lives between your two ears, but you know what? Your best, most encouraging friend can live between your two ears, too. Right now, I want you to get very familiar with what you are saying to yourself throughout the day. You can write those thoughts in this book, a journal, or your phone or tablet. You can do this exercise for a day or a week—it's up to you. It is a wonderful way of tuning in and recognizing the messages you are sending to yourself.

Starting now, every two hours, you will stop and spend just a couple of minutes checking in with yourself and answering the following questions.

Write down what you've been telling yourself about:

- What you've been doing for the past two hours:

  _____

  _____

  _____

- Your intelligence.

  _____

  _____

  _____

- Your competence.

  _____

  _____

  _____

- Your skills and abilities.

  _____

  _____

  _____

- Your worth—both self-worth and your value to other people.

  _____

  _____

  _____

- Your appearance.

  _____

  _____

  _____

If you prefer to write things down as you hear yourself saying them instead of every two hours, then by all means, do so. The point here is to develop a really clear understanding of one day's internal dialogue, but without disrupting your daily schedule.

Exercise 2: What do you say to yourself when the pressure is on?

Imagine now that you will be giving an important presentation at work tomorrow. Several key customers or clients, several of your coworkers, and your boss will all be present and watching you. It's the night before. You're lying in bed, in the dark, thinking about the presentation. What are you saying to yourself?

Take the time to honestly and thoroughly consider the kinds of messages that would be going through your head. You'd be having a conversation with yourself, so what would you be saying? Write down as much of this conversation as you can. Dig deep and really imagine this situation as if it were actually happening.

_____

_____

_____

_____

_____

Exercise 3: What are some common themes in your internal dialogue?

Look back at what you wrote down for both Exercises 1 and 2. Do you see common themes or threads running through both sets of information? If so, what are they? Describe them here:

_____

_____

_____

_____

_____

Exercise 4: What's the tone of your internal dialogue?

When you look back over what you wrote in Exercises 1 and 2, how would you describe the overall tone or mood of your internal dialogue?

- Is it generally positive, upbeat?

- If it is positive, is it rational? In other words, are the positive messages you're sending yourself realistic?

- Is it pessimistic or defeatist?

- Are there particular areas where your internal dialogue sounds particularly harsh or critical?

- Does your internal dialogue sound extremely optimistic or complimentary in some specific areas, but not others?

- Circle anything you wrote that illustrates especially positive or especially negative internal dialogue.

Exercise 5: What's your locus of control?

Glance back over your writing for Exercises 1 and 2 and ask yourself this question: what does your writing tell you about your locus of control, or the degree to which you believe you have control over what occurs in your life?

- Does it appear that you're telling yourself that **you** are in control of your life (**internal locus of control**), or that your life is dictated by **outside forces or individuals (external**

locus of control), or that everything is basically up to **chance**—it's the luck of the draw as to whether you have a good or bad day?

- Write down your answer:

_____

_____

_____

_____

Exercise 6: What kind of coach are you to yourself?

There is only one last thing I want you to do with this valuable data you collected about your internal dialogue. Since the goal is for you to develop your own internal life coach, as I won't be by your side every day, we want to build the skills of that coach within you and listen to what he or she has to say. Is your inner life coach a mean one who beats you up when you get off track? Or is your inner life coach encouraging? As you look at what you wrote, answer this question:

What kind of a coach are you to yourself throughout the day? Looking at the messages you recorded in Exercises 1 and 2, notice if you are the kind of coach you can count on to lift you up and encourage you? Or does your inner coach tear you down and reinforce your worst fears about yourself? *You're* the one who talks to you, all day, every day. Are you actively creating an unhealthy internal environment for yourself, and negatively influencing your experience of the world? Or are the messages that you tell yourself characterized by a rational and productive optimism? For example, if you were to decide to eat some pizza and ice cream late at night, do you say to yourself—"look at you, at it again, eating all the stuff you're not supposed to—you have no willpower, you loser!" or do you think, "Hey, don't beat yourself up. It tasted good, and you don't eat pizza or ice cream that often. It's not like you're going to wake up five pounds heavier tomorrow." Or, do you say, "Well, you already fell off the wagon; you might as well order another pizza! Round two!" Another thought you may have is, "Next time let's make it a pizza and ice cream party and have some people over!" You get the point—you can choose to talk to yourself about any given activity or decision in one of numerous ways. That voice is your inner life coach, and the goal is for your coach to lovingly help you align with your Best Self.

What kind of coach are you to yourself? Be specific:

_____

_____

_____

_____

By completing those exercises, you've just gained very useful insight into how you're talking to yourself. We all have a constant conversation going on in our heads, and by acknowledging that and really listening to what we say to ourselves, we can begin to rescript that conversation. Now that you've identified areas in which you are sending yourself unkind or discouraging messages, you can begin to root out those thoughts and replace them with your mantra or another self-affirmation. The next time a negative thought about yourself begins to form, imagine an alarm bell dinging in your head. When you hear the alarm, stop immediately and choose to reject that thought, and then choose a new message.

For example, let's say you are preparing for a social event with networking opportunities. As you go through the motions of getting dressed and ready to walk out the door, you might catch a glimpse of yourself in the mirror and you think, *I don't know why I bother with these things. I never know what to say to new people.*

I'm so awkward. Or, you may think, *Wow, I look old and tired. And what is that new roll doing around my waistline? Ugh.* Now, the second a thought like that flashes across your mind, imagine that you hear an annoying dinging or buzzing sound in your ears. Look at yourself in the mirror and say out loud, "I'm confident in my ability to socialize. I will smile, be friendly, ask questions of others, and I will create valuable new connections and friendships." Do this again and again until the positive, affirming thoughts become tape loops that just naturally play in your mind. In so doing, you will form new neural pathways in your brain. The result is that you will essentially go on autopilot and create the new reality that you've envisioned, from the inside out. As I've explained, I constantly talk to myself in the mirror because I want to be the best version of myself. If that still feels strange to you, find another method—just do something that gets the negative self-talk out of your head! We want to find what authentically works for you!

Self-Care

Life can move at a furious pace—sometimes like a raging river after a massive storm. We can find ourselves being swept away in the day-to-day rush from one thing to the next, and that's exactly why I want us to spend time now focusing on self-care. Self-care is usually the first thing we throw overboard when we're trying not to sink in the pressures of work, family, friends, and other responsibilities, but I want to caution you against that. Self-care is foundational to living your ideal life.

Self-care boils down to being compassionate toward yourself. Many people find it easier to be compassionate toward others than toward themselves, but I believe the more compassion you have for yourself, the more you will have to give to others. If your tank is full and overflowing, you have more to give away.

There are some practical ways that you can become more compassionate toward yourself. The first is to manage stress properly. I'm going to give you some practical tools and a system whereby you can prevent yourself from becoming stressed out, but first, let's get a gauge on your current stress level. Answer the next twenty questions honestly, and then we'll work together to understand your score.

Stress Quiz

1. How often do you feel that you are not coping with the demands put on you?

    ○ All the time   ○ Most of the time   ○ Rarely

2. Do you have problems going to sleep and/or staying asleep?

    ○ All the time   ○ Most of the time   ○ Rarely

3. Do you find yourself spending less time with friends, family, and colleagues, even canceling plans or ignoring their phone calls because they just feel like something else you have to "deal with"?

    ○ All the time   ○ Most of the time   ○ Rarely

4. Do you feel you are working harder than ever before, but somehow getting less done?

    ○ All the time   ○ Most of the time   ○ Rarely

5. Do you find yourself afraid to make decisions?

    ○ All the time   ○ Most of the time   ○ Rarely

6. Are you feeling anxious? Is your heart beating fast, your palms sweating?

   ○ All the time   ○ Most of the time   ○ Rarely

7. Are you feeling tense? For instance, are your muscles tensed up, your shoulders up around your ears, and your neck and back muscles tight?

   ○ All the time   ○ Most of the time   ○ Rarely

8. Are you feeling nervous?

   ○ All the time   ○ Most of the time   ○ Rarely

9. Are you jumpy and unable to relax? Do you feel like if you sit down for a moment and take a deep breath, something bad might happen because you aren't worrying about it?

   ○ All the time   ○ Most of the time   ○ Rarely

10. Do you become hostile and angry about minor things?

    ○ All the time   ○ Most of the time   ○ Rarely

11. Do you blame others when things go wrong?

    ○ All the time   ○ Most of the time   ○ Rarely

12. Are you critical of others' efforts?

    ○ All the time   ○ Most of the time   ○ Rarely

13. When other family members are having stress problems, do you think you are responsible for them?

    ○ All the time   ○ Most of the time   ○ Rarely

14. Are you avoiding having conversations about potentially stressful issues with family and friends?

○ All the time   ○ Most of the time   ○ Rarely

15. Are you having fights about "everything and nothing" with loved ones such as a spouse or immediate family members?

○ All the time   ○ Most of the time   ○ Rarely

16. Are you sharing fewer satisfactions with family and friends?

○ All the time   ○ Most of the time   ○ Rarely

17. Are you aware that you're experiencing stress, and that it is affecting your life?

○ All the time   ○ Most of the time   ○ Rarely

18. Are you having physical signs of stress, such as high blood pressure, tense muscles, and fatigue?

○ All the time   ○ Most of the time   ○ Rarely

19. Are you not taking the time to restore your mind and body after stress? For instance, after a stressful event, are you neglecting self-care activities such as exercise, meditation, restorative sleep, and hydration?

○ All the time   ○ Most of the time   ○ Rarely

20. Are you sad and depressed for no reason?

○ All the time   ○ Most of the time   ○ Rarely

Stress Quiz Scoring

If you marked "All the time" or "Most of the time" to at least one of these questions, you may not currently have a good system in place for managing stress. It's important to take steps toward changing that now, because stress only snowballs into more serious issues if left unchecked.

If you marked "All the time" or "Most of the time" to **more than five** of these questions, there is an even higher urgency for you to build a strategy around stress management in your life. You don't have to live this way, but if you start to prioritize self-care and realize that it's not "selfish" to put yourself first, you can take control over the stress. It's never too late!

Building Your Stress Management System

The goal is to build a system for dealing with stress as it comes in, instead of creating a solution for when you're already overly stressed out. It's the difference between prevention and treatment; it's far easier to prevent feeling stressed than to destress—much like physical ailments.

1. Mindful breath exercises

When a stressful thought enters your mind, or when something occurs that would normally upset your balance, find a way to disrupt the feeling, such as changing your breathing pattern. By becoming mindful of your breath, and taking 3–4 deep, cleansing breaths in and out, you can keep the stressor from taking hold. The stressed-out mind is essentially like a neurological storm, and the most powerful and immediate antidote is mindful breathing.

Mindful, rhythmic breathing isn't a new practice, and the reason it's been a tool for centuries around the globe is that it works.

Make breath exercises part of your daily routine because the more you do them, the calmer your baseline brain functioning becomes. This way, if something stressful does occur, it doesn't turn into the final straw that sets you off into a frenzy. Your foundation is strong, the winds of life can't blow you over.

It's up to you how you practice your mindful breathing—you can set aside a couple of minutes in the morning before your day really gets started, and then do it again midday, and once again before you go to sleep. Or if you have a different schedule that works better for you, that's fine, too. Just make sure you're connecting with your breath at least once each day as part of your stress management system.

2. Physical Exercise

Secondly, if you spend even just 20–30 minutes per day, five days per week, exercising your body, you are chemically resetting your brain and adding to the strength of your stress management foundation. In the Health chapter, we will delve much deeper into all the benefits exercise offers your brain and every other organ in your body, but for now, just know that exercise is also an imperative part of your overall self-care plan. It doesn't matter what type of exercise you do—whether it's jogging, walking briskly around the block, biking, doing a cardio machine in the gym, lifting weights, or doing an at-home workout in your living room—it's all wonderful. Find something you enjoy, look forward to, and that makes you feel great. If you dread the activity, you will not feel the same benefit.

3. Celebrate Your Life

You don't need to wait until your birthday to celebrate your life. Each and every day that we get on this earth is truly a gift, and if you take just a few moments each day to experience joy and laughter, and to embrace all the good things in your life, you are telling your brain to choose joy instead of dwelling on the stress. There is therapeutic value to feeling joy and it can (and should!) come from within.

Whatever it looks like for you, have a little party for yourself each day. I personally like to turn up the music and dance in my living room. (My dog likes to join in the fun, too!) Even taking the time to be out in nature and recognize its beauty and complexity is a celebration. Sit on a park bench and smell the air, study the petals of a flower, or feel the soft grass on your feet. Smile and allow a feeling of joy to wash over you. In order to deeply appreciate all that you have in your life, make some time to be in solitude, so that you can reflect on positive attributes of your life and the world around you. Or, treat your friends or family to a fun dinner . . . just because!

Another way to celebrate your life is to offer your time to someone else who is in need. Giving of yourself in some way to others is always an impactful way to experience joy in your life. It's easy to forgo these kinds of activities, but these can be the most life-affirming and sometimes inspirational moments in our lives.

4. Clean Up Your Sleep Routine

Physicians often talk about sleep hygiene, which refers to the habits and routines we create to get proper sleep so that we can maintain alertness in our waking hours. In terms of stress-proofing your brain, sleep is essential. If you're sleeping well on a regular basis, you are checking one of the biggest boxes in the self-care checklist. If not, the ripple effects can be detrimental. Lack of sleep has been shown to negatively impact cognition, reflexes, and even your emotional state. If you're trying to exist in a constant state of sleep deprivation, you make it very difficult for you to be your Best Self. It's kind of an all-or-nothing proposition, so I really encourage you to figure out how to consistently get the sleep your body and mind need.

Conduct a little experiment over the course of three nights to figure out just how many hours of sleep you require in order to feel your best the next day. On the first night, go to sleep as soon as you feel a little sleepy, and don't set an alarm—wake up naturally. Write down how many hours you slept. Then keep track of how you feel throughout the day—did you need a lot of coffee or stimulants to stay focused? Or did you feel clearheaded and focused? On the next night, go to sleep thirty minutes earlier than the night before, and wake up naturally. Write down how many hours you slept, and how you feel throughout the day. On the final night, stay up for one hour past the time that you begin to feel groggy, and set an alarm for one hour earlier than you woke up the day before. How many hours did you sleep, and how did you feel? What did you learn from the experiment? Were you able to pinpoint about how many hours of sleep you need in order to function at your best and brightest the next day?

Some people say if they get more than seven hours of sleep, they feel groggy and disconnected the next day. Other people can barely function if they get one minute less than eight hours. Figure out your optimal amount of sleep and then create a realistic routine that gets you into bed on time each night so that you can wake up when you need to and feel refreshed. There are all kinds of techniques you can try to improve your sleep—from lavender essential oil on your pillowcase to a white noise machine or fan—so take the time to really consider what makes your sleep environment the coziest for you.

I have learned that I need at least eight hours of sleep. When I don't get that much sleep, I feel like I need naps throughout the day; I feel more anxious, I am less focused, I'm moodier and less patient, and essentially, I'm less than my Best Self. I also tend to rely on caffeine as a stimulant throughout the day, which eventually leads to a crash. Even my skin suffers when I'm not getting enough sleep.

For my own nighttime routine, I first make sure that I don't eat anything for two hours before I go to bed—I know that if my body is working on digesting food, it will disrupt my sleep pattern. Then, as I'm winding down for the night, I bring my dog's bed into my bedroom, I play ten minutes of online Scrabble, I then review my day and what I really liked about it, and I ask myself if I owe any amends to anyone. I view my day from an angle of contentment. Then I turn out the light and go to sleep.

5. Unplug from Tech

It's a tech-obsessed world we live in, and it's reducing our ability to manage stress. If you're getting constantly barraged with dings, pings, and chimes from your phone, tablet, or computer all day long, you're endangering your ability to properly handle stressful incidents when they occur. The reason is that our brains aren't designed for the kind of constant interruption that technology creates. Focus is important, and if you're always splitting your focus between tasks and communications, your brain never gets a chance to calm down.

Take time each day to just completely unplug. No screens, no sound effects or vibrating devices. Just *be*. (This is also a good time to practice your mindful breathing exercises.) It might be tough at first, but soon you will come to look forward to your unplugged time, and your brain will thank you.

6. Connect with Your Relaxation

What makes you feel deeply relaxed? Your answer will be unique, and what's important is that you really understand what relaxation feels like and what induces it for you. Some people can just look at a massage table and already feel their heart rate and blood pressure dropping. Others feel Zen'd out when they're swimming or soaking in a warm bubble bath. I've met plenty of people who say they feel the most relaxed when they're riding a bike or going for a stroll outside in the sunshine. Or in my case, it's when I've set aside specific time for playing videogames.

I often ask folks if they meditate and many times they tell me they just don't know how—sometimes they even feel intimidated by the idea of it. Meditation is simply about relaxing the mind, connecting with your breath, and feeling present within your body in the moment. Meditation is a simple, quick method of relaxing yourself and tapping into your Best Self.

If you're unsure of how to get yourself into a relaxed state, or if you want to try something new, I encourage you to try a guided visualization technique, which is a form of meditation. There are apps that you can download on your phone for this, and listen on headphones, or you can try something simple like this:

Sample Guided Visualization Technique

1. Sit in a comfortable, quiet place, and focus your eyes on something directly in front of you or an object that makes you feel peaceful.
2. Tune out all the thoughts that come into your brain as much as you are able, and just keep your eyes focused solely on that object.
3. As you feel your heart rate slow down, begin to let your vision blur and then slowly close your eyes.
4. Imagine yourself doing something that you love or that makes you feel at peace. It could be strolling along a white, sandy beach, the sun beaming down, a light breeze in your face, and the sound of the gentle waves lapping

up onto your feet. It could be you sitting on top of a mountain, staring out at the gorgeous view all around you. Or lying in a hammock on a big, wooden porch, with a field of wildflowers stretching out in front of you. Any image that warms your heart and soothes your soul, that's what you should imagine.

5. Stay as still as you can, and as present as you can in that moment. As other thoughts try to take over the image, just imagine gently swatting them away with the back of your hand.

6. When you're ready, slowly open your eyes, take three deep, slow breaths, and then say your personal mantra out loud. (In chapter 4, you created your personal mantra.)

Regardless of what gets you there, take time each day to relax, and then once or twice a month, create time in your schedule to go deep into that quiet, relaxed state for a longer period, like one or two hours. For example, occasionally I will force myself to leave my phone behind and go out into nature—whether it's the beach, the mountains, or just a beautiful park. This practice will reduce stress in the moment as well as prevent an epic meltdown when a stress trigger hits. Again, it's about bringing your baseline stress way down so that you're not always operating at an 8, and any little thing sends you flying past 10 at warp speed. If you're constantly in the 0–2 range on the stress scale, you're better equipped to handle what comes.

Passions

The third component of your Personal Life SPHERE is your passion. What is it that makes you feel like you are plugged into the river of life and you are vibrating at your highest frequency? If you're not sure anymore, or you haven't asked yourself that question in a long time, there's no time like the present to look inward and rediscover your passion. Once you've uncovered it, your job is to find a way to express it—whether that's in the form of a hobby, volunteering, or some form of play. Perhaps you have a wide range of passions that you can express in different ways. I say, go for them all!

If you're not sure where to start, then have a little fun by trying out some new things you've never done before. Challenge yourself and step outside your comfort zone. Sign up for a dance class. Volunteer at the homeless shelter or the animal shelter. Buy some art supplies and try painting. Go see a play or musical at the local theater. Learn a new language while you're commuting. The list of activities here is limited only by your own imagination. The point is that you think about the last time you felt truly alive doing something, and then re-create that sensation on a regular basis in your life.

I once worked with a woman named Deborah who lived on the Upper East Side in Manhattan, she had a huge inheritance, was divorced with several grown kids, but she just had zero passion in her life. She had gotten to the point where she almost never left her apartment—she ordered everything in. She even had a mini salon in her home, as well as maids, personal shoppers, and so on. She'd programmed her environment in such a way that she literally never needed to walk out her front door. As a result, Deborah had ceased to connect with the outside world. When I met with her, I challenged her to not only leave her apartment for the first time in months, but to also leave her cell phone and wallet behind (other than enough cash for a taxi if she needed it) so that she could spend a few hours going to a part of the city that she'd never been to before.

I went with her on that first excursion and showed her by example how to be curious about the people around her and how to discover the magic of living in Manhattan, one of the most eccentric, interesting, and diverse cities in the world. It didn't take long for her to realize just how disconnected she'd become from life. It was a little overwhelming for her at first, but by the end of the day, she was literally coming alive again. It was like she'd put herself on pause, and the simple act of getting out into the neighborhood, talking to strangers, and soaking in the diverse sights, sounds, and sensations helped her hit the play button on her life again. You see, when we're disconnected, it's impossible to feel passionate about anything. She had allowed her life to become smaller and smaller; she was shriveling up from lack of passion. It's so easy to get into a pattern where you do the same thing over and over again, and in that repetition, passion can't thrive. But you have the ability to shake things up, break out of your routine or patterns, and connect in new, exciting, and enriching ways.

You deserve this. It will make you a more well-rounded person, and it will strengthen your new bond with your Best Self in ways you can't even fathom. I've even had clients who, once they gave themselves permission to explore their passions, realized that there was a way that they could create income around it. That doesn't need to be your primary goal, but what an exciting possibility that you could end up creating a career around something that lights you up from the inside! Remember, you can have many different passions in life. For instance, I have certain employees at CAST Centers whose job it is to greet potential clients when they walk in the door. This is a very important role, as these people are the first representation of our company. I always make sure these individuals are passionate about connecting with others. I like each of them to be a "people person," not because it makes them better at their job (though it certainly helps), but because I know they will enjoy this work. I want them to tap into their love of people and find true enjoyment in their career as a result. You spend about half of your life working and earning a living. Why on earth would you be in a job that doesn't make you feel alive? Simply knowing something about your personality and things that you love in life can tell you a lot about the types of jobs that will be the most rewarding for you. Aligning your SPHERES in this way (personal life + employment) can be a game changer. Talk about realizing your Best Self!

If you're reading this and thinking to yourself, *Yeah, right, Mike, I'll get right on that. In between doing piles of laundry, cooking dinner, earning a living, and trying to get a few hours of sleep, I'll do something I'm passionate about.* I would encourage you to go back to chapter 3 and take a look at your schedule. I'm willing to guarantee that there is enough available time in your routine that, within a thirty-day span, you could explore something about which you are passionate. I've worked with some of the busiest people in the world—they are hitting it hard from 5 a.m. to 10 p.m., and yet every one of them can carve out time for their passions. You can, too.

Living as your Best Self means you make time for your passions, because very often, they are a reflection of your art. No one ever regrets spending time pursuing their passion—there is truly *no* downside. So, don't let the sun go down on one more day without you connecting with your passion and acting on it. Seize the day!

For Those of You in Pain

Before I close out this chapter about your Personal life, I do want to talk to you about deep, emotional pain. From what I have seen in my work, there are two types of pain—the pain of rejection and the pain of loss. When you experience rejection, whether it's by a family member, an ex-partner, or even your own child, part of why it's so brutal is that the one person you believe could remedy this pain is alive, walking around, and seemingly happily living his or her life without you in it. With the pain of loss that comes with the death of a loved one you can feel like your life has shattered in the moment that they leave your side forever. This is true whether the death was expected, and you had time to prepare, or comes suddenly, as a shock.

I want to spend a moment speaking to both forms of emotional pain, because when you are living in a painful season of life, you can feel like you're all alone, and like it will never end. But you are *not* alone. And the pain you're feeling right now *will* subside.

Sometimes we feel so much pain and so much heartache that we don't know what to do with it. We want desperately to put it away, hide it from ourselves, lock it somewhere deep in our minds, and throw the key into the ocean. There are going to be times when you answer the phone and the news you receive seems impossible, like it can't possibly be happening to you and your loved ones. There are going to be questions for which you'll never receive an answer. There are going to be unspeakable moments when the only thing you are capable of doing is breathing in and out, and even that will feel like an insurmountable task. You're going to want so desperately to be able to hit the rewind button and go back in time. There may even come a day when you think you hear the sound of your whole world cracking in two, and know without a doubt that your life has been forever changed in one, fleeting instant. The blink of an eye—that's all it takes for a life to be altered.

My friend Cindy was what many would label as a "feeler"; she was highly emotional. She always looked up to her big brother, Wayne, just two years her senior, but acted as her protector. When they were young, Wayne included Cindy in all of his social outings. He took her to block parties and to hang out with his friends. He was the kind of big brother any kid would want.

During their high school years, Wayne would drive his sister to school every day when she was a freshman and sophomore. Cindy, who never fit in with the "cool" crowd, always felt cool when she was with Wayne. He knew what she needed emotionally. She could be herself in his presence. When it came time for Wayne to head off to college, he didn't go far away, and he still saw her on the weekends. She held him up on a pedestal and felt so blessed to be his sister.

In her junior year, Cindy was sitting in her English class when she received a message from the school to immediately go to the administration office. She knew in her gut that something was wrong, but she could never have imagined what the principal would say to her in the moments that followed. Her beloved brother had taken his own life that morning. Cindy didn't recognize her own voice when the primal, bone-chilling scream escaped her lips. She clenched her fists, looked toward the ceiling, and screamed, "Why?!" She felt as though she couldn't breathe, and her chest involuntarily heaved. Everyone around her tried their best to calm her.

Months later, Cindy recalls writing in her journal about an emotional firestorm that'd been raging inside of her since Wayne's passing—she would manage to get it contained, shrink the flames down to just a candle, and then without warning, it would explode again. She wrote, "This feeling—it's so real. It's as if it's actually happening to my body, and yet, I sit at a desk in a perfectly safe place. It's incongruent. It doesn't match up. How can I walk around and appear perfectly fine to everyone else whilst I'm being burned alive from the inside by these emotions? It's too much. Too much. Yet, deep down, way, way, down, at my core, protected within my heart, there is peace. There is an unshaken part of me—a part that remains still, quiet. The eye of the firestorm. This piece of sacred land, cordoned off from the rest of me—it is *powerful*. It may be silent, but it holds so much power concentrated in its tiny size for one reason—because it is directly connected to God through my faith. 'Yea, though I walk through the valley of the shadow of death,' just like we always said in church, 'thy rod and thy staff, they comfort me.' I can still feel it all, and the tears stream from the deepest rivers of sadness in my soul, but I can rest because I know God holds me in the palm of His hand."

Sometimes we don't get the answers that we yearn for, and very often with suicide, we can't understand or even begin to know the reasons why. But Cindy was able to make peace with the loss of her brother nonetheless, and even though her life wouldn't be the same as it was before, she knew she would be able to move forward. She also understood that her brother would not want her to be grieving his loss all the time—he would want her to continue living her life.

Pain is inevitable, and sometimes you're going to feel like you must surrender to it. That doesn't mean you're letting the pain win; that means you're human. This isn't about winning or losing. Life is a series of experiences, and pain is part of your experience of life.

If you are suffering today, allow yourself to be comforted. Accept comfort from God, from your family, from your friends and colleagues—and if you prefer to speak with someone anonymously, there are resources for you. You can even go online right now to www.doctorondemand.com and talk to a mental health professional in your area or call your doctor and ask for a therapist referral—whatever is going to make you the most comfortable. Or, if you feel the darkness closing in and like you are out of options, call or go online to www.suicidepreventionlifeline.org. There is help for you, no matter how much anguish you feel.

The desire to comfort is a universal Best Self attribute. We want to comfort one another. As hard as it may feel in the moment to accept sympathy, empathy, and care from others, do so anyway. Your soul will be soothed.

Your Personal Life Inventory

PART 1: **Rate your personal life on a scale of 1–10. A "1" would mean that you feel your personal life is in dire straits and in need of your immediate attention. A "10" would mean you feel that your personal life is in fantastic shape, and requires little or no improvement.** Aspects of your personal life to consider when assigning your rating include:

- Internal dialogue—what messages you're sending yourself each day
- Self-care—your stress management system, how you treat your body and your mind
- Passions—your hobbies, playtime

Personal Life Rating: _____ as of _____ (date)

PART 2: Now, list out some behaviors that are working in your personal life and why they're working.

Examples:

- I am actively modifying my internal dialogue so that it is positive and realistic.
- I prioritize self-care activities day to day.
- I make time to have fun and enjoy my life.

Behaviors that are working in my personal life are:

_____

_____

_____

PART 3: What are some behaviors that you know are keeping you from what you want in your personal life?

Examples:

- I spend too many hours numbing out in front of the TV or doing other activities about which I'm not passionate.
- I allow my internal dialogue to reinforce negative beliefs about myself and my abilities.

Behaviors that are not working for me in the area of my personal life are:

_____Why? _____

_____Why? _____

_____Why? _____

PART 4: Based on everything you just wrote down, I want you to think about what you need to do in order to go from your current rating to a rating of 10 in this area of your life.

The way you'll do this is to look at behaviors you need to *continue* doing because they're working for you, behaviors you need to *stop* doing because they're keeping you from what you want, and behaviors you need to *start* doing.

In order for my social life to feel like it's at a 10,

I need to continue: _____

I need to stop: _____

I need to start: _____

Coming Up Next . . .

Now that you've become better acquainted with your relationship with yourself, and with your emotions, *and* have a good handle on any areas that you need to improve in terms of your Personal SPHERE, we're going to move on to your Health SPHERE. If your health is out of alignment, or if you're not prioritizing your physical well-being, then every other SPHERE will *absolutely* be affected. Let's get your Best Self physically healthy, so you can live each day to the fullest!

7

Your SPHERES health

Your Best Self wants you to do whatever it takes to preserve, protect, and promote your physical health. Why? Because if you're unhealthy, you simply cannot show up fully in any of your SPHERES. Your health is fundamental. When you're feeling good, you might hardly ever think about it. But when there's a problem with your health, it can take over everything else in your life. In this chapter, our goal is to ensure that you are acting in your own best interest when it comes to your health. To *be* our best, we need to *feel* our best, and to feel our best, we need to keep our health in check. When our physical health is operating at its highest level, the possibilities for what we can accomplish in this world are endless. That's how I want you to feel.

I want to start things off by sharing a story with you about a good friend of mine. He had some major health struggles that you might relate to on some level. James says he grew up always being the "chubby kid." He remembers putting so much butter on his mashed potatoes that it would form a little lake, and then he'd ask for more. He'd scream for a hamburger and fries every time his family passed a fast-food restaurant. One of his earliest memories is the summer before he started first grade, when he was standing next to his mom at the department store as she requested the "husky"-size jeans for him. He hung his head in embarrassment and shame.

Unlike a lot of overweight kids who are tortured at school, James was never bullied for his weight. That's because he was always two steps ahead of any potential insult—he'd sit down at the lunch table and proclaim, "Move over everyone, fatty is coming in!" Humor was his shield, and it worked beautifully. He was popular, to the point of beloved, and was even elected class president year after year. His house was where all the kids congregated on the weekends and he had a group of very good friends. He was extremely active—he lived on the East Coast and was able to go skiing pretty much every day of the week. It was his favorite thing to do.

This is James's depiction of his Anti-Self, "Self-Destructive Steve," whose passion in life is lying around, watching TV, and eating junk food. Steve is totally self-absorbed, uncaring about others, and indulges in self-punishment.

Around the age of thirteen, James had a skiing accident and suffered a serious knee injury. Due to this, his lifestyle became more sedentary. As you might imagine based on his eating habits, his weight ballooned. His mother, a recovering alcoholic, sat him down at one point and told him that she believed he was a compulsive eater. She saw in him the same addictive personality she'd grappled with in her own life, and she thought the sooner he became aware of it, the less of a hold the addiction might get on him. Certainly, she'd been coming from a place of love and wanted only the best for her son, but instead of her intended result, her approach caused James to form feelings of guilt and shame around food.

This is James's depiction of his Best Self, "Jolly Janitor James," who derives happiness from helping others, giving of himself, and selfless acts.

He then began stashing food away and eating behind closed doors. He'd slather butter on a bagel and then cream cheese on top of it, just so he could pack in as many calories as possible at once. His mom stopped serving dessert because she was so afraid of the excess calories for her family, and especially James. James would just go over to a friend's house and eat six desserts behind her back. He says that eventually, he started to weaponize food and use it as a tool against himself.

Once puberty set in and people in his school started coupling up, he quickly became the guy without a girlfriend. That hurt. His buddy took him under his wing and they started exercising together. He also educated James about how college athletes ate, so he could start making healthier choices at mealtime. James lost sixty pounds pretty quickly, dropping down to around two hundred pounds at that time. The plan worked—he got his first real girlfriend. But as fickle high school love usually does, their love burned out quickly, and he once again turned to food for solace. He hadn't solved the real issue underneath the weight; his motivations for losing it were still purely aesthetic.

This yo-yo dieting continued for years, and he stopped getting on the scale at 406 pounds, though he continued to gain. At one time, he managed to white-knuckle his weight all the way back down to 175 pounds through a militant approach to diet and exercise, and then something would happen in his life—a broken bone, for example—and he'd swing back the other way, usually adding more to his previous all-time high. He recalls one night when he stood by his kitchen sink and unwrapped and devoured eight chocolate bars, one right after the other.

After twenty-plus years, James had grown extremely weary with the dangerous cycle, and despite the wealth of knowledge he'd acquired about nutrition and exercise on his journey, he simply couldn't find a solution that would last. He was on two blood pressure medications and had been diagnosed with non-alcoholic symptoms of hepatitis (NASH), which meant he had a fatty liver. He had pain in all of his joints, had very little energy for everyday life, and just felt bad all around. His lifestyle had taken a huge toll on his health and well-being, and his life was truly in jeopardy. He couldn't do any of the activities he'd once loved, like skiing (he recalls how much it hurt when he tried to squeeze his leg into a ski boot), everything in his body hurt, and he felt dejected. His wife was supportive, but there was only so much she could do—ultimately, it was going to have to be James's decision to get control of his health once and for all.

At thirty-five years old, he knew he was standing on a precipice; he could do something drastic or he could give up altogether. His fears ran wild—he wondered if he was a failure. He questioned whether he was enough. He had bottomed out. Finally, he made a decision. He had gastric sleeve surgery.

It's been a year and change since he had the procedure, and James is now at a perfectly healthy weight. More important, he's healed his toxic relationship with food, and his entire outlook on life has shifted. He realizes now that his Anti-Self had been running his life for a long time, and once he allowed his Best Self to take over, he experienced an awakening. He'd been living his whole life in a self-interested state of mind; his only motivation to do something for someone else had been for personal gain. He remembers a time when the only reason he would clean up around the house was to gain "brownie points" with his wife, and he never would have dreamed of volunteering or giving back to his community in some way—he was simply too self-absorbed. Now he takes joy in doing for others, and he's much more plugged in with his relationships across the board. He's thoughtful, patient, and kind—all qualities of his Best Self.

As for his health, he's in amazing shape, not because he's obsessively hitting the gym like a Navy SEAL. James exercises a few days a week and makes smart food choices. As a result, his liver is now healthy and he's off all medications. His doctor is very pleased that his blood tests have all come back perfectly normal. James is living proof of the power of the human spirit to prevail over seemingly impossible circumstances.

I share James's story with you because it's a prime example of what can happen when our Anti-Self gets a chokehold on our health. What's going on internally can manifest in our bodies—it's unavoidable. You create a healthy (or unhealthy) body first with your *mind*. And like James, you can make a choice and take control. Your challenges may or may not be as significant as his, but no matter where you're starting from, you *can* take charge of your health and make it a priority in your life.

Now, I am not a doctor and I don't pretend to have all the answers in this realm. But as you know, I have spent a lot of time curating my overall team, and one of my valuable teammates is the medical director at CAST Centers, Dr. Jorge E. Rodriguez, or "Dr. Jorge," as he's affectionately known. Dr. Jorge has a real gift for taking complex medical information and distilling it in such a way that the layperson can easily grasp. That is exactly what he's done for you in this chapter; he's translated in-depth medical studies and research into bite-size chunks that you can start using immediately in your everyday life.

As we all know, there have been millions of books, articles, blogs, and other content created on how to reach and maintain optimal health. Plus, medical information is constantly evolving as scientists conduct new research and make new discoveries. In this chapter, rather than trying to cover everything you need to know about your health (since that would make this book *way* too long, and it would instantly go out of date the minute it was printed!), I'm going to be realistic in scope.

First and foremost, you are going to assess your health and discover areas where you can make either small tweaks or big changes so that you can ensure your Best Self is in charge of your health. The most important piece is awareness, and that's what I want to help you achieve.

We're also going to zero in on some specific, new, and exciting health-related topics and tools that I believe can help you feel your very best. That includes:

- the interconnectivity between our brain and gut,
- "newtrition," what I call the right approach to nutrition that supports you in living as your Best Self,
- exercise as it relates to your mind, body, and spirit,
- alternative options for disease prevention and wellness.

All of the information within this chapter can have a direct and highly beneficial impact on your quality of life and give you the functional, physical framework needed to operate as your Best Self across all your SPHERES. Buddha once said, "To keep the body in good health is a duty . . . otherwise, we shall not be able to keep our mind strong and clear." I know I've seen it in my own life—when I'm not taking good care of my body, my mind is neither strong nor clear.

So, let's discover how you can keep your body in good health!

HEALTH RED FLAGS

Before we go any further, I want to put something on your radar. If you have a specific health issue that you know you need to address or that you need to approach in a new way, I encourage you to work on it starting today. Too many people freeze for fear of dealing with a medical issue because they worry about uncertain outcomes. That inactivity can be worse than the health issue itself. So, push your fear aside. Be proactive. Take control. Go to the doctor. Seek a specialist if necessary. Get a second opinion, look at your issue from different angles, take whatever steps necessary, but *never* let a health problem linger. That should be your number one priority, always.

How Do You Feel?

Now, I'd like to do something with you called a body scan. We're often not connected to our bodies—we don't take the time to really check in with how we feel. Close your eyes and take an inventory of your physical body. Start with the top of your head down to your toes and check in with yourself. Do you feel fullness in the gut, tightness in the neck, a headache? We become conditioned to accept small degrees or even larger degrees of pain, but that pain is our body telling us there's an underlying issue. In a lot of ways, we can treat our bodies like a house—and wait until our structure practically collapses before we address the underlying issue.

Body Scan Results:

My head feels . . . _____

_____

_____

My back feels . . . _____

_____

_____

My legs feel . . . _____

_____

_____

My head feels . . . _____

_____

_____

My hands feel . . . _____

_____

_____

My stomach/digestive system feels . . . _____

_____

_____

My breathing feels . . . _____

_____

_____

Overall, I feel . . . _____

_____

_____

Many of our health issues are just part of who we are. But some are a result of our habits. Let's take an inventory of some of the behaviors that may affect our health. Circle the ones from the list below that apply to you and add any that may be unique to you but aren't listed here.

Behaviors That Affect Your Health:

Smoking   Lack of sleep
Abusing alcohol   Stress
Recreational drugs

Food and Beverages That Affect Your Health:

Sugary drinks   Processed foods
Overeating   Not enough fruit and vegetables
Eating late at night   Eating out too often
Salty foods   Too little water
Fried foods

Physical Health Issues

Chronic pain   Organ issues (such as
Prone to illness   cardiovascular disease/
Bad allergies   pulmonary disease/breathing
Muscle pain   issues/kidney or gallbladder
Joint pain   problems, etc.)

Fitness

Not working out or exercising in any way
Doing workouts that could hurt you
Doing workouts that are not rigorous enough

If you are dealing with an issue with your physical health that is not
listed above, write it here:

_____

_____

_____

_____

Now look back over the items you circled and honestly ask
yourself, "Do I want to change this?" If the answer is yes, you're

going to take that with you into the Goals chapter, and craft a plan around it.

If your answer is no, write down what it would need to look like for you to change it. In other words, what is your line that you don't want to cross? Or, if you're resistant to thinking about at what point you would want to change it, ask yourself why you feel that resistance. Perhaps you are in a state of denial? If you are not concerned about changing your health issue now, at what point would you want to change it?

You've committed to being curious about yourself, as well as honest, open, willing, and focused on achieving the changes that are for your Best Self. This chapter isn't about striving to be in *perfect* health; this is about striving to be healthier. As we can tell from James's story, by yo-yoing back and forth and only making superficial changes rather than getting to the root cause of his health challenges, that caused more health issues and more suffering and thus made his road to recovery that much more difficult. So, we want to raise your bottom—and by that I mean, you don't have to wait until you hit the "rock bottom" stage we've all heard about before. Rather than waiting until your health is so far gone that you're in need of hospitalization or something extreme, let's find a way to "raise your bottom" to a more acceptable level when you can still really take action and have an effect.

With health issues and the need for change, people often say, "I'm working on it," but when I ask them what that change looks like, they truly don't have a plan. It's just become a thought that they're a little more willing to ponder, but there's no action attached to that. I want you to be the best version of yourself, and what you need to do is to ask your Best Self to look at your health issues closely. Have that conversation with yourself, because you are likely avoiding something, and by so doing you are going to cause yourself more suffering down the road—and face it.

Gut Feelings

Dr. Jorge has taught me a lot about how there is a connection between the brain, your emotions, and your intestinal tract. How many times have you been so anxious or scared that your "stomach" has been tied up in knots? There's a reason you can literally feel fear or anxiety in your digestive system—your gut and your brain are tied together in interesting ways.

In the past several years, there has been some fascinating research coming out about the connection between the gut microbiome and the brain. In case you're wondering, the gut microbiome refers to the flora (bacteria) within the gastrointestinal tract. You have trillions of bacteria that live within your gut, and we now know that those bacteria play a massive role in your overall health. Those bacteria are necessary for us to be balanced, or for our health to be optimal. When found in the correct proportion, they keep us healthy. But if that delicate balance is altered, your immune system is impacted. If you're prone to or suffering from illness (even just colds or allergies), inflammatory diseases or autoimmune diseases, one of the first things to do is to improve the balance of bacteria in your gut through probiotics and prebiotics.

Perhaps an even more mind-boggling discovery in terms of the gut microbiome is that some of those bacteria actually have the ability to control your mind. I'm not kidding! There's a specific class of bacteria known as psychobiotics, and they play a huge role in the gut-brain axis, which is the communication between your gut and your mind.* In fact, in the not-so-distant future, it's quite possible that doctors will be prescribing specific pre- and probiotics to treat depression and anxiety via the gut instead of

---

* *The Psychobiotic Revolution: Mood, Food, and the New Science of the Gut-Brain*, eds., Scott C. Anderson et al., National Geographic, Washington, DC, 2017.

the drugs so commonly used today, the SSRIs and other dopamine-enhancing drugs that treat them via your brain/neurological system.* But having an issue with depression or anxiety isn't the only reason you should keep your psychobiotics in balance—anyone's mood can improve simply by balancing these bacteria. The power that those tiny little bacteria living in our gastrointestinal system have is truly astounding. Of course, these gut microbes are not the only thing that can contribute to anxiety, depression, or even Alzheimer's, but science does indicate that they play a role. And now that we have this knowledge, we can feel empowered over our health in a brand-new way.

The authors of *The Psychobiotic Revolution: Mood, Food, and the New Science of the Gut-Brain Connection* write, "Gut issues like irritable bowel syndrome and inflammatory bowel disease are highly associated with depression and anxiety, but the connection is often missed. Curing the underlying GI [gastrointestinal] problem can often resolve the mental issues. But without a clear signal from the gut, people don't always get the proper treatments. If you go to a psychiatrist for anxiety or depression, the doctor rarely asks you about your gut issues—but that is likely to change as the connection between the gut and the brain becomes better understood."

Without getting into the weeds on the science behind all of this, here's what you need to know right now: the foods and supplements that you are feeding your gut are directly feeding your mind, and thus your mood, and quite often, your behaviors. You not only *are* what you eat—you also *feel* and *do* what you eat! Researchers studying psychobiotics have isolated several specific strains of bacteria that can improve mood, and it's an area of study that continues to develop. The great news is that many of these strains (and the prebiotics that "feed" those important bacteria)

---

* David Kohn, "When Gut Bacteria Change Brain Function," *Atlantic*, June 24, 2015, https://www.theatlantic.com/health/archive/2015/06/gut-bacteria-on-the-brain/395918/.

can be found in foods such as unsweetened yogurt, kefir, and fermented foods. So, let's talk about your current diet and see where you can make some tweaks in order to help stabilize your mood, unfog your thinking, and give you all the energy you need to be your Best Self.

"Newtrition": How to Think about What You Eat

With the endless array of information that's out there in the nutrition and diet space, I aim to simplify as much as possible for you, so that you can in turn simplify your own diet. It is so easy to get caught by the contradictory information that comes out, almost on a daily basis, about what to eat, what not to eat, when to eat, and how much. Therefore, in the same way you are reexamining all of the seven SPHERES of your life in order to live as your Best Self, I want you to be willing to reexamine your diet and your beliefs around nutrition. The reason I call it "newtrition" is that you are going to approach it in a new way—a simpler way. You are going to think about food as fuel for your Best Self. With every meal, you have a choice—are you going to choose to fuel your Best Self or your Anti-Self?

The big takeaway I have for you is this: what you put into your body has a direct correlation to your output. If your diet is high in sugary, processed foods (who knows what is really in those?), you're going to feel sluggish, tired, moody, and disconnected from your daily activities. Sounds a lot like your Anti-Self, doesn't it? The reasons: foods that have been processed often contain chemical additives that your body can't deal with as easily as compounds naturally found in food, and the refined sugar causes huge spikes in blood sugar. Those blood sugar spikes result in your body releasing insulin, a fat-storing hormone, which results in tiredness or sluggishness. It's quite a roller coaster you put your body through when you consume highly processed foods or beverages. If you prioritize whole, nutrient-dense foods you'll perform better in every area. You'll be alert, alive, connected, and balanced. The reason those foods help you be your Best Self is that they provide your cells with the energy and hydration they need without adding in all the extras. They are absorbed slower, too, so you don't feel hungry all the time.

To help you better understand the types of foods you should be eating in order to maintain your alignment with your Best Self, let's start with the basics. There are three forms of nutrition: *carbohydrates, fat, and protein*. You need all three. The end. Moving on. I'm kidding! But it's true—you do need all three of these nutritional building blocks in order to be healthy. Let's look a little closer at each form.

1. Carbohydrates

Carbs are compounds in foods that your body uses for quick energy—they're sugars, starches, and cellulose. I know there have been various diet fads that say *all* carbs are evil, but it's just not true. Your body needs carbohydrates because it converts them to energy you can use for all of your activities, so if you try to cut them all out, you're not going to feel good or be able to function well for the long haul.

Processed foods like white bread, pasta, dessert foods, packaged foods like chips, pretzels and popcorn, candy, and anything else that isn't a whole food are going to slow you down, especially as we get older. Although they are very tasty, our bodies do not require any of those foods. The same goes for beverages—your body does not need sugar-laden or artificially sweetened drinks. We can fully function by drinking only water—and there's always the option to change up the taste by adding a squeeze of citrus fruit, cucumbers, strawberries, etc.

Healthy, nutrient-dense carbs, on the other hand, help fuel your brain and body. Organic vegetables, fruits, whole grains, nuts, seeds, and legumes are all great choices for carbohydrates. When it comes to veggies, lightly cooking them or eating them raw is the way to go, rather than cooking them at high heat or frying. You will get more of the built-in nutrients the less these foods are cooked.

WHEN I WAS YOUNG . . .

I've shared with you in earlier chapters that as I child, I struggled in school. Looking back, I think part of the problem was that I was always exhausted. I remember feeling so much more tired and lethargic than other kids in my class. I had no idea at the time that the donuts and fast-food breakfasts I was eating were affecting me. My diet was standing in the way of my ability to function as my Best Self. I had brain fog all the time, couldn't focus, and I was always yawning. All those unhealthy, simple carbohydrates did me no favors, and they won't for you, either, so make better choices than I did!

2. Fat

You may still be caught up in the old-school thinking that a low-fat diet means you'll lose body fat, but that's been proven inaccurate. Recent studies have found that fat is not the enemy* and,

---

* https://www.eurekalert.org/pub_releases/2018-08/esoc-coh081618.php.

in fact, the low-fat diet trend that held a tight grip on us for many years may do more harm than good. Fats are crucial for hormone regulation by feeding our hormones the nutrients they need to function. When hormones aren't getting the proper fuel they need, a host of health problems can occur—everything from fatigue to lack of mental clarity, hair loss, a dysregulated menstrual cycle in women, vitamin deficiencies, and dry skin. Remember, your body and brain need fat to function!

The key here is the type of fat you're consuming. Fats that are highly processed (think vegetable oil, cottonseed oil, canola oil, shortening) can cause inflammation throughout your body, leading to memory deterioration and weight gain.[*] (Are you seeing a theme here? Processed foods do not help you in being your Best Self!) Always look for healthy, naturally occurring saturated and unsaturated fats like avocados, coconut oil, grass-fed butter, pasture-raised chicken eggs, and olive oil. These healthy fats will keep you feeling satiated, focused, sharp, and in a better mood.[†]

3. Protein

Protein is made up of amino acids and is vital in keeping your organs, hormones, and tissue functioning. Protein makes up our muscle and cells, including the brain and heart muscle, so it plays a major role in keeping your whole body in top form. You'll find the best forms of protein in grass-fed, organic eggs and meat, beans, legumes and nuts, all of which are readily available now at all mass retailers, along with organic fruits and vegetables—these are no longer luxury items! If you choose to add a protein powder into a smoothie, I'd urge you to select a brand that has no additives in the ingredients—it should be made purely of organic

---

[*] https://www.nature.com/articles/s41598-017-17373-3.
[†] https://www.sciencedirect.com/science/article/pii/S0166432816302571.

protein sources without any sweetener. If you need to sweeten the smoothie, use organic honey, dates, or banana.

Other Best Self Foods to Incorporate

To help keep your gut microbiome healthy, it's a good idea to work in some fermented foods such as kombucha (there are multiple brands available in mainstream grocery stores these days—try them out—they're delicious!) or sauerkraut into your diet. These foods and beverages have a ton of probiotics in them, which can help reduce inflammation in your body, decrease bloating, and improve digestion and weight loss. I also recommend finding a good, high-quality probiotic supplement to take each day. Working in one serving of unsweetened yogurt or kefir each day is also a great idea, as they contain many of the strains of good bacteria that can help balance your mood. And, finally, fiber is an important key to good gut health as well, but make sure it's coming from whole foods rather than over-the-counter fiber mixtures. This is because your body can use more of the nutrients from high-fiber foods like blueberries, raspberries, beans of all kinds, and legumes, so stick with those. Fiber is key because it helps your body absorb sugar more slowly, and as a result, it can help you maintain a healthy weight. Fibrous foods also help clean your colon, thus reducing your risk of certain cancers. And you know what they say—an apple a day keeps the doctor away. Whether it does or not is up for debate, but eating a whole, organic apple each day is never a bad idea. (Even Dr. Jorge agrees!)

Interval Fasting

While "newtrition" is about eating nutrient-dense, unprocessed (whole) foods, it's also about choosing when to eat and when not to eat. There's a lot of new science suggesting that fasting, or eating in intervals, can induce something called autophagy—the body's consumption of its own tissue, by recycling waste produced inside your cells to create new materials to aid in cell regeneration.* One of the most exciting findings is that autophagy encourages the growth of new brain and nerve cells, thus improving cognitive function.† It's even been shown to improve your mood.‡

If the idea of fasting sounds scary to you, consider that you're already fasting for many hours each night while you sleep (hence the name breakfast—break the fast). If you simply stop eating after dinner at 8 p.m. each night, and then start eating again at 10 a.m. the next day, that's a fourteen-hour fast right there. Seems pretty doable, right? And it gives your body time to spend its energy on cleaning up cells rather than digesting. Plus, it will prevent you from eating foods late at night, which can disrupt your sleep pattern, and cause weight gain.

When you're filling your plate with satiating whole, nutrient-dense foods, you'll be amazed at how your body adapts and utilizes those resources. It might take a week or so to get the hang of it, but your body will adjust.

Exercise

There's more research than I could possibly quote indicating the positive results of daily exercise for the human body, brain, and even spirit. Don't overthink exercise, though. The best kind of exercise is the kind you'll do. Find something that you enjoy that will get your heart rate high enough to make you sweat (obviously

---

* https://www.ncbi.nlm.nih.gov/pmc/articles/PMC2990190/.
† https://www.ncbi.nlm.nih.gov/pmc/articles/PMC2647148/.
‡ https://www.sciencedirect.com/science/article/pii/S0165178112008153?via%3Dihub.

talk to your doctor before you start a new regime—especially if you have preexisting health challenges) and do it daily, or as often as you possibly can!

I like to go to the gym, and that's often where I get hit with inspiration. That's because my blood is pumping, and my brain is getting nourished with oxygenated blood. You might find when you're in a funk, or feeling blocked in some way, that getting some exercise will click you back into "on" mode.

If your job requires you to be seated for long periods of time, you might experience pain or tightness in your hips or lower back. I highly suggest dynamic stretching for just ten minutes a day. Simple things like plank walkouts, toe touches, hip hinges, and squats next to a chair can make all the difference to combat this pain. You can easily go to YouTube and plug in the exercise names above to see videos for proper body placement for each of these movements.

Should you want to do further research on the most effective exercises you can do (how to get the most bang for your buck in the time you spend), then I'd direct you to high-intensity interval training and high-intensity resistance training. These have become the gold standard in exercise these days, and you can apply their principles across a large variety of movement—running, biking, swimming, resistance bands, weights, and so on.

Exercise is a key component of your Best Self, and I encourage you to find a way to work it into your routine. In the Goals chapter, you are going to look more closely at how you're spending your time, so be thinking about how you can fit regular exercise into your schedule.

Prevention/Wellness

What are you doing in terms of preventative health right now? In other words, what steps are you taking to preserve your good health and to become aware of potential issues before they become real problems?

Back in the Personal Life chapter, we discussed the idea that it is not selfish to take care of yourself first. That notion applies 100 percent to your health. But where I think there's still a disconnect for many is that they assume they don't have to address their health unless instructed by a doctor. But your doctor doesn't know the whole picture of your life—only *you* do! Listen to your own intuition, and if you think something more is going on than your doctor is finding, by all means, seek a second opinion or an alternative point of view or treatment. And, if you want to prevent having to go to the doctor at all, take your health into your own hands and be proactive—put your health first as much as you can.

You need to be your own advocate when it comes to your health. There are lots of options in today's world for alternative means of disease prevention and wellness. It's important that you do your research, and not just go to any practitioner you find online. Make sure that whomever you see has the proper licensure and certifications. And be sure to schedule a consultation before having any actual treatment. This is true for traditional Chinese medicine (TCM), platelet-rich plasma therapy (which I've had done on my shoulder and is pretty cool—they take some of your own blood, spin it in a centrifuge, and then inject only the plasma-rich platelets into the problem area, which can help speed your body's healing process), acupuncture, herbal treatment, reiki, functional medicine (a biology-based approach to medicine that focuses on identifying and addressing the root cause of various health problems and diseases), cold laser therapy (which uses spe-

cific light wavelengths to speed healing in targeted areas), cryo-
therapy, infrared sauna (which uses infrared light to create heat,
and can help your body in detoxification), and the rest of a list
that really goes on and on.

THE BIOHACKING TREND

In case your curiosity is piqued, and you want to dig deeper into
ways that you can take control of your health so that you can
function at a higher level, you might want to look into a trend
called *biohacking*. There are numerous podcasts and books
that fit into this category, but the basic concept is looking for
shortcuts, or "hacks" to increase our body's productivity and
performance. Now, there are people who consider themselves
professional biohackers, and they are essentially acting as human guinea pigs, testing new products, supplements, diets,
and so on. I urge you to let them do the testing, rather than
subjecting yourself to something that is potentially dangerous.
Be smart.

But biohacking can be a fascinating rabbit hole in which to
go down and you'll learn about all kinds of different ways you can
boost your brain function from certain glasses that combat the fa-
tiguing effects of blue light, to MCT oil to give mental clarity, vibration plates to detox the body, sensory deprivation tanks, and the list
goes on! Do some research online or in your podcast app and see
what you find interesting.

In an earlier chapter, we agreed that openness is essential in
your Best Self journey. When it comes to your health, and making sure that you feel incredible, you need to keep an open mind.

Know that there are lots of options out there, and if you do your homework, you can find something that works for you and makes you feel great.

Health Inventory

Now it's time to determine what you'd like to accomplish in the area of your physical health. These questions will help you.

PART 1: First, rate your physical health on a scale of 1–10. A "1" would mean that you recognize that your health SPHERE needs your immediate attention because you are facing health challenges, and a "10" would mean that you are already taking excellent care of your overall health and you have little to no room for improvement in this SPHERE. Aspects of your health SPHERE to consider when assigning your rating include:

- how you feel physically,
- which behaviors you feel you need to change because they are negatively impacting your health,
- how your body is helping you align with your Best Self.

Physical Health Rating: _____ as of _____ (date)

PART 2: Now, list out some of your behaviors that are working well for your health and why they're working.

Examples:
- I regularly exercise in a way that feels good for my body.
- I eat foods that I know are supporting and preserving my physical health.
- I go in for checkups on a routine basis.

Behaviors that are working to protect, promote, and preserve my health are:

_____Why? _____

_____Why? _____

_____Why? _____

PART 3: What are some behaviors that are not working for your health, and why?

Examples:
- I am abusing some substance that is harmful to my health.
- I am neglecting some aspect of my physical health out of fear or denial.
- I am avoiding exercise because I feel that I have too far to go to achieve any degree of health.

Behaviors that are not working in the area of my health are:

_____Why? _____

_____Why? _____

_____Why? _____

PART 4: Based on everything you just wrote down, I want you to think about what you need to do in order to go from your current rating to a rating of 10 in this area of your life.

The way you'll do this is to look at behaviors you need to *continue* doing because they're working for you, behaviors you need to *stop* doing because they're keeping you from what you want, and behaviors you need to *start* doing.

In order for my physical health to feel like it's at a 10,

I need to continue: _____

I need to stop: _____

I need to start: _____

The Next of your Seven SPHERES

My hope is that you feel empowered about your health, and that you understand that if you're not feeling great, there are a multitude of options out there to help you feel better. Allow your own intuition to be your guide and take your health into your own hands today. Going forward, I hope you make a pact with yourself to be honest about your behaviors, because the truth is that everything we do, eat, think, and feel has an immediate and direct impact on our physical health, and thus, your longevity. Later, when we're talking about setting specific goals to improve each of our SPHERES, include at least one health goal. Deepak Chopra says, "If you consciously let your body take care of you, it will become your greatest ally and trusted partner." Remember that as you go forward!

Next, we will tackle your SPHERE of learning. I'm really excited to show you how to remain in a lifetime learning mode. Knowledge is power, and it's what helps us avoid stagnation and continue to evolve.

8

Your **S P H E R E S** ducation

I sat in the back of the classroom, notepad and pen at the ready, trying my absolute best to keep up with what the teacher was saying. I started out by furiously writing down every word I could, but after a few minutes went by, I tuned out and just started doodling cartoon faces. I squinted my eyes, shook my head, and told myself, "Listen. Come on. You can do this." Then the teacher announced it was time for a pop quiz. As I stared down at the questions in front of me, I felt like my throat was closing. I didn't know a single answer. Even though it ran completely contrary to my character, the thought of looking at the kid's answers next to me flashed across my mind. I was desperate. Everyone knew that if you flunked your classes, you would have to go to the dreaded summer school. I'd seen those kids many times during summer basketball league, and they all looked like zombies. No thanks!

Walking out of the classroom after the bell rang, I couldn't have told you one detail from the lesson my English teacher had just taught. The only thing I knew for sure was that I'd failed that quiz. Ugh.

"What am I doing wrong?" I asked myself. I felt like everyone had the playbook for how to do school. I just was guessing. I swapped out books at my locker and realized that the next class was history. I had left my history book at home. I knew I'd need my book today. I'd even created a special cover for my history books, with maps all over it. Standing there in the hallway of my junior high school, I felt like I just wanted to give up. I was always a step behind. I just couldn't compete academically no matter how hard I tried. School was torture for me.

I also had no idea why I had to learn the specific lessons taught at school. How was I going to use any of this in my real life? Even now I wonder why on earth I needed to spend time learning cursive or algebra.

Sports and friendships were what I loved most about school. My social circle and basketball carried a lot of the self-esteem that was completely missing from my academic life. I loved the camaraderie and teamwork. Looking back, I can see now that I've always thrived in team settings—when we had group assignments or presentations in class, I always did well. On my own, I floundered.

I usually knew what days the report cards were coming, and I'd try to get home early enough to intercept them in the mail. That day I'd been too late. As I walked through the front door of our house, I could already hear my brother and sister celebrating their latest straight-A report cards with Mom and Dad. (Actually, let me be clear because they would take offense my saying they had straight A's—they both had 4.3 GPAs or higher. Who on earth gets higher than a 4.0?! WTF!) I, on the other hand, had completely forgotten about report cards. Wonderful. I rounded the corner into the kitchen and I could practically hear the record scratching and falling silent as all eyes were suddenly trained on me. An unopened envelope sat on the counter, with my name front and center. My brother and sister were practically glowing and they didn't have to say a word—we all knew how this was going to go.

Trying my best to distract, I said, "Hey, guys! What's for dinner?" My attempt fell flat, as my mom picked up the ominous-looking envelope and handed it over to me.

"Michael, your report card came today!"

Through gritted teeth and a fake smile, I replied, "Oh, how amazing!" Of course, I knew in my gut I would be disappointing her and my father once again, but I ripped into the envelope anyway. Two B's, two C's, and one D stared back at me. My shoulders hunched over, I left the report card on the counter and slinked silently off toward my room.

Later that evening, my parents sat me down for a serious talk. I was no rookie when it came to this kind of discussion. I braced myself for the guilt trip, for the advice on how to improve my grades; maybe they were going to hire another tutor. But this conversation went differently, and not in a good way.

"Mike, we think it's in your best interest if you repeat the eighth grade." My parents went on to explain their reasoning—that it would give me an advantage playing high school basketball—but I knew the truth. I simply wasn't keeping up. At the sound of those words, it felt like my whole life had just cracked in two. My parents were holding me back. In *junior high*. All of my friends would be heading off to begin their high school careers, and I'd be stuck with a bunch of younger kids, taking all the same miserable classes as I had for this entire year. It was as if I'd be living in a perpetual state of Groundhog Day—repeating the same cycle of twenty-four-hour misery again and again. This couldn't be happening to me. I simply nodded my head, my eyes cast down toward my feet, unable to utter a response, and went to bed.

My parents chose to enroll me in St. John the Baptist Catholic school in the hopes that I would get more attention from the teachers there than I had in my public school. But it only just served to confuse me more, because on top of understanding the new environment, I had to figure my way around the Catholic faith. When I arrived, everything was different than public school. We wore uniforms (which kept me from having to shop at the big-and-tall store, thankfully), for one, and I quickly learned that everyone was intimidated by a nun who ran the school. That was quite confusing to me as I wasn't sure why people would be scared of a tiny, old lady in black-and-white. I had only ever seen nuns in movies like *Sister Act*, so my understanding of nuns was clearly limited. I was a kid who'd never done a Hail Mary in his life—nor did I understand the point of all of it. I had a ton of catching up to do, but I did have some success on the basketball team, and my grades improved a tiny bit.

I went on to attend Mater Dei High School, the largest Catholic school west of the Mississippi with more than five thousand students. Mater Dei was known for their athletics. I was the oldest freshman in my class, and I had a great social life all four years there. By my senior year, I was captain of the basketball team and we were ranked in the top twenty-five schools in the nation, so the pressure on the court was intense.

Despite having tutors from Princeton Review and being as disciplined as I possibly could, my grades remained poor and I performed badly on the SATs. Luckily, because of my basketball skills, I was able to go as a walk-on at Fordham University in the Bronx.

Once I arrived at college, I just wanted to have fun. By that time, my addiction had started to spiral out of control, and I was addicted to crystal meth. I stopped sleeping, doing more and more meth, and even convinced myself that in addition to it being a fun drug, it would also help my studies. Boy, was that completely wrong.

I can remember a time when I did a line of meth in the bathroom before philosophy class. I hadn't slept in about three days. The longest I went without sleep was seven days and that was toward the end, before I made a decision to change my life. In class, the teacher was lecturing about Descartes and I raised my hand. I started to debate the teacher. It was like an out-of-body experience. I thought I was so smart. I thought I was running the class. That's the thing about drugs, they make you lose touch with reality completely. I was talking nonsense, which only became apparent to me when I saw all the students in class turn around to stare at me in the back of the room. I remember feeling so embarrassed that I packed up my bag and left class early.

I just felt so out of place in college. I eventually dropped out of school and made a decision to get sober.

Once I was clean, I attended Metro State University, in Minnesota. It is amazing the things we can do when we aren't abusing drugs. It was in my psychology courses and the drug and alcohol counseling courses that I came alive. What had shifted? I had finally been able to connect my authentic self with my studies— I was focused on what I actually wanted to learn. I became a straight-A student practically overnight, and it felt amazing.

When you change your story, and when you pursue what you love, incredible things can happen. The fact that I got straight A's, frankly, was a miracle, but when you are living right, miracles become real.

While I was an undergrad at Metro State, I interned at two different treatment facilities, and worked at two others. We focused a lot on helping people get off and stay off drugs and alcohol, but what I realized was that their real struggle wasn't with substances; their struggle was with life. It seemed to me that there was too much emphasis on the diagnosis and very little to do with teaching folks how to become the best version of themselves. The recidivism rates were terrible; people couldn't manage to stay off drugs and alcohol after leaving the facility. Even the prestigious rehab I went to didn't have great results—of the twenty-two men I was there with, only two of us remained sober within one year of treatment.

During my internships, I learned so much. I came to understand that I was driven to help people, not just addicts but everyone, who struggles to improve their lives. When I realized this, I read and read and then read some more. When you're happy with your life, you don't abuse drugs and alcohol. If I could help people discover happiness, the rest would take care of itself.

As I've shared, I ultimately opened the CAST Centers, a treatment facility that focuses specifically on aligning people with the lives they want to live as a method of dealing with addiction and other mental health disorders. We often say that by the time our clients are done at CAST, they practically have a master's in psychology because of the wide range of best practices we teach and incorporate in our program. We spent years creating the CAST Alignment model, which I am sure you can guess is focused on a person's Best Self and operating from a place of authenticity. Our results have been powerful, and I continue to be inspired by our clients who are able to turn their lives completely around. At CAST, we don't follow what other treatment centers are doing in the industry unless it somehow helps free our clients to be a better version of themselves.

The reason I share my own educational journey with you is this: once you discover the topics about which you are passionate, you can and *will* love learning. I am not saying that you will have my experience. You will have your own experience. Ever since I chose to work in the mental health profession, I have never stopped learning. I listen to podcasts, I watch YouTube videos by people who inspire me, I push myself to evolve and become more knowledgeable, and I enjoy every second. Education is what helps us evolve, grow, and get better.

Even if you never liked school, if you believe you have a learning difference or you think you just don't like the process of taking in new information, your Best Self is *thirsty* for knowledge—your job is simply to figure out what interests you on a deep level. What quenches your unique thirst for knowledge, and, importantly, what is the best method for you to learn? These are the questions we are going to explore together within this chapter. Let's go for it.

Exercise: Your Current Education Picture

Part 1: What do you want to learn?

Right now, I want you to write down three things that you'd love to learn about, or that you've always said you wanted to learn one day. These can be any topic that's ever been of interest to you, so reach deep inside yourself for this one. What topics is your Best Self interested in?

If you always thought you'd like to speak another language but you just haven't taken the time, put that on the list. Maybe you've wondered if taking a pottery class would be a fun way of expressing yourself creatively. Add it to the list. Perhaps you've daydreamed about getting your motorcycle license, but just never took the plunge. Maybe you saw a documentary on a specific topic, person, or point in history that really fascinated you—take that as a cue to learn more through research, books, podcasts, and more.

Whatever it is that sounds intriguing and can give you a new skill or set of information—those are the items that you should include on this list.

I would like to learn . . . .

1. _____
2. _____
3. _____
4. _____
5. _____
6. _____
7. _____

Part 2: Why aren't you learning these things?

Now, why *aren't* you currently spending time learning new things? Maybe you think you're too old to learn a new language. Perhaps you believe you can't create time in your life, or that you've never been smart enough to grasp new information.

Write your reasons for not learning more about the topics you wrote down in the first part of this exercise here:

1. _____
2. _____
3. _____

Part 3: Are your reasons valid or true?

Let's test your reasoning. Go through your list of reasons for why you are not currently committing time to learning more about your areas of interest, and test if those reasons are true.

For instance, if one of your reasons is that you're too old to learn something new, ask yourself if anyone your age or older has ever learned a new skill. The answer to that question is yes, of course they have! Consider Priscilla Sitienei, a midwife from a rural area of Kenya. She received no education growing up, and thus did not know how to read or write. But she had a desire to record some family history to pass down to future generations, so she began going to school with her six great-great-grandchildren . . . at the age of ninety!* Vera Wang didn't become a fashion designer until she was forty years old. Joy Behar was an English teacher until she started her career in showbiz when she was in her forties. Harland Sanders, whom you know as Colonel Sanders, opened his first Kentucky Fried Chicken restaurant when he was sixty-five years old. If these people learned and put into practice brand-new skills at an older age, so can you. Therefore, your "I'm too old" reason is neither true nor valid.

If one of your reasons is that you cannot create time in your schedule for learning about one of these items, look for thirty minutes per week to devote to your new skill. If you can find half an hour, and everyone owes themselves half an hour, then your reason is not true, and you would circle "Invalid."

Rewrite your reasons for not learning more about topics that interest you here, and then circle Valid or Invalid after each one:

Reason   *Circle one:*

1. _____ Valid or Invalid

2. _____ Valid or Invalid

3. _____ Valid or Invalid

Part 4: Commit to Learning

This exercise can be very enlightening, if you allow it to be so. The point is for you to realize that the only thing stopping you from learning something is your own excuses.

---

* http://www.bbc.com/future/story/20170828-the-amazing-fertility-of-the-older-mind.

Remember, you don't have to enroll in a formal class to continue to be educated. There are endless options for learning out there. If you like the structure of a curriculum, you can do online classes at your own pace. Or, if you want a more casual process, you can listen to podcasts, watch videos online, and read books or articles. Or perhaps you know someone who is an expert in something—you could ask them to help you in learning more about that topic or skill.

There is a lot of research backing the idea that seeking new information, building new skills, and using your brain in new ways on a regular basis is one of the best ways to preserve the long-term health of your brain. It can slow aging, reduce your risk of dementia, and keep your brain nimble and clear for the future, but also for now.* The more you use the brain, the more you *can* use your brain. It's interesting how that works, right?

Learn out of Love, Not Duty

Now that you have a fresh outlook on the type of information your Best Self wants to learn, it's time to ask yourself if you're engaging in learning about something that actually does not interest you on any level.

I've worked with plenty of clients over the years who attended college and majored in something because their parents demanded it, or even went to law school or graduate school at someone else's urging, or because they believed it was necessary to have the career expected of them. I can tell you firsthand that

---

* Matthew Solan, "Back to School: Learning a New Skill Can Slow Cognitive Aging," https://www.health.harvard.edu/blog/learning-new-skill-can-slow-cognitive-aging -201604279502.

sometimes we get notions in our heads about advanced degrees we think are needed in order to pursue something we love, but very often, there's another way in if school is not for you. Twelve years ago, when I decided I wanted to open a treatment facility that focused specifically on aligning people with the lives they wanted as a method of addiction and mental illness treatment, I thought the next logical step I needed to take was to get my master's degree in social work. I spent hundreds of hours researching and visiting the best schools. Then I started studying for the GRE, the entrance exam for master's programs.

I studied constantly; day and night, nonstop, I lived and breathed the GRE. I was going to ace that thing, come hell or high water (or, in this case, snow). Test day arrived. I was in my apartment in Minneapolis and there was a damn blizzard outside. I got in my car, turned the key in the ignition, and found that it wouldn't start.

As I sat there in the driver's seat, helpless, unable to take the test I'd prepared so much for, it hit me like a ton of bricks. I was on the wrong path and the universe was telling me to stop—grad school was not for me. Right then and there, I decided I was going to find a different way to accomplish my goal. Even though I had no clue how, I knew in my spirit that I was going to do things radically different from how everyone else in the mental health space was doing things and help people the way I believed they would best be helped. And that's exactly what I did! I questioned the status quo, the way that everyone else was doing it, and then blazed my own trail. All along this journey I've been on, my parents have been thrilled that I've discovered my niche, my passion in life, and are very proud.

Here's one more example I want to share with you—I recently met someone who had a marketing career that he didn't find satisfying, so he decided to go to law school in his mid-thirties. It was a grind for him, and he did not enjoy the process in the least.

But he followed through nonetheless, while also fitting in as much time as he could playing beach volleyball and swimming in the ocean—two things he loved dearly and that made him feel truly alive. He'd been a junior lifeguard in his youth, and he always thought of those times as the best in his life.

Immediately upon law school graduation, he joined a well-respected firm in Los Angeles. After less than a year of working as an attorney, he came to realize that he was wasting his precious time on earth doing something that he wasn't passionate about, and worse than that, it ran contrary to the fundamental elements of his Best Self. So, he quit. And then he drove straight to the beach and started training for a new skill—that of being a lifeguard. Now he spends his days doing exactly what he loves, and he hasn't looked back.

I know he'd tell you the biggest lesson to take away from his experiences is to not wait as long as he did. If you're unhappy in your educational path, make a change. I'm not talking about crumbling under the pressure of a difficult course or a tough professor—I'm talking about a feeling in your gut that you're not connecting with the information being taught, or that you can't force yourself to care about it. Those are signs that it's not aligned with your Best Self, and that the issue is not something that will ever resolve on its own.

If you're currently in school or investing a lot of time learning about a specific topic, and you're not feeling fulfilled, is there another means to your end goal you haven't yet considered? Try to approach your studies from multiple angles so you can see new possibilities.

The Most Important Lessons Are about Yourself

Education is the driver behind your evolution as your Best Self, and a very important part of that is learning more about yourself. Self-awareness is key. By remaining curious, you can always find out more about what makes you tick. You'll also uncover certain triggers that might lead to your Anti-Self stepping in, and as you do, you will gain control over those triggers.

Right now, ask yourself these three questions so that you can continue to learn about who you are and who you want to become:

How have you evolved in the last year?
How are you choosing to evolve today?
What do you want to evolve into a year from now?

If you were going to teach a room full of fifteen-year-olds a course called "Life," and the students were totally motivated to learn—like total sponges—what would you teach them? Write it here:

_____

_____

_____

The point of that exercise was for you to discover your most fundamental beliefs about life. Those beliefs are going to change over time, and they might already be shifting simply because of the work you've been doing in this book. This is very telling about your own story up until the current moment.

PART 1: First, rate your educational life on a scale of 1–10, where "1" means that you need to prioritize this SPHERE and give it some immediate attention because it is severely lacking, and a "10" means that you have little to no room for improvement in the SPHERE of education. Aspects of your education SPHERE to consider when assigning your rating include:

- Your evolution in terms of learning aligns with the interests of your Best Self.
- Do you learn more about yourself every day?
- Do you go to bed each night feeling more knowledgeable than when you woke up that morning?

Work/Education Rating: _____ as of _____(date)

PART 2: Now, list out some behaviors that are working well in your educational life, and why.

Examples:
- I push myself to learn a lot, while keeping my life in balance.
- I feel passionate about what I'm learning every day.

Behaviors that are working in my educational life are:

_____Why? _____

_____Why? _____

_____Why? _____

PART 3: What are some behaviors that you know are keeping you from what you want in your educational life?

Examples:

- I work all week, and I just want to shut my brain off on the weekends!
- I am untrusting of new information.
- I end up watching the news and believe that is a way of educating myself when in reality, it is simply a distraction.

Behaviors that are not working for me in the area of my work/educational life are:

_____ Why? _____

_____ Why? _____

_____ Why? _____

PART 4: Based on everything you just wrote down, I want you to think about what you need to do in order to go from your current rating to a rating of 10 in this area of your life.

The way you'll do this is to look at behaviors you need to *continue* doing because they're working for you, behaviors you need to *stop* doing because they're keeping you from what you want, and behaviors you need to *start* doing.

In order for my work/educational life to feel like it's at a 10,

I need to continue: _____

I need to stop: _____

I need to start: _____

Evolution of Your Best Self

I believe if you're living each day with an open mind, a curious spirit, honesty, a willingness to take action when needed, and an extreme focus on the tasks at hand, then your mind will become fertile ground for learning vital new information. Those are the elements needed to continue to evolve and grow within your Best Self. The incredible thing is that each new day affords you new opportunities to improve yourself, and thus the lives of those around you. Ensure that you're always in "learning mode."

Moving ahead within your SPHERES, the next area we'll investigate is your relationships. Who you are at your core will be apparent in all your close relationships—with family, friends, and romantic partners. It's completely possible to be your Best Self with all of the people in your life.

9

Your Relationships

The truth is, as much as we'd like to think that some relationships are so "complicated," most are really quite simple. If everyone shows up as their Best Self at all times, for most interactions in a relationship, it's going to be relatively smooth sailing. Will you disagree from time to time? Naturally. Do people evolve and sometimes shift away from one another as they enter new seasons of life? Definitely. Those are normal, expected occurrences. But long periods of disharmony or even toxicity between two people simply do not need to happen. The "it's complicated" option really does not need to exist for your relationship status.

The tricky part is that you can't control whether other people operate as their Best Self in their interactions with you. The only person you can control is yourself, so in this chapter we're going to talk about ways you can control your authenticity, and what you can do when those around you aren't reflecting their own. Relationships can get out of balance from time to time, but with the tools I'll give you here, you can be proactive about doing your part to get them back to equilibrium.

Your Best Self does not ever want you to become a doormat in an unhealthy relationship, so sometimes you may need to make tough decisions and part ways with someone. But in this chapter, we will go through some steps you can take in your troubled relationships before you get to that point.

I've divided this chapter into three main sections: Your Values (which have an impact on all of your relationships), Family Relationships, and Intimate Relationships. At its heart, however, this entire chapter is about *you* and how you can stay connected to your Best Self across every relationship you have with other people.

Your Values

In order to have a meaningful conversation about all of the relationships in your life, we need to start with answering this key question: what are your core values? This is because conflict generally arises in our relationships when our values are at odds.

Values are principles or standards of behavior we hold as very important in life. It's your personal code, your measure for right and wrong. Keeping your values aligned with your Best Self helps you to make better decisions in life, but also in relationships. You might already have a basic understanding of your own set of values, or perhaps you've never given them much thought. The family you grew up with had certain values, and some of them may be part of who you are today, and others may not.

You will notice that not all of the values on the list are positive ones. Many of them have negative connotations such as anxiety, bitterness, and regret. Sometimes people do value negative feelings like that—for instance, someone who believes things won't work out unless they worry about them constantly, if they're being honest with themselves, would say that they worry is one of their values. That certainly wouldn't be a value that your Best Self holds dear, and the hope is that, by this point in the book, you have shifted your values to only include positive feelings or attributes.

Values Exercise Part 1:

Here is a list of core values. Circle the ones that resonate with you.

Authenticity	Growth	Reputation	Appreciation
Achievement	Generosity	Respect	Forgiveness
Adventure	Honesty	Responsibility	Perseverance
Authority	Humor	Security	Anger
Autonomy	Influence	Self-Respect	Discouragement
Balance	Inner Harmony	Service	Hostility
Beauty	Justice	Spirituality	Regret
Boldness	Kindness	Stability	Anxiety
Compassion	Knowledge	Success	Disinterest
Challenge	Leadership	Status	Humiliation
Citizenship	Learning	Trustworthiness	Rejection
Community	Love	Wealth	Bitterness
Competency	Loyalty	Wisdom	Embarrassment
Contribution	Meaningful Work	Zest	Jealousy
Creativity	Openness	Self-Regulation	Resignation
Curiosity	Optimism	Intelligence	Condemnation
Determination	Peace	Teamwork	Failure
Fairness	Pleasure	Humility	Judgment
Faith	Poise	Perspective	Rigidity
Fame	Popularity	Social Intelligence	Criticism
Friendships	Recognition		Fear of [specify]
Fun	Religion	Prudence	Lethargy

Sadness	Futility	Suspicion	Guilt
Cynicism	Misery	Despondency	Poverty
Frustration	Sorrow	Greed	Worry
Loneliness	Despair	Pessimism	
Self-Doubt	Gloom	Withdrawal	
Depression	Ostracism	Disappointment	

Now that you have circled all the values that apply to you, rank your top seven values from most important to least.

1. _____

2. _____

3. _____

4. _____

5. _____

6. _____

7. _____

All of the positive values on the list you just created above represent your character strengths. These are behaviors that should energize you and what you offer to others in relationships. However, if there are some negative values on your list, realize that those are coming from your Anti-Self, and your goal is to move away from values like that and embrace the positive values you listed.

Values Exercise Part 2:

Next, in another color circle the values that were your family of origin's. These may differ from your values, and that's okay! The idea here is to see the overlap, and the differences.

Authenticity	Justice	Wisdom	Rigidity
Achievement	Kindness	Zest	Criticism
Adventure	Knowledge	Self-Regulation	Fear of [specify]
Authority	Leadership	Intelligence	Lethargy
Autonomy	Learning	Teamwork	Sadness
Balance	Love	Humility	Cynicism
Beauty	Loyalty	Perspective	Frustration
Boldness	Meaningful Work	Social Intelligence	Loneliness
Compassion	Openness	Prudence	Self-Doubt
Challenge	Optimism	Appreciation	Depression
Citizenship	Peace	Forgiveness	Futility
Community	Pleasure	Perseverance	Misery
Competency	Poise	Anger	Sorrow
Contribution	Popularity	Discouragement	Despair
Creativity	Recognition	Hostility	Gloom
Curiosity	Religion	Regret	Ostracism
Determination	Reputation	Anxiety	Suspicion
Fairness	Respect	Disinterest	Despondency
Faith	Responsibility	Humiliation	Greed
Fame	Security	Rejection	Pessimism
Friendships	Self-Respect	Bitterness	Withdrawal
Fun	Service	Embarrassment	Disappointment
Growth	Spirituality	Jealousy	Guilt
Generosity	Stability	Resignation	Poverty
Honesty	Success	Condemnation	Worry
Humor	Status	Failure	
Influence	Trustworthiness	Judgment	
Inner Harmony	Wealth		

Now, rank the top seven values that you grew up with as a child.

1. _____
2. _____
3. _____
4. _____
5. _____
6. _____
7. _____

Values Exercise Part 3:

In order to see the differences between your current values and those of your family, let's compare them side by side.

MY CORE VALUES	MY FAMILY'S VALUES
1.	1.
2.	2.
3.	3.
4.	4.
5.	5.
6.	6.
7.	7.

Values Exercise Part 4:

Becoming more aware of your own values will help you identify people in your life whose values sync up with yours, and help you become more aware of why you may have issues with certain people in your life. To help you dig deeper, answer these questions:

What do people tell you are your strengths? For instance, do people tell you that you are a loyal friend? Or that you are an optimist? Or that you're a great teammate? Think about the positive feedback you've received from friends, family members, coworkers, bosses, subordinates, etc., and write it all down.

How do those strengths sync up with your core values?

Do you feel you need to work to exhibit more behavior in your life that reflects your values?

Sticking to and following your values is not always easy. It's a lifelong journey that has many bends in the road.

I once worked with someone who said, for his entire life, "fun" had been one of his core values. He was a cameraman who specialized in drone footage and other specialized camera work. He wouldn't take on a project unless he knew he'd have fun doing it, he traveled around the world seeking out fun adventures, and he judged how good a day had been by how much fun he'd had. He even found the perfect counterpart—a woman who equally valued fun. And then they decided to have a child, and he couldn't believe how quickly—seemingly overnight—after the baby was born that his values shifted and suddenly all that fun galivanting around the globe lost its luster, and a new value replaced it—love. He still valued fun, though, and his challenge was to find a way to make these values sync up so that one was not at odds with the other. Part of the solution was to redefine what "fun" meant for him—whereas before it might have translated into spending a weekend shooting drone shots of Coachella, now it might mean going with his family to the park up the street. The point is: you may need to redefine how you live up to your values as your life evolves and changes. As your priorities in your life change, your values likely will, too.

Another way in which your values may be challenged is when you or someone you love is wronged in some way. When the unexpected occurs—whether it's losing a home to a natural disaster, being wrongly accused of something, or if illness strikes—that's when our core values are tested the most. But it is when we are facing adversity that we most need to connect with and exercise our core values, as they are what will help see us through to the other side.

SECTION 1: Family Relationships

Our relationships with our blood relatives/family of origin are the first ways that we learn how to connect with others. No one thrives in isolation; we come to know ourselves through others. Secure and healthy connections with family are one of the main ingredients for having a resilient life. Our bond with our family begins to shape our beliefs and behaviors, teach us what we need from others to proceed in feeling safe and responded to in our early childhood. These first relationships form our behavioral patterns for the rest of our lives.

Our capacity to give and receive love has deep roots in our earliest experience and process of attaching to and connecting with others. As does an incapacity.

At the CAST Centers, using the CAST Alignment Model, we explore our attachment patterns of behavior and the impact they have on our lives today. These patterns of bonding and attachment behaviors are activated when our individual needs surface requiring safety, security, and closeness. When these needs are met, we would describe this as a secure attachment.

A secure attachment implies a system in which the attachment figure, usually a parent or major caregiver, is seen as accessible and responsive when needed, providing a secure base from which you can explore the world.

On the other hand, insecure attachment implies a system in

which the responsiveness of the caregiver cannot be assumed, and the child's needs are not met, which drives the child to adopt a strategy for the perceived unresponsiveness of the parent or caregiver. This may manifest as disruptive, or attention-seeking behavior, all aimed at regulating a relationship with a caregiver to have the child's needs met. Or, interestingly, an insecure attachment can lead a person in a positive direction. For example, Beth's dad was an alcoholic while she was growing up, but because of her dad's lack of taking care of her, she learned at a young age how to take care of herself. Now as an adult she knows how to take care of herself and take on responsibilities because she's been doing so for most of her life.

The bad news may be that we did not all experience a secure attachment when we were young, but the good news is that you can develop the right strategies and good habits in your adult relationships—and this is true within intimate relationships, friendships, and even relationships with family members. There are several ways to do this: you can create more awareness around identifying your needs in any given relationship, you can engage in healthy communication with the other person, you can set healthy boundaries with others so that you never feel taken advantage of, and you can work on managing the feelings that arise when you might not get what you want from others.

To get you thinking about your family relationships, both when you were a child and now, here are some questions to ask yourself:

- When you were younger, who did you believe your family wanted you to be?
- What pressure did you feel from your family to behave in a certain way?
- What was important to your family? (Academics, chores, babysitting your younger siblings, all of the above?)

- How important is your family to you on a scale of 1–10? Why did you choose the number you chose?
- How good is your relationship with your family on a scale of 1–10? What makes it good? What is your struggle?
- What are strengths that you developed from growing up with your family? (Examples: you're hardworking, disciplined, focused, honest.)
- How do you handle conflict, and how is it similar or dissimilar to your parents? Does it work for you?
- Do you still worry if your parents are going to like something you decide, whether they are going to approve or not approve of your behavior?
- Are there negative moments from your childhood that still haunt you? What are they? Can you reframe those memories into something you can appreciate now?

TIPS FOR EMPTY-NESTERS

When you've spent so much of your time, love, and energy raising children, and find that one day, they are just gone—off to college, the military, or just flew the coop to live on their own—your life can feel like one giant void. Dealing with an empty nest can be very emotional, but you can find peace in your new quiet space. Here's how:

1. Know that it's normal to feel emotional at first, and don't try to stash those emotions away. Cry when you need to but try to end each crying session by reminding yourself that you've done a good job raising your kids—that's why they feel confident enough to leave home in the first place!

2. Your child is moving on, and you need to as well. This is a great time to reassess your life, reconnect with your Best

Self, take on some new hobbies and responsibilities, and live each day to the fullest. Find ways you can give back such as volunteering, connecting with old friends, or joining a new exercise class. Find joy in other things besides your child.

3. Though your child may not be living with you, remember that you are still a parent. Now, you may not be making the hands-on, day-to-day decisions, but you are still a resource to your child. You will still need to be there for him or her, no matter what. You are still valued.

4. Remember, your child isn't moving away from you—they are moving toward his/her own life. Take time to celebrate your accomplishments as a parent rather than focusing on your sadness that they are gone.

5. Do not call your child constantly, demand visits, or pour on the guilt. In so doing, you will hold him or her back and make them feel responsible for your happiness. They can't be. Do not sabotage his or her success by asking them to fill a void for you.

If You're Angry with a Family Member(s)

We may allow a family member to say or do certain things that are hurtful to us because they are "family." If a friend or stranger did these same things to you, you would likely have a very different reaction. A fight in a family system typically happens when somebody says or does something that directly or indirectly hurts you. Because we don't have a family therapist sitting with us in our living rooms growing up, we are left trying to make sense of these often painful or hurtful situations, and very often there's a lack of forgiveness that lingers. By the way, it is perfectly okay to choose not to have certain family members in your life. I have certain family members with whom I just don't have great chemistry, and I'm sure you do, too. Just because you are related by blood, that doesn't mean you are required to have a relationship with them.

If you're in an ongoing argument with a family member (sibling, parent, aunt, uncle, cousin, etc.), or you've developed a rift over the years, or you're still angry at him or her over something that happened in the past, whether it was last week, last year, or ten years ago, it's time to either start working on healing the relationship or dissolving the relationship.

If you have bitterness and guardedness with a family member, it's important to ask yourself if those emotions are spilling over into other relationships. Even if they originated with one person, these are powerful emotions and they can start to affect every area of your life and other relationships if you allow them. For example, you can't be one kind of sibling and another kind of mother, wife, or friend. In order to truly live as your Best Self, you need to show up as your Best Self within all of your relationships. It's impossible to compartmentalize, so I encourage you to take steps to mend a troubled relationship with a family member, so it doesn't pollute other parts of your life.

Here are some tools to help you tap into your Best Self to get to some healing in this space.

- If every time you think about confronting your family member, you get scared or anxious, and worry about their reaction, ask yourself if the problem could really be with you.
  - Trust yourself to come out from behind your wall, deal with what happens no matter what, and then love them through it.

- Are you afraid of being vulnerable? If you miss having a relationship with your family member, tell them, even if that means allowing yourself to be vulnerable. You might be afraid of getting hurt, but aren't you presently in pain because you're withholding your feelings? Isn't that course of action keeping you in conflict? Take the risk; don't let fear of vulnerability stand in your way.

- If you're competing in some way with those you love, you are competing with people who are on your own team! Ideally, your family members should be a part of your support system, not the people with whom you are at odds. If a competitive spirit is at the core of your issue with this person, resolve to stop competing with him or her, and it's very likely that when you stop, they will, too.

- If you have feelings of jealousy toward your family member, ask yourself if you're really resentful of his/her success—or whether you just have a need that isn't being met by that family member. If you need your family member to acknowledge, explain, or apologize for something, tell him or her.

- Accept your differences with your family member and love him or her anyway. You don't have to be the same, and you don't have to like the same things or have the same priorities. You simply have to love each other in the best way you can.

- In the most difficult relationships, decide to take the Best Self high road by saying, "I'm going to love you, whether you like it or not." If that's how you both approach the situation, something good will come.

- Whatever your justifications for the conflict, ultimately, they aren't worth it. If you lost that family member today, how much would you be focused on your complaint against them? Would you be proud that you wasted this time? Don't let another day go by without letting your family member know what's truly in your heart.

ABUSE WITHIN FAMILIES

If you were a victim of any type of abuse at the hands of a family member, I would highly encourage you to seek professional help because it's going to affect your life today unless it's truly healed. Those relationships deeply impact our life, and if there was abuse, neglect, or a combination thereof, then it's important that you take appropriate action to get the healing that you may need. These are complex issues that aren't going to be solved just by reading this book.

SECTION 2: Intimate Relationships

Let's begin our discussion about your intimate relationships with revisiting your values and comparing them to people with whom you are intimate. That could be your partner, spouse, someone you're interested in dating, and so on.

Intimate Relationships Values
Exercise Part 1:

Circle the values that apply to your partner. Again, there are both positive and negative values in this list. Your partner may hold some negative values, and if he or she does, then you'll need to decide if that works for you or not.

Autonomy	Boldness	Citizenship	Contribution
Balance	Compassion	Community	Creativity
Beauty	Challenge	Competency	Curiosity

Determination	Pleasure	Perspective	Fear of [specify]
Fairness	Poise	Social Intelligence	Lethargy
Faith	Popularity	Prudence	Sadness
Fame	Recognition	Appreciation	Cynicism
Friendships	Religion	Forgiveness	Frustration
Fun	Reputation	Perseverance	Loneliness
Growth	Respect	Anger	Self-Doubt
Happiness	Responsibility	Discouragement	Depression
Honesty	Security	Hostility	Futility
Humor	Self-Respect	Regret	Misery
Influence	Service	Anxiety	Sorrow
Inner Harmony	Spirituality	Disinterest	Despair
Justice	Stability	Humiliation	Gloom
Kindness	Success	Rejection	Ostracism
Knowledge	Status	Bitterness	Suspicion
Leadership	Trustworthiness	Embarrassment	Despondency
Learning	Wealth	Jealousy	Greed
Love	Wisdom	Resignation	Pessimism
Loyalty	Zest	Condemnation	Withdrawal
Meaningful Work	Self-Regulation	Failure	Disappointment
Openness	Intelligence	Judgment	Guilt
Optimism	Teamwork	Rigidity	Poverty
Peace	Humility	Criticism	Worry

Now, what if you have a relationship with someone who has different values from you? Well, that depends on what they are or how the priorities line up. If honesty is your number one priority in a relationship and your partner does not have it on their top six, it might be a deal breaker! But a good, open discussion about what you need/expect and value in a relationship is a great one to have in the beginning. You don't want to discover down the road that you've become deeply involved with someone who doesn't feel the same way you do about honesty. Communication and openness are key.

Awareness of who you are and what you need in order to grow in a relationship is imperative. So, answer these questions, and I encourage you to ask your partner to do the same—I find that when couples do this work together in a supportive way, it can be empowering and productive and either create a deeper connection or answer questions that you both may be avoiding in the relationship.

1. What you are willing to accept in a relationship?
2. What you are not willing to accept in a relationship?

As you form new intimate relationships in your life or continue to shape and evolve within your current one, keep these questions in mind so that you can be sure you're never connected to someone who does not share your core values.

Myths vs. Reality in Intimate Relationships

Have you ever thought about how the media shapes our perceptions and beliefs around what romantic relationships are supposed to look like? Earlier, I shared with you a story about one of my clients whose Anti-Self was nicknamed Rapunzel. Her unrealistic ideals and ideations about intimate relationships were born out of messages she'd received through television shows, movies, music, commercials, and pop culture in general. Yes, she experienced some dysfunction growing up and she was trying to fill the void left by a strained relationship with her father, but the media machine just fueled her fire. I think that's true for a lot of people, especially women.

Weddings are a $72 billion industry. That's some serious money! And what's sad is that as a result of all the endless television shows, magazines, and social media focus on the "big day," a lot of couples lose sight of the *big picture*. A wedding is one day. A marriage is "supposed" to last a lifetime. But in many cases, the primary focus shifts to the pomp and circumstance of that one day instead of the rest of the couple's lives. That certainly hasn't done anything to help the 50 percent divorce rate.

Almost every part of the wedding ceremony is designed to tell you that the couple is going to last forever, although in the back of your mind you may not always be so sure it's going to be permanent. Of course, you should *never* talk about that—at least not to the couple's face. (I've overheard wedding guests discussing the over-under on whether the blissful bride and groom would last a year—and that was at the reception!) The audience gasps as the beautiful bride walks down the aisle all in white, the officiant talks about God and love, about the couple being there for each other in sickness and in health, then we party—which may or may not include getting intoxicated (because what better way to celebrate holy matrimony than to get trashed afterward?). When mirrored back to us, the whole modern take on weddings can seem a little . . . shallow, don't you think? How did we get here?

For a moment, let's look at the typical timeline in terms of our exposure to society's definition of romance. As children grow up, they read books and see movies and television programs that include romanticized love stories, and this continues well into adulthood. Show me any summer blockbuster (that isn't based on a comic book franchise!) and I'll show you a glamorized love story, with all the romance and none of the compromise, rough patches, bad moods, or midlife crises. It's no wonder our expectations are completely skewed as adults—we're subjected to unrealistic depictions of love from a very young age.

Moreover, generally, these stories would have us believe that the *only* way to truly be happy in our lives is to have a partner. You're essentially told that if you're single, something is wrong with you, and you must make it a priority to find your soul mate. And it's quite challenging to overcome these subconscious beliefs when they bombard and surround us.

By the time we hit puberty, our sexuality comes into play and we realize who we're attracted to and we often develop our first crush. Most folks see a big future with that first crush—it feels like a "forever" love. There's a lot of excitement and passion, until we learn (often in a painful fashion) that it doesn't last forever. As a result, we begin to see the difference between infatuation and intimacy. Then we have the cultural norms, like school dances, where young men are expected to ask their dates with some big, romantic gesture (have you heard of "promposals," by the way? They're like marriage proposals but for the prom, and they are becoming more and more over-the-top), and everyone is just hoping someone asks them because the idea of coupling up starts young. If you're LGBTQ, it's often an even more confusing process and makes you feel even more left out. That's because there aren't significant role models kids can look to, or a consistent conversation or framework for how to navigate through social circles that may not accept you. If you're left out for whatever reason, you probably end up feeling rejected which can be extremely damaging to your self-esteem. These wounds can stay with us for decades if we let them.

I may be the oddball here, but I categorically *do not* believe something is wrong with you if you are single. The theme I defined at the very start of this book is that everyone is unique. There is no one-size-fits-all answer for people in *any* category, and that includes relationships. So, let me be clear: you can absolutely be your Best Self without being in an intimate relationship. Period. You have permission to reject all of the "you must find and marry your soul mate as soon as possible" propaganda that's being peddled to you by all corners of our culture, but especially the people who sell engagement rings, wedding dresses, and tuxedos for a living. It's a fallacy. And what's worse is that people who are trying desperately to live up to society's definitions of what their relationships should look like are often left feeling disappointed, despondent, and believing something is wrong with them, rather than with the system. That equally infuriates and saddens me. It's time we become accepting of ourselves and others, regardless of relationship status.

Stepping slowly off my soapbox now, I'll share with you what I've come to realize even in my own life is this—if you are yourself, and you have faith, then you're exactly where you're supposed to be, whether you're in a relationship or not. You can try to force things, but if pieces aren't meant to fit together, it's going to lead to heartbreak.

And here's the other important point—let's say, hypothetically, you were to get married and then divorced eight years later—there's a social stigma that says that was a bad marriage. But what if most of it was great but you just fell out of love at the end? Why can't you just celebrate those great years you had together? There shouldn't be a rule that you have to define an entire relationship based on how it ends. Cherish the good memories. Life is impermanent, and you cannot control it. I don't believe people who do get divorced are quitters or that something is wrong with them. Everyone is on their own journey. With that said, I do believe that you owe it to your Best Self and to your partner's Best Self (and certainly to your children if you have them) to try to work on a relationship before you decide to split. If you feel you've tried everything and it is simply time for the relationship to come to a peaceful end, then you can part ways knowing that everyone did their best.

Depending upon where you are currently in terms of intimate relationships—single, casually involved with someone, in a long-term committed relationship, or anything in between—the most important thing to think about is whether you are able to operate as your Best Self within that relationship. And yes, that still stands if you're single because you need to be showing up as your Best Self each and every day for yourself—remember, that's your most important relationship no matter what your relationship status. You can flip back to the Personal Life chapter for a refresher on that topic.

There are some really damaging myths around intimate relationships that I want to dispel right now. If you are subscribing to any of these myths, you are making it nearly impossible for you to live as your Best Self within your relationship. After each myth, I'm giving you some Best Self truth that you can take away and apply to your relationships. No matter how your current relationship feels to you right now, and no matter how long you've been together, you still need to be aware of these myths.

Let's take a look:

MYTH #1: A great relationship requires like-mindedness on all issues.

BEST SELF TRUTH:

- You and your partner are two different people, on every level. It is not a requirement that you think the same way about everything.
- When you do have issues in your relationship, you won't solve them by aligning your thinking exactly with your partner's, because that could actually mean betraying your core values.
- Remember that the joy of intimate relationships comes from being with someone who enriches your life, not just reflects it. Embrace your differences.

MYTH #2: A great relationship requires a great romance.

BEST SELF TRUTH:

- We already touched on this when we discussed the notion of the wedding day versus real life but there is more to it than that. If you have some deep need for being swept off your feet with movie moments constantly, you are setting yourself up for disappointment because it's simply not sustainable.
- Understand the difference between falling in love and being in love. Just because the passion and excitement of the first phase of love fades as you settle into a secure, realistic relationship doesn't mean something is wrong. It's simply a new phase, one in which you can experience a new depth of connection.

MYTH #3: A great relationship requires excellent problem solving.

BEST SELF TRUTH:

- I think a lot of people believe that in order to be in a functioning relationship, you have to solve every problem that comes your way. False!
- The majority of problems that arise in a relationship are, in fact, not solvable.
- The key is not to let these problems fester inside you and start to breed resentment, and touch upon qualities of your Anti-Self.
- Learn how to agree to disagree and find the emotional closure that you need and refuse to relive the same issues over and over or use them as a weapon against your partner.

MYTH #4: A great relationship requires common interests to eternally bond you together.

BEST SELF TRUTH:

- Sure, it's great if you both enjoy windsurfing on the weekends or going to football games in the fall. But if one of you enjoys an activity and the other does not, no one needs to go out of their way to try to learn to love it or, on the other hand, to give it up.

- Again, your differences teach your partner, so it's perfectly fine if you have divergent interests.

MYTH #5: A great relationship is a peaceful one.

BEST SELF TRUTH:

- It's unrealistic to think that you will have peace every single day of your life. Do not be afraid that arguing within a relationship is a sign of an unhealthy bond. Even the healthiest couples fight.
- Arguing is all in the approach. If done correctly, arguing can strengthen your bond by allowing you to release tension that might have built up, and by affording you the peace of mind that you can have discord between the two of you, without fear of abandonment or humiliation.

Here are some Best Self arguing techniques:

- Do ask yourself during any conflict what your Best Self would do or say, rather than indulging in emotions spun up by your Anti-Self.
- Don't attack the worth of your partner during an argument—there's never an appropriate time for character assassination.
- Do keep your voice at a normal volume—yelling does not help the other person "hear" your point.
- Don't engage in or start conflict because it's stimulating to you. That kind of behavior has Anti-Self written all over it.
- Do keep the argument on topic. Shifting to other unresolved issues just makes everything more fraught.
- Don't pursue a take-no-prisoners approach in your arguments—where you need to be right so badly that you completely shut down any kind of open conversation.

- Do tell your partner you hear and understand his or her points by repeating them back.
- Don't walk away from the issue. Even if it cannot be resolved, seek to find emotional closure you can both live with.

MYTH #6: A great relationship allows you to vent all your feelings.
BEST SELF TRUTH:

- Even in moments when you are all wound up, under huge amounts of pressure, exhausted, frazzled, or fried, remember that you still love your partner and you still owe him or her the respect of not spewing unfiltered emotion that could be extremely hurtful.
- Forgiveness is important in relationships, certainly, but don't set yourself up for having to beg for forgiveness because of something awful you said in a tense moment.
- Before you open your mouth to say something when you're feeling heightened emotions, stop, take a deep breath, and ask your Best Self what you should do. You may even want to take a pause and repeat your ritual or personal mantra. I'm not kidding! It doesn't matter if it's in the heat of an argument—you can call a time-out and go center yourself, then come back and continue.

MYTH #7: A great relationship has nothing to do with sex.
BEST SELF TRUTH:

- In relationship surveys, couples who report that they have a satisfying sex life say that sex rates at only 10 percent on the "importance scale." On the other hand, couples who report that their sex life is unfulfilling say that sex rates at 90 percent on the importance scale. In other words, sex doesn't matter in a relationship until you're not having it.
- Sex allows us to experience a quality level of closeness, vulnerability, and sharing with our partners.

- To be clear, sex doesn't simply refer to the actual physical act. Any means by which you provide physical comfort to your partner can all be viewed as part of a fulfilling sexual life.

MYTH #8: A great relationship cannot survive a flawed partner.
BEST SELF TRUTH:

- We all have two things in common: each of us is unique, and none of us is perfect. You can have a great relationship despite the fact that both of you are flawed individuals.
- Instead of obsessing about your partner's shortcomings, remember the qualities that attracted you to him or her in the first place. Perhaps some of these idiosyncrasies were part of the attraction? Just because a behavior isn't mainstream, that doesn't mean it's toxic to the relationship.
- However, there's a really important point here. Be careful to distinguish the difference between a partner with quirks and one with a serious problem. Serious problems that are destructive and abusive include substance abuse and mental/physical abuse. Unlike idiosyncrasies, these are not behaviors you should learn to live with, and you need to take steps to protect yourself and your children if something like this is going on.

MYTH #9: There is a right way and a wrong way to make the relationship great.
BEST SELF TRUTH:

- There is no definitive "right way" to be a good spouse, good parent, or to handle all the relationship challenges life throws at you. There is the way that your Best Self would do all of those things, though, and only *you* know if you're drawing from your Best Self or if you're allowing your Anti-Self to run the show.
- Do what works for you and what feels authentic to you rather than following arbitrary standards you might have read in a book, seen in a movie, or heard from a well-meaning friend.

If what you and your partner are doing is generating the results you want, stick with it. If both of you are comfortable with the current structure and values, you can write your own rules. For example, on the topic of secrets within a relationship, some couples practice complete, unvarnished openness, with no secrets being kept on either side. If that works for you, great. However, if your relationship operates just fine with a few secrets that meet specific criteria (such as no secrets that affect the health of either partner or a child, etc.), that's okay, too. The key is that you and your partner need to be on the same page about it.

- Remember not to be rigid about the way in which you accept your partner's expressions of love. There is no "right way" for someone to love you. The fact that your partner expresses feelings differently from you, or from how you might expect doesn't make those feelings less genuine or of less value.

MYTH #10: Your relationship will only be great when you can fix your partner.

BEST SELF TRUTH:

- I've said it before and I'll say it again—you only have control over yourself and your behaviors, no one else's, including your partner's. You cannot change him or her. So this means you must own your part in any issues you're facing in the relationship. And if there are aspects about your partner that you absolutely cannot accept, then don't fall prey to the belief that you can change him or her. Deal breakers are just that—reasons to end the relationship.

- One thing we talked about earlier in the book was that, once you change yourself and are living a life that is authentic to your core, to your Best Self, then you might be surprised how the immediate world around you will begin to adjust to what you're putting out there. In other words, you can't change your partner, but if you change yourself, with time, your partner may begin to react to you differently. If you change, the dynamic has to change—it doesn't mean it will change for the better, but it will change.

- You cannot expect your partner to take responsibility for your happiness; you are responsible for your own happiness. And remember that love is reciprocal—the more you give, the more you get. You must be loving and attentive to your partner in order to receive love and attentiveness.

There's no such thing as the perfect relationship, because we are all imperfect. Each relationship has its own dynamics that work or don't work. If there's an area in your relationship that's not currently working, then I hope you'll have an honest, open, and curious conversation about it. The underlying goal in the work we've done together is to learn and really understand what's important to you in your intimate relationships.

Parenting as Your Best Self

If you're a parent, there's no more important area in your life where you need to be connected to your Best Self. And from what my clients and friends who are parents tell me, there's also no other area more challenging than parenting to act from your Best Self! Remember, parent is a noun, a verb, and a 24/7 job.

If you are not currently a parent and don't plan to become one, please feel free to skip over this section. With that said, some of these tools might still prove useful in relationship with the "big kids" that you might have in your life, so it could be worth a skim.

What follows are some specific tools designed to help you with your authentic journey as a parent so that both you and your children can thrive.

Best Self Parenting Tool #1: Purposeful Parenting

One of the most important and exciting decisions you can make as a parent is to define success goals for your child. Choosing, communicating, and pursuing clear and age-appropriate goals will give your children a sense of purpose that brings them the experience of mastering their world as they achieve the designated benchmarks in their lives. Your definition of success for your child must reflect your child's interests, skills, and abilities—not just yours.

Remember—your child is not you—he or she has her own, unique personality and they must learn from an early age how to connect with *their* Best Self. Therefore, one powerful goal you can set with your child is helping him or her discover who they are, what interests them, and how they interact with the world. Nurture his or her individuality along the way so that they will be encouraged to connect with their Best Self. We teach our children by doing, so model what living as your Best Self looks like—if they see you being authentic, they'll be more apt to do so themselves. One of the primary responsibilities you have as a parent—and one of the greatest gifts you can give to your children—is to teach them to develop their gifts fully to build their lives around whatever it is that fulfills them.

Another amazing goal to work on together is socialization, which is helping your child to become a responsible citizen, work in harmony with other people, and develop intimate and trusting relationships. Within that sphere, it's important you equip your child with the ability to turn off the noise of life and not let any negativity from others affect them deep down. Encourage them to communicate with you so that you can work together to decipher what's important and what's just "noise." One of the ways you can do this is to set a nightly routine where the family goes over the good and bad parts of everyone's day. This can be over dinner, or whenever makes sense in your routine. Everyone shares at least one good thing that happened in their day and one bad thing. The idea is to share in each other's joys and encourage each other through the tough stuff. If your child was bullied or mistreated in some way, you can help them overcome that and build them up emotionally.

Finally, if you can instill the ability to practice purposeful gratitude, you will help them immensely in understanding that true happiness occurs when we're living in the moment, present, and deeply grateful for everything we have. Create a fun way to exercise gratitude as a family each day, whether that's going around the table at dinner and sharing something you are grateful for and why, or pulling something out of your family "gratitude jar" talking about why you're thankful for that thing—and bookend your day with it. It can be just a few seconds, or a longer discussion, whatever works in the daily rhythm of your family. But if you can wake up with an attitude of gratefulness and end the day that way, too, you are giving your children a gift that will serve them for a lifetime.

Best Self Parenting Tool #2: Parenting with Clarity

Parenting with Clarity is based on the principle that communication between parents and their children is essential for building and maintaining a loving and productive relationship. As a parent, your goal is to create a home environment that fosters feelings of safety, security, belonging, self-confidence, and strength for the entire family unit. In order to achieve this, you must communicate with total clarity.

Children need to feel that they have certain power and influence within the boundaries that you've created in your family. The primary way to promote that feeling is to give them your full, undivided attention when you are communicating with them, and weigh very carefully what they're seeking to convey. Listening is key. Too often, the only communication that takes place between you and your child is when a crisis has erupted or when negative feedback is being given. It's important to talk about critical issues outside of stressful situations. The time to discuss curfew, for example, is not when he or she comes home thirty minutes late. You need to clearly communicate those rules *before* your child goes out for the night. If he breaks curfew, save the discussions of consequences until the calm of the next morning when you are less likely to react out of anger. Or, if you have a younger child, and he or she sometimes refuses to brush their teeth at night, create consequences so that the next time they refuse, you can calmly and quietly remind them that their decision has specific consequences. Yelling and screaming in the heat of the moment is the poorest form of communication you can practice.

Often when it comes to communication, timing is everything. Children want to be heard, to be acknowledged and know that their feelings are being considered. They want to know that they can earn certain rights and privileges if they do what is expected of them. They want to have a perception of some power, some ability to create what they want through their behavior. This begins at a very young age—even in the earliest months of your child's life. But when he or she wants something that they shouldn't have, and you say no, it's important that you make eye contact and tell him or her that you acknowledge that they are upset, that they're having big emotions, and that you love them. Don't back down and give in if what your child wants is not something they should have. Make sure you take the time to tell them that you hear them and acknowledge their feelings. Explain the logical reasons why they cannot have whatever it is they are asking for, but don't feel the need to overly explain, as you run the risk of getting into a conversation in which they think they can convince you. State your reasons, make sure they feel heard, and then move on. If you get into the habit of doing this from the beginning, or from whatever age your child is now, then it will be easier for you to continue to handle it in this way, and it will pay off as your child grows and matures into a less demanding or recalcitrant teen.

Best Self Parenting Tool #3: Parenting by Negotiation

Life requires lots of negotiation, and parenting is no exception. As a parent, you need to identify your child's personality type and negotiate according to that.

If you've got yourself a highly rebellious kid, you don't necessarily want to approach negotiations in a heavy-handed way. One of the first steps in teaching your child the basics of negotiation is to make sure he or she can foresee the consequences of their actions and develop a sense of responsibility for the outcomes their actions generate. Then he or she will feel empowered and you will be more likely to have successful negotiations every time.

Best Self Parenting Negotiation Steps

- Narrow the area of dispute.
  - Focus only on the current dispute at hand—don't throw in other areas of discord or disagreement, recent or in the past.

- Find out what it is your child really wants.
  - You may already know what that is, but make sure it lines up with what you feel they should have. If it's something that endangers them in some way, it's off the table.

- Work to find a middle ground.
  - *Compromise* is a magic word in all households, but especially those with children. Being able to find a middle ground in which everyone feels like they've won can defuse problems quickly and prevent a battle of wills.

- Be specific in your agreement and the negotiation's outcome.
  - Make sure your child understands the final decision completely.

- Make negotiated agreements, shorter term in the beginning.
  - For young children, it's hard to refer back to an agreement made even a few hours ago. Use age-appropriate timelines when you're negotiating.

Best Self Parenting Tool #4: Parenting with Currency

If you want your child to behave appropriately, you have to set the standards for the behaviors you want. Too often, parents focus solely on their child's undesirable behaviors and as a result, their parenting styles can dissolve into complaining and reacting.

Instead of focusing on trying to change unacceptable behavior, if you focus on developing positive behaviors in your child, then the negative behaviors won't be so overwhelming. A great way to accomplish this is by understanding your child's currency. Currency is a system of rewards or acknowledgment for good behavior. If presented during or immediately after a target behavior, the likelihood of that behavior occurring again increases. Figure out a way for your child to receive as much currency as they can through appropriate behavior.

There are many different currencies and they can vary with your child's age. Star charts work very well for young kids—they get a star for specific positive behaviors, and after a certain number of stars, they receive a small gift—stickers, bubbles, sidewalk chalk. Avoid rewarding with food of any kind, so that you don't set up an unhealthy relationship with treats/candy that could be harmful later in life. And don't start off with rewards that are expensive, or else you might set expectations that are unrealistic or too high! With older kids, they can earn certain privileges or extra time for fun activities because they've shown that they are responsible and they can choose positive behaviors. Once you understand what is valuable in your child's life, you can mold and shape his or her behavior.

Best Self Parenting Tool #5:
Parenting Through Change

You must be willing to adopt a whatever-it-takes mentality when it comes to parenting. This may mean that you take two weeks off from your job and stay home with your child who is ill. You might have to make sacrifices like driving a less expensive car, moving to a smaller house, cutting back on eating out, or vacationing closer to home to afford to pay for private school when public school isn't working out. The future of you and your children is precious. When and if there are drastic issues, they will call for drastic solutions.

When changes occur in a child's life and thus the life of the family unit, it can help everyone deal with their new normal, if you write an expression of commitment together. That way, you are able to develop a communication system around everyone's new expectations, anticipate resistance, and put a plan in place for any bumps in the road.

Best Self Parenting Tool #6:
Parenting in Harmony

Creating harmony in your household starts with you making sure you are not competing with anything or anyone else for your child's attention, and vice versa. I've heard of young kids having to physically turn their parent's head away from their cell phone to get them to look them in the eye and listen to them talk. And we all know kids can plop down in front of the television and just zombie out, staring at the screen, completely oblivious to any conversation their parents may be trying to have with them. If the TV, cell phones, video games, or other tech-related activities are keeping you from having harmony within the household, it's time to seriously evaluate your family's priorities.

Start by creating your Best Family top ten Priorities. Then list the top ten things that waste time in your household. Once you compare these two lists, determine whether or not the way your family is living and investing their time is congruent. If you find the priorities and values at the top of your first list reside at the bottom of your time allocation list, you need to consciously start reordering your family's time and energy commitments so that you can all honor your Best Family Priorities.

Best Self Parenting Tool #7: Parenting by Example

The most powerful role models in children's lives are their parents. It's a fact that children learn vicariously by observing the behavior of others and noting the consequences of their actions. They watch what happens to family members when they succeed or fail, and those experiences become a reference for how they will live later in life. This is known as modeling. Through your actions, words, behavior, and love, you can direct your children to where you want them to go.

As you're parenting by example, tune in to your thoughts, feelings, and behaviors and evaluate them against how you were raised. Ensure that you are making conscious, purposeful decisions, not ones based on a negative family legacy—in other words don't allow contamination into your family system. If you experienced abuse, neglect, or questionable parenting as a child, decide that it ends with you—do not "pay it forward" to your own children. We have no choice in who our parents and family of origin are, but when it comes to how we raise our kids, we have all the choices. There are infinite ways we influence our kids, both consciously and unconsciously. It is a lot of pressure, but everything you say and do matters. Remember this.

Show your kids how to be happy, well-balanced, and fulfilled adults. Show them that you live as your Best Self, and they will learn to do the same.

Relationships Inventory

Now it's time to rate your relationships, which I've separated into three categories.

YOUR FAMILY RELATIONSHIPS: First, rate on a scale of 1–10. A "1" would mean that your family relationships are seriously troubled, affecting you negatively in your daily life, and require your immediate attention. A "10" would mean that your family relationships are supporting you living as your Best Self and require little or no improvement.

What are some behaviors that are working for you in this arena, and why? Examples:

- I set boundaries with relatives who take advantage of me.
- I am honest with my relatives, but respectful in my delivery.

What are some behaviors that you know are keeping you from what you want?

- I give in to the demands of relatives even when doing so does not serve me.
- I allow relatives' comments to cut to the quick of my feelings and I harbor guilt and resentment toward family members.

YOUR INTIMATE RELATIONSHIPS: First, rate on a scale of 1–10. A "1" would mean that your intimate relationship(s) are not functional for you and do not support you living as your Best Self. A "10" would mean that your intimate relationship(s) feel healthy and rewarding to you and do not have much room for improvement.

What are some behaviors that are working in this area, and why? Examples:

- I listen to the needs of my partner and communicate my needs.
- I am honest with my partner.

What are some behaviors that you know are keeping you from what you want? Examples:

- I cheat on someone whom I really want to honor with faithfulness and honesty.
- I have a hair-trigger response pattern, and often lose my temper with my partner.

(If this applies to you):

YOUR PARENTING LIFE: First, rate on a scale of 1–10. A "1" would mean that your parenting life is suffering, and you know it needs your immediate attention. A "10" would mean that you feel truly great about your parenting life, and you are parenting as your Best Self the majority of the time.

What are some behaviors that are working in this area, and why? Examples:

- I create positive family traditions or rituals.
- No matter how stressed out, tired, or frustrated we are, I make sure to tell my kid(s) I love them every night.

What are some behaviors that you know are keeping you from what you want? Examples:

- I raise my voice and/or argue in front of my kids.
- I demean my kids when they disrespect me.

As We Enter Your Employment SPHERE . . .

You've done a lot of work in this chapter! Good for you. Relationships are at the center of our souls and can "fill our buckets" with joy. Up next, we're going to continue by taking a look at what you do for work—and considering how much time most of us spend on work, this will be a very important conversation. So, let's make sure you're able to be your Best Self while doing your job.

10

Your Employment

SPHERES

vividly remember when my third-grade teacher at Valencia Elementary School, Miss Takahashi, asked our class what we wanted to be when we grew up. That's always how the question is phrased—*what* do you want to be? Kids' responses generally fall along familiar lines—astronaut, firefighter, doctor, president of the United States. From an early age, we are led to identifying the work we want to do, not who we want to be as people.

Imagine if we offered personal development as a course in schools. What if we taught children to focus on discovering their authentic selves, and then allowing life to dictate what type of career best suited their passions and gifts? I believe we'd see a lot less depression and anxiety among the general population if we did that instead of focusing so much on what we want to be when we grow up.

My belief in that ideal runs deep, and it's the theory upon which I've built the dual-diagnosis treatment program upon which CAST Centers thrive. Our tagline is "We create the freedom to be your Best Self," and we accomplish that through the CAM-CAST Alignment Model—which we spent years designing. I think that everyone, not just people dealing with addiction or some degree of mental health issues, deserves to discover this kind of freedom in their life. We want every person who comes to CAST to have the best, most cutting-edge therapies and fully customized treatment programs, concurrently with the most thoughtful and compassionate care. The challenge in helping people achieve this goal lies in the need to tailor our programs to everyone.

Each person's journey is different. Would it be easier to conform to more common treatment paradigms? Sure. But I didn't set out to create a cookie-cutter experience—that wouldn't have been authentic to me, my passion, or my vision. In my life, I've found there are no shortcuts, but if you're truly enjoying the journey, you prefer to take the scenic route anyway. Over the years, I've employed hundreds of people at various companies and start-ups—from attorneys to therapists, physicians, office managers, receptionists, cleaning staff, and so on—and what I've learned is that there are two types of employees—those who clock in and out to earn a paycheck, and those who are passionate about their job. There's no crystal ball in a job interview that will truly tell you whether that person is the wage earner or the passionate employee. No amount of schooling or training can tell an employer about what type of employee that person might end up being. But those who are deeply passionate about the work they're doing, and connected to their Best Self at work, are hands down the best and happiest employees.

Several years ago, I was building out the team at CAST Centers, and as the company was growing and succeeding, I started hiring people who had been in the industry for twenty-plus years. I was specifically hiring for a role that would build a bridge between our administrative work and our clinical work—and that person would be our executive director. She was beyond experienced, truly a superstar. She came in and said to me one day, "Mike, are you aware of what's going on with your clinical director?" Through the conversation that ensued, I learned essentially that the inmates were running the asylum. Our clinical director at the time was showing up to work at 11 a.m., bringing his dogs to work (and these dogs were disruptive, smelly, and not workplace-friendly), and was even seeing private patients at our offices during his work hours. When I talked to him about his behavior, he got belligerent and even believed that I was going to take his side, but ultimately he decided to resign. Once he moved on, my new executive director was able to fully turn things around within the company. And here's the key: someone who was just there for the paycheck would have never taken those steps or risked shaking things up—but because she cared so deeply about her work and was so passionate about our mission, she was able to make changes that made the whole system work better. Her enthusiasm for her work is contagious, and she's beloved by all of us at CAST.

In this chapter, my primary goal is to help you discern whether you're acting as your Best Self at work just as you are at home. I have found both in my own career history and with my clients, that if you can't be yourself at work, then you are wasting valuable time in your life. A lot of people seem to lose themselves in a fear of trying to be something that they aren't while on the job; they have trouble syncing up who they are at work with who they are in the rest of their lives. The idea is to be your Best Self at all times.

Here are some telltale signs that you're not your Best Self at work:

- You worry about whether people at work like you.
- You feel completely exhausted at the end of your workday.
- You fight feelings of boredom at work.

- You feel uncomfortable in the clothes you're required to wear at work.
- Your coworkers avoid you or don't want to spend time with you.
- You feel like the boss always promotes other people ahead of you.
- You feel you aren't using your true talents in your job.
- You clam up or just remain silent in meetings.
- You don't feel like you're in "sponge mode," learning new skills, ideas, and information on a regular basis at work.
- You can't wait to leave at the end of your workday.
- You don't feel inspired by your work.
- You can't be honest with your colleagues or boss about what needs improvement within your organization.
- You don't like your colleagues.
- When you leave work, you attempt to forget your work completely. You compartmentalize.
- You don't feel proud of yourself at work, or of the work you're doing.

If you have to essentially fake it all day long while earning a living, you are eventually going to drain yourself dry. But don't despair, you aren't trapped forever. Let's determine if your job matches up with your authentic lifestyle and make the necessary shifts if not.

What Is Your Art?

Remember in the beginning of the book when I said that we are all artists? It is true—we simply need to discover our unique art forms. I think of your art as your "why." If you haven't heard of Simon Sinek, check him out online—he created something known as the Golden Circle. It looks basically like a target—with the outer ring being "what," the middle ring being "how," and the inner circle being "why." The function of the golden circle as he sees it is primarily for businesses and branding. But in the context of my work and my life, my golden circle would be:

What = I am a life coach
How = I guide people through various exercises and modalities
Why = To give people the freedom to be their best selves

All of the projects I'm involved in, from the work we do at CAST, to the appearances I make on *The Dr. Phil Show*, come back to my why. When I am operating in my why, my work *never* feels frustrating, time-consuming, or burdensome in any way. The "why" is where your art lives.

I tell everyone I work with that they are an artist. I've worked with some of the biggest pop stars on the planet, but they are no more or less an artist than you. Our art is that connection between our Best Self and the world. Going back to who you are down deep and operating from that place is the first step to solving any problem you face within your employment SPHERES.

Here's a question for you: what is your current definition of work? I encourage you to challenge yourself here, especially if you do not enjoy your work or if there are elements of your job you truly dislike. The dictionary defines work as "a mental or physical activity as a means of earning income; employment." I can guarantee that if you don't love your job, it is because it is not aligned with your why and hence not aligned with your artistic expression.

The people who feel this way often can't wait for Friday afternoons—the end of the workweek and the start of the weekend. These folks also dread Mondays and suffer from the Sunday night blues. In some social circles, I have overheard people saying,

"Let's not talk about work." There is this sense like somehow work has to be tiring in order for it to be considered work. Americans especially seem to believe that if you're not stressed beyond belief and physically exhausted by Friday afternoon, you haven't worked hard enough that week. There's much more emphasis on the number of hours you put in than what you've actually achieved or accomplished within your work. And there's little to no emphasis on how much you've enjoyed your work or how much fun you had at work. That's not even a thing in most industries—fun at work?! And when it comes to vacation, people often talk about completely unplugging from work, ignoring emails, turning off the work phone, etc. because by the time there's a vacation rolling around, they are just completely burned out on work. To me, that's an indication that their SPHERES are out of balance. When I sit down and talk with someone who is experiencing job burnout, usually the reason isn't the job itself. It's more that they're lacking passion and fun in their life and it's easy to blame their job for that. But if your career is a reflection or manifestation of your art, then you will feel energized rather than exhausted by your work.

Here's a little quiz to help you look at your work less as a job description and more as an art.

Write down three times in the last few months that you loved your job.

1. _____
2. _____
3. _____

Why did each of those experiences make you love your job?

1. _____
2. _____
3. _____

Is it possible to have more of those experiences in your current job?

What might one of your arts be?

Are you currently in your art when you are at work?

When I work with clients, it can sometimes take several hours before we really define who someone is as an artist, so don't be surprised if those questions were a bit tough. You might be thinking, for example, that your art is to help people. Well, that is not necessarily an art so much as something you enjoy. That's a little broad, so what specific way do you enjoy helping people, and what type of people do you enjoy helping? How you do it may be through customer service. If this is the case, then think of your art as "creating space for people to feel heard."

Once you identify your art as creating space for people to feel heard, there are many various shapes that can take. What's important is that you have identified your art. If your current job is giving instructions over the phone on how to set up a computer, that may not line up with your art, so you may not be feeling fulfilled within that job. Use what you've learned about your art to find ways to express yourself within your work. There may be possibilities for that within your current job, or you may need to start thinking about making a move.

My brother, David Bayer, is the perfect example of someone who spent a lot of time doing work that fulfilled him in terms of financial security but left him feeling like he had a lack of purpose. He has a degree from an Ivy League university and worked in digital marketing. When he'd finally had enough at the age of thirty-seven, he changed his career and became a personal development coach. He's now the CEO of one of the leading self-improvement seminars in the country, called the Powerful Living Experience. In essence, he built a business around helping people connect their art, passion, and purpose with their careers and he's never looked back.

Making Money

People tell me all the time that they wish they were making more money. This is a common and understandable desire, to say the least. Let's explore your relationship with money through the following questions.

1. What does money mean to you?
2. What were your earliest experiences with understanding money?
3. Did you have any traumatic events or major stressors that were related to money?
4. What limiting beliefs have you developed around money?
5. Do you believe that money can come easily to you?

I have employed some very talented people through the years, and when a conversation about money was necessary, the energy in the room instantly became awkward and uncomfortable. Our source of income can be a particularly sensitive area to explore. This is a common place for fears to take hold. It makes sense, really. No one wants to feel like they can't make ends meet. For some, it's a matter of pride—being able to provide for our family is important. For others, it's a fear that developed in childhood if they were raised in poverty or in a family that struggled with finances. I've worked with many who can recall having to wear shoes with holes in them to school, or even going to bed hungry at night. These experiences become deeply engrained in our emotional memories. As we get older and become responsible for making our own living, sometimes we're still acting as that helpless child, and we choose jobs we don't love simply for the paycheck, or the first job offered for fear of nothing else coming along. This makes sense, but at some point, you must give yourself permission to consider other possibilities. Ask yourself: if money were not a consideration, what would you enjoy doing?

It might be tempting to say you'd like to just veg out on a beach somewhere and watch the sun go down from the comfort of a hammock day after day. But here's the thing—it's not realistic and I can tell you that the people I know who do live this way very often feel empty and untethered because they're not serving a purpose other than their own indulgence.

So, now let's revisit the question. This time, I want you to think as if you're operating from your Best Self. What would your Best Self love to do for work? What type of employment would make you feel like you're using your gifts, doing your art, in a way that is productive and rewarding? Allow your imagination to run wild, set no limits. As you look inward, allow all of your fears to melt away. You are unencumbered, free. Your life is your own, and you can choose whatever your heart desires. Ask your Best Self what you seek.

- After creating this vision, what were you thinking?
- Did anything get in the way of your vision? Do you think that your vision is impossible, or doesn't exist?
- Next, take that vision from your mind's eye and imagine how you might be able to translate it into the real world.
- How can you take the essence of the career you really want and create a realistic starting point?

As an example, if you love spending time in your garden on the weekends, and all your friends enjoy the bounty of fresh fruits, vegetables, and herbs that you grow, then maybe there's a local nursery where you would thrive? Or perhaps visual art has always been a passion of yours. Even if you're no Picasso, you could still work at the neighborhood art supply or craft store and be surrounded by what you love (and even get a discount on some new paints and canvases!). If you're a good writer and have always excelled at grammar and punctuation, there are freelance jobs online that would allow you to express that writing, editing, or proofreading interest and make money while doing so. Maybe you're in retail and it's as simple as moving from the shoe department where you aren't feeling satisfied to the makeup department, which might align more with your interests. Or if, for example, you are in finance, but you're not stimulated by the type of work you're doing because you're a people person and your job is just you and a computer most days, it could be that you can take your skills and apply them toward becoming a financial advisor, where you interact with clients on a daily basis. There are many ways that you can effectively connect the inner desires of your heart to your income. You just have to get a little creative.

What's Your Lifestyle?

What type of lifestyle do you want to live? For example, perhaps it's important to you in this season of life that you're able to work a very flexible schedule on your own terms. There are a lot of ways now that you can make money online and through apps where you can control your availability. Anything from dog-walking to graphic design, at-home spa and salon services to running errands or handyman work for those in your town—there are apps and websites looking to hire in all of these arenas, and many more. Sometimes you're on the right track with your current career or job, but you just need to make a minor pivot. When I was training to become an alcohol and drug abuse counselor, it was not at all what I envisioned. I was spending hours on end doing documentation. We were required to write out every detail of our interactions with patients. The reasons for that make perfect sense, and I knew it was important work, but it just did not jive with my personality. So I pivoted. I moved from counselor to interventionist, and I loved it. I am not a paperwork person; I am a people person. That was the best move I could've made and it set me on the right path for my authentic self, for which I am so grateful.

Another important aspect about your lifestyle that you should consider when you're looking at your employment is your commute. If you're spending hours on end commuting from home to work, and it's impacting your relationship with your family, then you need to seriously weigh what's important to you and determine if you need to find a job that is closer to home, or even consider moving closer to your workplace. You don't want to run the risk of building up resentment toward your work because you feel somehow forced to spend less time with your family as a result of it. Remember that you and you alone hold the power to make the necessary changes in order to create the lifestyle you want.

The bottom line is that you might need to shift your perspective on employment. Work isn't just about money and doesn't have to be something you dread. It is also something completely within your grasp to reframe. You can, and should, make your work fit into your overall authentic life. Once you truly believe that, the rest will come.

Ready to Make a Change?

You may currently be in a job that you don't like for a variety of reasons. I think it's smart to first take a look at the truth of why you are unhappy. Here is a little assessment I've used many times to help you gain some insight into whether it's time for a job/

career change, or time to somehow show up differently at the job you currently have. In other words, does the job need to change, or does your approach to it need to change?

- What do you not like about your job?
- Do you think your life is going to be far better and most all of your problems will be solved if you can quit your job and find a new one? ○ **YES**   ○ **NO**
- Have you had similar problems in past jobs? ○ **YES**   ○ **NO**
- Does this job, more so than ones you've had in the past, make you feel like you aren't able to be your Best Self?
  ○ **YES**   ○ **NO**
- Do you feel worse about yourself and your life while you are at work than you do when you're doing other activities in your life? ○ **YES**   ○ **NO**
- What, if anything, did you like about the job when you first started it?
- What does your Best Self think you should do about the job? **(i.e., quit ASAP, make adjustments within it, have a discussion with your supervisors about your concerns, etc.)**
- Is it really the job that's the problem? ○ **YES**   ○ **NO**

If you answered "yes" to that last question, do you think it's possible that the issue lies with you, rather than in the jobs you've had? For instance, do you consistently butt heads with your boss? Or, have you been disciplined over and over for the same things, such as being late, not complying with company policies, etc., within different organizations? If you're able to see a pattern of problems from job to job, then do you think it will be different if you go work somewhere else? Or do you think it might make more sense to look inward and discover why you keep repeating the same behavior over and over again at work?

Alternatively, is it possible that you're trying to work in an industry that just doesn't match up with who you are? Maybe the general morals and ethics of the industry you're currently in just don't sync with your authentic self, so you're in a constant state of cognitive dissonance. For instance, if you're working in mortgage loans but you don't feel great about some of the loans your customers have signed up for, you might be experiencing some ethical dilemmas. Or let's say you sell some kind of health product and you find out that they use animal testing practices, and you have an ethical problem with that—so now you're at odds with your company. If any of that rings true, then the answer might be to broaden your scope and consider other industries that might interest you.

If, on the other hand, you haven't been able to get promoted up the ladder at the organization where you work because you're lacking certain education or certifications, then now is a great time to invest in your future! If you want to reinvent your relationship with employment, then you will have to do the work required. But the effort is more than worth it in the long run. Another possibility, and one I've heard over and over, is that you like your job, but not the people with whom you work. If you're dealing with individuals who act inappropriately or somehow make your work life more difficult than it should be, I encourage you to set a meeting with your human resources department and lean on them to help you sort out the issues with your colleagues. One of the key functions of HR directors is to help smooth out personnel issues, and act as mediators on your behalf. And you might even discover through that process that some aspect of one of your Anti-Self personalities has snuck into your work life, and you're experiencing issues with coworkers as a result of your insecurities. Always keep an open mind and be willing to own your part in any work conflict, so that you can more effectively find a resolution.

If you've conducted exhaustive research and you conclude that it is, indeed, time for you to move on from your current employment, then first you must create a detailed plan. How much savings do you have in place? Are you financially able to walk away without another job lined up? If not, then you need to create a goal to find a new job that you feel will be rewarding for you, and then follow the seven steps in chapter 13 for attaining that goal.

Finding a new job can feel overwhelming at first, and that might even be the reason you've stayed in your current job as long as you have. But once you program your strategy for landing your dream job, it will feel much more realistic and within your grasp. Just remember that you deserve to have a career that lines up with your authentic self, so don't sell yourself short. Persevere by getting creative and casting a very wide net. One day you will look back and be so glad that you did.

The Out-of-Work Scenario

All of us have found ourselves out of work at one time or another in our lives. Unemployment is part of the journey in this SPHERE. So, if you're out of work right now or you know for sure that you're ready to leave your current place of employment, the key is not to confuse activity with productivity in terms of your job search. Emailing out your resume to hundreds of hiring managers that you found online is certainly a good place to start, but you need to go the extra mile to actually land the job you desire. That means getting on the phone and following up. Rather than calling and requesting a job interview, consider requesting a general, informational meeting first. Go on a fact-finding mission about the company's needs, and then while you're there, let them know how your skills line up with their current needs.

If you're currently out of work and feeling the pressure of a dwindling bank account or your credit card debt is piling up, then you need to be spending as much time each day of the week actively looking for a job as you would be spending at a job. Get up each morning, get dressed as if you're going to work, and then spend eight hours looking for work. I always tell my clients to create a spreadsheet to track all the companies that they've contacted, with the name, phone number, and email of the person with whom they communicated. Do this until you have a job offer that you are excited to accept.

If you're in financial dire straits, then freelance, do odd jobs, or work part-time in whatever way you need to keep the lights on, and then continue the job search in your off hours. If you have to deliver pizzas, work at a coffee shop, or answer phones at a customer call center, do it. No job is "beneath you"—a belief like that comes purely from ego. Don't let your ego get in the way of your ability to be your Best Self and find your perfect career. True happiness down the line will be worth the struggle.

You might even be surprised at the incredible contacts you can make at one of those entry-level jobs. I worked at two different coffee shops while I was in college, as well as at the YMCA as a referee, and those experiences were so valuable. In addition to lessons about how to work on a team, how to deal with the public, and how to talk to just about anyone, I also discovered something important about my authentic self—I could never thrive in a corporate structure. Knowing what does *not* work for us is part of the journey toward discovering what *does* work for us. Fold all of that information into your overall mission to reinvent your Employment SPHERE.

HOW TO STAND OUT ABOVE OTHER APPLICANTS

I have interviewed hundreds of people for jobs at CAST Centers, and the number one criteria I consider is how much they have researched our organization in advance of the job interview. If someone hasn't done the research on our facility and our philosophy, how on earth are they going to be able to represent us or know if their fundamental value system matches up with ours? It boggles my mind that literally 80 percent of applicants have not spent the time to thoroughly comb through our website and come to an interview armed with an understanding of our values. Takeaway: the next time you're applying for a job, make sure you've learned as much as possible about the company for which you wish to work.

What Kind of Employee Are You?

The best thing you can do to ensure that you're the type of employee who stays on the boss's radar in a good way is to put yourself in the boss's shoes. Ask yourself what he or she might need in order to make things run more efficiently. Think about the owner of the company and his or her top goals and priorities, and ways in which you can be an essential part of the plan for achieving those.

Speak up! Send them your ideas and your insight on what might be missing that you could bring to the table, or problems that you can help solve.

Be proactive. Don't just have your hand out each year, looking for a raise because you've been a loyal employee. Your proposal for a pay increase should be focused on the company, not on yourself. If you have an annual performance review, focus on ways that you've gone above and beyond the call of your particular job description, and brought fresh ideas and solutions to the table as ways to increase revenue or productivity. No idea is a bad idea—even if only one out of 100 of your ideas pan out, that one could be the game-changer for the company and for your future growth.

I'm consistently blown away by the productivity and creativity of my current team. But there are some people who worked for me in the past who have been more focused on themselves than on what more they could do for the company, the clients, the brand, the vision. They have viewed their time at CAST as merely a job, not as being a vital part of a team.

It's a simple shift in perspective, but it's a powerful one. The "I" guys do not get the positive attention, the quick promotions, or the big raises. Bosses and owners naturally want to reward those who are showing up with fresh ideas, with a problem-solving mentality and with a team orientation. Let that be you!

The Biggest Lessons from My Own Employment Journey

Looking back across the evolution of my career, I am deeply grateful for all of the job experiences I've had—and they've been good, bad, and ugly for sure. I've tried my hand at everything from bartending (with zero training—*that* was interesting), to being a barista (another kind of learning curve), waiting tables at a five-star restaurant (and breaking more than my share of wine bottles), and being a soccer referee (without knowing any of the rules of soccer). I've even done temp jobs for hourly wages, too, where I pulled up old flooring, painted walls, and on and on. Overnight shifts at a rehabilitation center where I had to do room checks on people who had been convicted of a crime and were awaiting sentencing stands out in my mind for sure. My job history runs the gamut, to say the least, and I'm willing to bet your own work experiences do, too.

As I've told you, when I was twenty-two I got sober and re-booted my life. My family had cut me off financially—I mean *really* cut me off. I had intended to go back to New York City after thirty days, but I had no way to get there. I might have known how to act like an entitled person with money, but I was flat broke. So I took what is often referred to as a "sober job." This is the type of job you use to get back on your feet. I was scraping by and counting my pennies in order to buy a sandwich at a local deli. It was within that job that I really learned to do the right thing.

Up to that point, I had played by my own rules and my rules were, frankly, immature and unprofessional. But in my first sober job, I really tried to be the best I could possibly be. I learned to mop, clean, how to greet people, and I learned that coffee shops play the same songs over and over again. (I also learned that when you steam soy milk, it screams at you. Little-known fact.) The point is: there's no easy way to the top. There are no shortcuts.

On day one of working in a treatment center, I had a mentor who told me that when you work in self-help you have to "grow or go." You either evolve in life or you check out of life. And it is a choice you have to make. To this day, I still live by that belief. Always be in "sponge mode." No matter what your job is, soak up lessons and information from those around you so that you can continue to evolve as your Best Self.

Employment SPHERE Quiz

The time has arrived for you to take inventory of your Employment SPHERE. Now that we've done some thinking together and hopefully you have a fresh perspective, answer these questions honestly.

PART 1: First, rate your employment life on a scale of 1–10. A "1" would mean that you realize your employment SPHERE is in poor shape and requires your immediate attention. A "10" would mean that you are quite pleased with your current employment SPHERE and status, and it has little to no room for improvement. Aspects of your work/education sphere to consider when assigning your rating include:

- Your enjoyment/rewarding nature of your job or school experience,
- how well your job provides financially for your lifestyle,
- your work relationships,
- how balanced your work schedule is compared to other aspects of your life.

Employment Rating: _____ as of _____ (date)

PART 2: Now, list out some behaviors that are working well in your work life and why they're working.

Examples:
- I push myself to do well at work, but while keeping my life in balance.
- I feel rewarded by my work.
- I encourage others in my workplace and have built positive relationships there.

Behaviors that are working in my employment are:

_____ Why? _____

_____ Why? _____

_____ Why? _____

PART 3: What are some behaviors that you know are keeping you from what you want in your employment life?

Examples:
- I am lazy with my work assignments and always wait until the last minute to finish them.
- I am a "workaholic"—I work myself to death and have no balance between my work and personal life.
- I have formed some toxic relationships with colleagues due to my competitiveness or jealousy.

Behaviors that are not working for me in the area of my employment life are:

_____ Why? _____

_____ Why? _____

_____ Why? _____

PART 4: Based on everything you just wrote down, I want you to think about what you need to do in order to go from your current rating to a rating of 10 in this area of your life.

The way you'll do this is to look at behaviors you need to *continue* doing because they're working for you, behaviors you need to *stop* doing because they're keeping you from what you want, and behaviors you need to *start* doing.

In order for my employment life to feel like it's at a 10,

I need to continue: _____

I need to stop: _____

I need to start: _____

Love Your Living

I believe that if you stay rooted in your authenticity while earning your living, life will surprise you beyond your wildest dreams. There are going to be hard days—that's true in all careers, for all people, across all time. But not every day has to be a hard day. If you once loved your job but it's become mundane, choose to revisit what you used to love about it, and reignite that fire within yourself. In the perfect scenario, your job should make you feel energized, fulfilled, and vital.

Make it your mission to create for yourself a rewarding career that is a reflection of your Best Self. It can be simple tweaks, or it might mean a whole employment overhaul—but commit to the journey, and then do everything in your power to *enjoy* that journey. Choose to have an optimistic approach each day, and things will begin to happen that align with that outlook.

You've covered a lot of ground so far, but the journey isn't over yet! In fact, everything we've discussed to this point has been leading up to the last of your seven SPHERES of life, your spiritual development. You see, underneath everything—our jobs, relationships, our education, and even our physical health is our spiritual life. Who are you, on a spiritual level? In what ways does your spiritual life contribute to and manifest in your overall life? These are big questions that we're going to explore together in the next chapter. I'm excited, and I hope you are as well!

11

Your Spiritual Development Life

In this chapter, we're going to delve into your spiritual life. I purposely saved this for the last of your seven SPHERES because I felt it was important for you to gain a very clear understanding of who you are in all the other areas of your life first, before diving into this arena. I believe that your spiritual life forms the underpinning for all your other SPHERES.

Let's define what spirituality means within the context of our work together. The dictionary defines spirituality as: "the quality of being concerned with the human spirit or soul as opposed to material or physical things." I believe our spiritual life underpins everything else in life. I think of your Best Self as actually being your spiritual self. Your spiritual self is the place within you from which all goodness and light radiates outward. It is where you form your integrity, values, and how you treat other people.

In my experience, people tend to neglect their spiritual life in their day-to-day hustle, and yet it's what they cling to when life throws a curveball. Faith is very often the solid ground that people seek when their universe is shaken by crisis, major fears, extreme regrets, or anything outside of their normal. I would argue that instead of waiting until something implodes in our life, it's more beneficial to maintain a connection with our spiritual self always. Here's why.

We always hear that we should try to avoid the topic of religion at dinner parties, unless, of course, we're seeking an intense argument. People's religious beliefs are very strong, and they run deep. There are thousands of different types of religions across the world, and every one of those religions believes that its faith is the right faith, which makes sense because if you're going to trust your eternity to someone or something, you want to believe it's real and true. To be clear, I'm not looking to dive into the particulars of various belief systems to which you might subscribe. And so, for the purposes of this chapter, we are going to separate out your spirituality from religion.

Regardless of any specific religious affiliation, your spiritual journey is unique to you—we each have our own way that we plug into our spirituality. For me, I did not grow up in a religious household. We were one of those families that celebrated both Hanukkah and Christmas, because my mom is Lutheran and my dad is Jewish. The way that I now choose to connect with my spirituality is through practices like meditation (which I express in different ways depending on the day or circumstance), self-affirmations, and the ritual and mantra I shared with you previously. I didn't learn those growing up; I've discovered them over time. They all help me align with my spirituality. This is a function of my personality—across the board, I tend to feel connected when I'm alone, and the way that expresses itself in my spirituality is that I prefer to practice it alone versus in a religious forum like a church, synagogue, or mosque. Of course, I understand there is a lot of value for many people when they come together as a community in like-minded beliefs, and I've certainly taken part in church or in a Shabbat dinner, etc., but for me, I choose to be alone when I practice my spirituality. That may change over time, or it could stay the same—I'm open! I think philosopher Dallas Willard put it perfectly when he said, "Spiritual people are not those who engage in certain spiritual practices; they are those who draw their life from a conversational relationship with God." In this chapter, we're going to explore what that relationship looks like for you, and how *you* can be most aligned with who you are spiritually.

Some people have completely shut off any belief or faith in God, a higher power, or bigger energy because a certain religion was forced upon them in childhood and that particular practice left them feeling cold, or uncomfortable. Now, as an adult, clinging to those ideas won't align with their Best Self. It's a common response to this situation to try to shut spirituality out altogether but I believe we are all spiritual beings and trying to ignore that will take more energy than embracing spirituality in a way that works for you. I want to help you define what spirituality means to you and determine why you might have reservations about it.

The central question we are going to focus on in this chapter is: How much of your Best Self is actively aligned with your faith? I look at faith as believing in something that you can't prove, and I think it is one of the most powerful ways to transform your life. I also believe in the notion that faith without work is dead, which for me means that it requires action to align with your faith, both internally and externally in the form of giving our time, talent, and treasures to others.

I also look at faith as a way of putting out into this universe something that you authentically want in your life, and then believing that it will come back to you. For example, about seven years ago, I realized that I loved working in the creative arts. I live in Los Angeles and there are a lot of people trying to "make it" out here. Because I wanted to work in the arts myself, I started to visualize what it would feel like, what exciting types of people I could connect to, and how I could help others have larger platforms, so they could send out positive, empowering messages to their millions of fans. I ended up attracting just these experiences into my life because I believed from my own most authentic place that it was my destiny. I had faith that it would happen.

Research backs up the idea that having a sense of spirituality has positive effects on our life, especially in our mental and physical health. People with faith have been shown to live longer and have a lower risk of heart attack.* They also report experiencing less anxiety and stress in their lives,† less depression and more contentment,‡ they suffer less physical pain,§ are less likely to panic under pressure,¶ and children who are taught about faith and whose faith is cultivated while they are young, are less likely to get involved with drugs and underage sex. There's really no question that faith can improve your life and enrich your days in powerful ways, many of which are really beyond our understanding.**

Our spiritual connection comes in and out throughout our day, as we're constantly reminded that we're not in control of what happens to us. Something bigger and stronger than us is calling

---

* Laura E. Wallace, Rebecca Anthony, Christian M. End, Baldwin M. Way, "Does Religion Stave Off the Grave? Religious Affiliation in One's Obituary and Longevity," 2018, http://journals.sagepub.com/doi/abs/10.1177/1948550618779820.

† Deborah Cornah, "The Impact of Spirituality on Mental Health: A Review of the Literature," Mental Health Foundation, 2006, www.mentalhealth.org.uk/sites/default/files/impact-spirituality.pdf.

‡ "Spiritual Engagement and Meaning," Pursuit of Happiness, 2016, http://www.pursuit-of-happiness.org/science-of-happiness/spiritual-engagement/.

§ Ozden Dedeli and Gulten Kaptan, "Spirituality and Religion in Pain and Pain Management," Health Psychology Research 1, no. 3 (2013): 29, doi:10.4081/hpr.2013.1448.

¶ Rudy Bowen et al., "Self-Rated Importance of Religion Predicts One-Year Outcome of Patients with Panic Disorder," Depression and Anxiety 23, no. 5 (2006): 266–73, doi:10.1002/da.20157.

** Lisa Bridges and Kristin Moore, "Religion and Spirituality in Childhood and Adolescence," Child Trends, 2002, https://www.childtrends.org/wpcontent/uploads/2002/01/Child_Trends2002_01_01_FR_ReligionSpiritAdol.pdf.

the shots and we can choose to align with that or we can unplug. When we unplug from it, we start to lose ourselves, we'll start to doubt life, attract people who aren't aligned with who we are, we'll start to believe things about our brothers and sisters in this life. There is more good than bad in this world—either you can ride the warrior wave of freedom and love or you can be your own worst enemy. We aren't built to do this life alone. When music speaks to your soul, when you feel free, when you breathe and find your truth and clarity, when you feel good helping others, you're living a spiritual experience. I agree with the French philosopher Pierre Teilhard de Chardin, who summed it up nicely when he said, "We are not human beings having a spiritual experience. We are spiritual beings having a human experience."

I want to share with you a story about a client who rediscovered and reconnected with his spiritual self because of a challenging circumstance he was facing in his life. It might seem at first like this story belongs in the Employment chapter, but I want you to see how your spirituality can have a positive effect across all of your SPHERES. Because he learned how to lean on his faith in new ways, his entire life changed for the better.

Handcuff Henry and His Spiritual Wake-up Call

When Henry and I started working together, he had a job as a junior advertising executive at a boutique firm. He'd been there four years. He was usually the first to arrive at work, and almost always the last to leave. He was hungry and passionate and had a deep determination to prove himself within a tough industry. But Henry was also very humble; unlike some of his more egotistical colleagues, he did not walk around beating his chest about his accomplishments. He'd never had a need to be the center of attention; he'd been raised in a big family, and as the eldest son, he took on a lot of responsibility for caring for the younger kids. He loved that part of his life, however, as his Best Self was a nurturer, a natural caretaker. He took joy in his role in keeping the household running and pleasing his parents. He was a people pleaser.

In his career, he was very skilled at working with clients one-on-one. He made them feel like they were an integral part of the process in creating beautiful and compelling ad campaigns that elevated their brand. He made them feel heard; his caretaking tendencies certainly helped him quickly gain the trust of his clients, and they always spoke highly of him. He had a true gift.

Henry was also a deacon in the church where he and his family attended, and he told me right off the bat that he prayed every day and he considered himself a man of faith. They were actively involved in the church community and known as a generous, loving family who would do anything for those in need.

Donald, the owner of the ad agency where Henry worked, had recently allowed his stepson, Ronnie, to take over a huge portion of the business so that he could step away to focus on a new project. Because Donald knew that Henry was so skilled with clients, he also gave him a more significant role in the company, and Henry was elated. Overnight, he'd become one of the youngest execs in his industry with his title and level of responsibility. Henry felt that he must step up to the plate because this kind of opportunity might never come around again.

The problem was that Ronnie did not know the first thing about advertising, so he was threatened by Henry. He wanted all the power for himself. He used company income to fund his extravagant vacations and torpedoed deals with big clients by demanding more money. On several occasions, employees even witnessed Ronnie engaged in violent outbursts, smashing items against the wall of his office in rage, slamming the phone onto the floor, drinking in his office, and sexting female colleagues. This guy was off the rails.

In the midst of all this, as the agency began to get a bad reputation, one of Henry's biggest clients moved to fire them and hire a new ad agency—a behemoth that had been a loyal client for decades. Henry was devastated. What he didn't know is that one of the key people at that company, Henry's former client, told the new ad execs about Henry and requested that they try to poach him and bring him on board to help manage the account. That would mean a gigantic leap for Henry to a Fortune 500 company with the executive-level salary and fringe benefits to match, but Henry had no idea this was going on in the background—he missed their calls.

When Donald, the owner, came in to question the staff about why they had lost the major client, he believed Ronnie's claims that Henry had been slacking off and delivering subpar work. He led his stepfather to believe that Henry was the reason that the company had lost the client and Ronnie even crafted a ridiculous allegation that Henry was having an affair with a client's wife. As a result, Donald demanded that Henry repair the situation, get back the clients they'd lost, and do everything to return the company to its previous standing—essentially make Ronnie look good.

Henry was so terrified that he'd never have a job this great, so he just accepted all of the blame, allowed everything to happen, and vowed to work even harder to bring in new, bigger clients. But his body started rebelling. He began suffering from debilitating panic attacks; he was sick all the time. He even started losing his hair from all the stress.

"I just can't see how I'm going to make this situation better," he'd said. "I'm doing everything I know how to do, but with Ronnie there, it's such an uphill battle."

"You told me that you're a man of faith, that you attend church.

Have you prayed about this situation?" I asked Henry, the first time we met.

"Almost nonstop. I feel like I'm in twenty-four/seven prayer mode, asking God to help me."

"It looks to me like you don't have much faith that the problem is going to work out, though." This statement hit Henry right between the eyes. I don't think he was expecting to hear that.

"What do you mean?"

"Well, it seems to me that you're letting people and the situation at this company manipulate you and take advantage of you. It seems like you believe life is happening to you, not for you."

"What's the alternative? I don't want to go backwards. I've been handed this amazing title and opportunity to essentially run the company—I can't blow it."

"Are you afraid?"

"Terrified."

Next, we did the Anti-Self exercise together, and the character Henry created was Handcuff Henry. He had metaphorically handcuffed himself to this job, and thus allowed the people in power to treat him however they wished. He was the only one of his peers with such a high position, and was deathly afraid that he wasn't worthy, and that he would never have another opportunity this great. Because he was so entrenched in his Anti-Self, he actually had convinced himself that he somehow deserved the mistreatment and character assassination.

"If someone else were sitting in your spot right now, what would you tell them about that fear?" He thought for a moment.

"To have faith."

"What does that look like?"

"Stepping out, taking a risk, not trying to control everything, and not accepting awful circumstances. God wants more for them." He paused. "And what God does once, He'll do again."

"Does any of that apply to you?"

"Yes. It absolutely does." He started to shift in his seat, sat up straighter—it was like the light was returning to his eyes. "I feel like I'm a kid who's been fighting over a beaten-up, old tricycle. There has to be something else out there for me."

Handcuff Henry had been running the show for him because fear had taken root. But once Henry took off the handcuffs and started believing, *really* believing in the strength of his spirit, that there was more for him than this tiny little ad agency, interesting things started to happen. He called me just two days later and said he'd found an email that had somehow gone into his junk folder—it was from that giant advertising agency I mentioned earlier. They wanted to meet him. He'd apparently also missed two calls from them—he'd been so hyperfocused on trying to solve and control his problems with Ronnie that he'd not even noticed the voice mails they'd left asking for him to come in and interview.

Fast-forward three years later—he did make the move to that big agency, and then he branched out on his own and created a nonprofit organization that is flourishing. Whenever we talk about that period in his life now, he says, "I'm never signing up to be Handcuff Henry again. Ever! I'm living from now on as Free Henry."

When we get connected, or reconnected to our spiritual selves, and lean on our faith, amazing things *can* happen in our lives. Handcuff Henry was blocking good things from coming. He was trying to control everything in Henry's life, but he was doing so with his hands tied behind his back. He was never going to get anywhere that way. It was when he took the handcuffs off, embraced his faith, and gave away his need for control that his life began happening *for* him, not *to* him.

Being spiritual means believing you deserve to feel fulfilled, you deserve to be treated well, and it means having an attitude of prosperity, not scarcity. God (higher power, spirit, the universe, life, or whatever word makes you feel safe and connected) wants more for you and all you need to do is accept that and receive it in your heart. Henry had created a false narrative for himself—he believed that if he pushed back against his abusive employers, he'd lose out on the one and only opportunity he'd ever get to run a company. He was so shortsighted, fearful, and doubtful that he was willing to sacrifice his own well-being in order to hang on to false security.

This is a common theme across human history; we have a way of putting ourselves in invisible boxes and refusing to see the great, big world of possibility around us. Rumi, a thirteenth-century Islamic scholar, wrote, "Why do you stay in prison when the door is so wide open?" Have you ever felt that way in your life? As if you're imprisoned, shackled, unable to make a move? Like you've lost all control and you're at the mercy of others? What you probably don't realize at those times is that the door really is wide open—you just need to make the decision to walk through it.

It's important in these moments to ask ourselves what our Best Self would do. Your Best Self is always looking out for you and can help you break free of your self-imposed handcuffs. But this can be difficult. I realize this. Buddhist monk and peace activist Thich Nhat Hanh once said, "People have a hard time letting go of their suffering. Out of a fear of the unknown, they prefer suffering that is familiar." I think that really gets to the heart of the issue. We're terrified to choose something different than our current reality, because we worry—what if it's worse? That's exactly why I want to help you build your spiritual life up in a way that can erode your fears and help you find strength and courage to face the unknown. The amazing truth about the unknown is that it's usually far better than you could have imagined.

Cultivate Your Spirituality

While your specific faith and belief systems, if you have them, may inform your spirituality, I want to help you connect with your spiritual self on a level that transcends the specificity of religion. In other words, I want you to peel back the layers of whatever it is you believe until you get to your spiritual center.

Here are some techniques for connecting or reconnecting with your spirituality in a meaningful way.

1. Create an intention around your spirituality

Start this process by deciding what you want to accomplish in your spiritual life. This looks different for everyone, but some examples include: to set more time aside for prayer, to start attending religious services that used to be fulfilling for you, but you got too busy to attend, to meditate on a daily basis, to find a spiritual practice you can share with a loved one, and so on. If you approach this with a solid intention, you'll be more likely to succeed.

2. Fan the flames of your spirit

There is so much wonderful material out there these days that can inspire you on a spiritual level. Whether that's in the form of inspirational quotes from people you admire, reading the Bible, inspirational books written by folks who have experienced miracles in their lives or a spiritual awakening, audio books from spiritual thinkers or gurus—find what resonates with you, and feed your spirit with that type of content. We spend much of our time being entertained by social media and entertainment that doesn't offer a deeper meaning, so make an effort to work in content that lifts you up.

3. Seek quiet

Life today is noisy. We've talked a lot already about turning down the noise of life, and when it comes to connecting with your spirituality, it's essential that you find that quiet place within yourself and just *be*. And I'm not referring to actual noise that you hear with your ears—in fact, if the way you connect with your inner voice is to pump up the rock music and dance in your living room, go for it. What I'm referring to is a quiet within yourself, when you've turned off all the other outside voices and influences. These are often the times in our lives when an answer we've been looking for will rise to our level of consciousness, or when we'll have a realization or see something in a new way. Ways that you can tap into that quiet place within your mind is to sit and say something that gives you a good, positive vibration. For example, you may have seen folks in the movies or on TV say "ommm" a few times or use some kind of chant, concentrating only on the vibrating sound it makes when they say the word and letting all other thoughts just slow down until they are still. If you pray, that can also help you to quiet the constant thoughts in your mind. Or if you have a photo or a piece of art that brings you peace, create time to just gaze at it. Make it a priority to spend this kind of "quiet" time with yourself at least once a week.

4. Be aware of signs

Keep your spiritual eyes as well as your physical eyes open at all times and be aware of signs being sent to you. As an example, I have a friend who was mourning the loss of her dog, and she'd been praying for peace. One afternoon, she saw a rainbow on her living room floor at the exact spot where her dog used to sunbathe in the afternoons. She took it as a sign that her dog's soul lived on, and that she could choose to be peaceful with that knowledge.

Another common type of spiritual sign is called a synchronicity. This is when you hear the same phrase over and over or see the same specific number in numerous places—it could just be a simple reminder that there is something bigger than you, than us, and that life is more than just your day-to-day activities—that we are all part of a universe that is beyond our understanding. I know someone else who said he actually had a profound spiritual experience while watching the film *The Lion King*. A certain scene in that film triggered his spirit to rise, and he suddenly knew what he needed to do in a situation with his son. Everything from a song on the radio to words spoken to you by a stranger to a beautiful sight in nature, all can be seen as signs if they move you, and your heart is open to receive them in that way.

Also, know that there are opportunities around every corner. Remain open to gifts the universe wants to give you so that you don't walk right by them. If someone offers to pay for your cup of coffee in line at Starbucks, receive that gift. Christian author Rob Bell once said: "This breath, and this moment, and this life is a gift and we are all in this together. We all have countless choices every day to close down or stand up straight and open up and take a big breath and say YES to the gift." Being open to receiving the gifts that life will bestow upon me has been a powerful decision in my life. If I'd tried to maintain tight control of any aspect of my life, make clear plans and stick with them no matter what, I would have missed the boat . . . big-time. I could never have predicted the trajectory life would take me on, and I'm so grateful that I let go and have stayed open to whatever has come my way. I had told myself previously that I wasn't going to do television work but when Dr. Phil asked me to do a few episodes, I said yes! I said yes because I thought maybe there is something in the bigger picture. Now that I've appeared multiple times on his television program, I know that I was right.

There are signs everywhere, and if you remain open, you'll begin to see them in the most unlikely of places.

5. Give credit

As you become more plugged into your spiritual awareness, if something positive happens to you or someone in your orbit, connect the dots to the work you've been doing. Don't chalk it up to chance or coincidence. Make a point to realize that your spiritual development will help you feel more fulfilled in amazing and often mysterious ways. Take a moment to acknowledge that connectivity, so that you will continue walking this amazing path. Even minor shifts, improvements, and seemingly insignificant moments of joy or peace are all part of this spiritual journey.

6. Share with others

Talk to other people about your spiritual journey and ask them to share theirs with you. This will enrich your experience and inspire others. Realize that not everyone will be open to these types of discussions, so if someone doesn't respond positively, don't take this personally. They aren't in a place for that kind of sharing— their journey is unique just like yours. Choose to shine your spiritual light on the world around you, and it will reflect back to your own life.

7. Have fun always

Laughter is the outward expression of inward joy. I encourage you to be playful in your quest for your spiritual self. Have fun with it. Laugh, even in difficult moments. Allow joy to bubble up from within your spirit. Even on our hardest days, we can choose to laugh, we can choose to find something to be happy about and a joy we want to share, and we can ride the wave of that contentment to get us through our challenges.

8. Pay it forward

In most religions, there is a fundamental belief that when we give generously, we generously receive. The Bible says, "Do not be deceived: God cannot be mocked. A man reaps what he sows. Whoever sows to please their flesh, from the flesh will reap destruction; whoever sows to please the Spirit, from the Spirit will reap eternal life." It's the same basic concept as karma. If you treat people in a hurtful, cruel, or vindictive way, in a way that is meant solely to help you or boost your ego, it does not matter how much you pray, or how often you attend religious services—you will not be rewarded. When I say rewarded, I simply mean that you will not be able to live as your Best Self. Treating others poorly is like throwing a giant obstacle in your own path.

Tap into your generous spirit and find ways to share goodness with the world around you. If you see someone having a rough day, offer a helping hand. Discover new ways within your community to help those in need. Ask your friends and family what you can do for them. Approach the world with an attitude of giving. This doesn't have to mean financially—there are so many other ways to give of yourself. You have talents you can share. You have time to give. And even if you hope to get something out of a volunteer or charity experience, I know you'll quickly learn that the greatest gift lies within the giving itself.

MORNING SPIRITUAL RITUAL

If you could carve out a few extra minutes at the start of each day, what would you like to include as part of your morning routine to align you with your Best Self? Maybe you would spend some time reading inspirational quotes. Or maybe you'd wake up and watch the sunrise? Would you choose to spend that time in prayer? One prayer that's been instrumental in helping me greet each day as my Best Self is the Third-Step Prayer from Alcoholics Anonymous:

> *God, I offer myself to Thee—*
> *To build with me*
> *and to do with me as Thou wilt.*
> *Relieve me of the bondage of self,*
> *that I may better do Thy will.*
> *Take away my difficulties,*
> *that victory over them may bear witness*
> *to those I would help of Thy Power,*
> *Thy Love, and Thy Way of life.*
> *May I do Thy will always!*

The idea behind this prayer is to step outside ourselves and allow a higher power, universe, or whatever we like to call it to take over. Where we cannot, it can. I find great comfort in that knowledge. The opposite of this is to take everything onto our own shoulders, to try to manage difficulties alone, and to be bonded to ourselves. That is like setting ourselves up to fail. Realizing that we don't have all the answers is not to admit defeat—it's actually what proclaiming victory looks like. Trusting in the universe, in a spiritual being or whatever we want to call it that we cannot see and that we don't understand, is hard. But it's in that surrender that we find freedom and peace. And as you have heard me say many times, the universe is working in our favor and we don't need to play God.

Defining Your Spiritual Life

Now that we've digested some ideas around spirituality, let's pause so that you can reflect on the current status of your spiritual life. This will help you understand where you are—and determine if there are any adjustments you'd like to make.

- What would a healthy spiritual life look like to you?
- Do you have reason to believe that life is working in your favor?
    - If yes, why? And when did you first start having this belief?

    - If no, why not? And what are your earliest memories of feeling this way?

- Are there aspects of your spiritual life that fulfill you and you wish were more prevalent in your daily life? If so, what are they?
- Who are your spiritual mentors and people you trust within your spiritual world?
- Do you believe that the way you were raised affects your approach to spiritual development?
    - What elements do you choose to keep?

    - Which elements do you choose to reject?

    - If you were lacking something in your spiritual life growing up, what can you do to bring it in now if you wish?

- What are your Best Self's tenets for living a spiritual life? Mine are patience, understanding for others, lack of worry, being inspired, feeling clever and creative, and feeling that the possibilities for my life are endless.

What Is Your Best Self Spiritual Mission Statement?

One way to maintain a strong connection to your spirituality and the faith and/or belief systems that inform it is to create your spiritual mission statement. To do this, look back at the tenets you wrote in the last exercise and craft those into an action-oriented statement. For example, here is mine:

Mike's Best Self Spiritual Mission Statement

> *I am a giving, patient, understanding, clever, worry-free individual, and I approach life each and every day with the fundamental belief that* anything is possible. *I remain open to the gifts that the universe gives to me by practicing humility. I purposely derive inspiration from unexpected places, I am uniquely creative, and my purpose and passion is to help others find the freedom to become their Best Self.*

That's what mine looks like, but yours will be different, of course. It can be as short or as long as you want, and it can change over time, so you should return to your spiritual mission statement often and see if it needs some refreshing. A mission statement facelift, so to speak.

You can write it down and put it on the refrigerator, paint it on canvas and hang it on your wall, have it embroidered on a pillow. Display it however you like to have a consistent reminder of your mission statement. Even if it's taped to your computer monitor or the visor in your car—that all works, too!

Spiritual Development Inventory

Now it's time to determine what you'd like to accomplish in the area of your spiritual development. These questions will help you.

PART 1: **First, rate your spiritual life on a scale of 1–10. A "1" would mean that you recognize that your spiritual life is suffering and requires your attention. A "10" would mean that you believe your spiritual life is functioning well and has little or no room for improvement.** Aspects of your spiritual sphere to consider when assigning your rating include:

- How developed you are in your spiritual life,
- how you're using your spirituality to bolster/support your pursuit of your Best Self,
- how rewarding your spiritual life feels for you.

Spiritual Life Rating: _____ as of _____(date)

PART 2: **Now, list out some of your behaviors that are working well in your spiritual life and why they're working.**

Examples:
- I regularly meditate, and I find the meditation helps me stay aligned with my authenticity.
- I practice religion or spirituality that is a source of fulfillment for me.

Behaviors that are working in my spiritual life are:

_____Why? _____

_____Why? _____

_____Why? _____

PART 3: **What are some behaviors that are not working in your spiritual life, and why?**

Examples:
- I'm going through the motions of a certain religion, but none of it feels real to me/it doesn't fulfill me.
- I am too angry from past hurts to engage in any type of spirituality.

Behaviors that are not working in the area of my spiritual life are:

_____Why? _____
_____Why? _____
_____Why? _____

PART 4: Based on everything above, I want you to think about what you need to do in order to go from your current rating to a rating of 10 in this area of your life.

The way you'll do this is to look at behaviors you need to *continue* doing because they're working for you, behaviors you need to *stop* doing because they're keeping you from what you want, and behaviors you need to *start* doing.

In order for my spiritual life to feel like it's at a 10,

I need to continue: _____

I need to stop: _____

I need to start: _____

Boldly Moving Forward

"Just as a candle cannot burn without a fire, men cannot live without a spiritual life." Those were words spoken by Buddha, and I believe them strongly. I am convinced that you cannot be your Best Self without having a vibrant spiritual life, whatever that might look like for you. It might be a yoga practice, meditation, prayer, deep connection to a church, and so on. Underneath any spiritual practice is a foundation and a belief that there is more to this existence than just us, that there is good for you, and a belief in the good and the beauty that you cannot see.

We have now worked through all seven of your SPHERES! Congratulations. Now we are going to make use of all the important data you've collected about yourself, all of the areas you know you'd like to tweak, change, or even overhaul, and plan your course of action. The last chapters of this book are very action-oriented, and I'm thrilled to share these tools with you. I've seen so many clients and friends use them successfully, and the best part is, when you implement them into your life, you will feel the positive results right away.

12

Assembling Your Best Team

The people around us have tremendous influence on our lives and in all of our SPHERES. Any successful person will tell you that they could never have accomplished what they have in their lives alone. Walt Disney did not create his empire alone. Steve Jobs did not create Apple alone. Martin Luther King did not ignite the civil rights movement alone and you have not built your life all by yourself. Though it may feel at times that we exist in this thing called life all alone, this is simply not true. The richness, depth, and complexity of our time here on earth is, in fact, defined by how we relate to others, by the connections we make with one another. We are all in this together, whether we choose to realize it or not, and I believe that we can and should work to elevate each other's experience of the world, to learn from each other's perspectives, and to be open to giving and receiving the amazing gifts each of us has to share. We can achieve so much more together than we can alone.

There's no question that we can and do have a plethora of different types of relationships with people in our lives, but there's an important distinction I want to make before we go any further. Not all of those people with whom you have relationships should be on your "team," which I'll also refer to as your inner circle. Your team is composed of individuals you have *purposely* chosen because you can more easily and fluidly be your Best Self around them, they inspire you and you inspire them, and your relationships with them are positive. We'll get into the specifics of evaluating and selecting your own team, but I don't want to risk sounding cold, detached, or like you're assembling a baseball team who is determined to win the World Series at any cost. This isn't *Moneyball*—this is your life. Unlike a sports team, your life team is about more than just winning—it's about enjoying the journey together. Remember, the journey is the destination, and you *and* your team should be thriving every step of the way.

I cannot stress enough the importance of this chapter. Every client I have ever worked with tells me that by analyzing their team, they were able to make changes or additions that have improved their lives tremendously. The idea is to create a team around you that inspires and encourages you to be your Best Self. We typically don't take the time to evaluate all the people around us, and we may not think very much about the idea of our "team" until we end up in crisis and need to lean on the strength of others to help us through. One of the reasons you might not have spent time really looking at the team you have around you is that you aren't convinced you really deserve to have people who support you play important roles in your life because you believe your primary function in life is to help, support, and serve others. Maybe you've become a bit of an island in that way—floating around alone, disconnected. If that is the case, then let me remind you that your Best Self believes you deserve to have an awesome team and your Best Self also knows that in order for you to give of yourself fully to others, you must be able to derive strength, knowledge, and assistance from your team. Alternatively, it could be that your team is a revolving door—you keep bringing people in and then, when they disappoint you, hurt you, or wrong you in some way, you push them out. That can be a slippery slope and a dangerous pattern and as you read this chapter, keep in mind that having a team is not about having someone to blame for your problems—instead, your problems need to be worked out within your SPHERES and via your Best Self.

From the previous work we have done in this book, you have utilized the Best Self Model and the seven SPHERES to see what areas of your life are in alignment and what areas have been neglected or are operating in dysfunction. In this chapter, we are going to conduct a thorough inventory of the people in your life. We will see who should be more involved in your life and you may want to pull away from or just shift the dynamic in subtle ways. As we know, no one is perfect, and if you haven't been approaching everyone on your team as your Best Self, we'll try that first and then we will look at the pros and cons of their presence and make some decisions.

You are at the center of your own life. Orbiting around you in this harmonious galaxy, there are partners, children, family, close friends, important acquaintances, colleagues, and so on. The size of your galaxy does not matter, but ideally you should have folks that support you in all seven of your SPHERES—which might be a new way for you to perceive your relationships. Some people may fit into several of your SPHERES, whereas others may only fit into one—and that's perfectly fine. I have worked with individuals who have very large teams and, as a result, carry a great deal of stress. They need to trim down their galaxies. I've also worked with people whose teams are tiny, and they found they needed more support. We want to find the unique team that gives you the best balance in your life by working through this chapter.

Over time, new people will emerge in your orbit, and some other people will disappear from it. There is a myriad of reasons why people come and go—from a geographical change, professional change, psychological change, to an epiphany, a newfound passion, loss, and much more. There are probably some people you have known for many years, but you only see once in a while. Regardless, these are the friends with whom you pick up the conversation right where you left off. You likely have your go-to friends in the neighborhood you can count on for a favor, and those you'd call in the middle of the night if there was an emergency because you know they'd throw on some clothes and head over to help out. And then there are those people you don't know intimately but on whom you depend for professional services—your accountant, landscapers, hairstylist, masseuse, personal trainer, nutritionist, and so on. And then you have people in your life who serve a different kind of purpose—like friends you play a sport with and that help you remain active, or people in a book club, people with whom you attend religious services, etc. The bottom line is that we all have your own, unique team of people in life and we want to determine if they are all helping you stay aligned with your Best Self.

YOU'RE A TEAMMATE, TOO!

One thing I want you to keep in mind is that you are a key player on someone else's team, and they are lucky to have you because you are working to be the best version of yourself. Someone who is on this journey, in my opinion, is a true gem in anyone's life. So, as you analyze your team, think about the role you play in others' lives, and how you can continue to grow. We will dig deeper into this concept of reciprocity later in the chapter, but I just wanted to put it on your radar early on.

Let's begin this process by looking at your team in terms of your seven SPHERES. Very likely, you will have some people who fall into several categories. That's perfectly fine; this is about figuring out what your life looks like and works best for you, and what may not be optimal at this time.

I remember talking to my friend Alexis not long ago about an issue she was having with her hairdresser. Now, your hairdresser or barber might not be the very first person you think of when you're looking at your own team, but to Alexis, her hairdresser, Cindy, served a much bigger purpose than just giving her a cute cut-and-color. She'd been seeing Cindy for nearly twenty years, and over that time, they'd become very close friends. They were both divorcees, and they helped each other in a lot of ways—from watching each other's dogs when they went out of town, to helping each other navigate their dating lives, and just being a shoulder to cry on when the going got tough. But Alexis started to notice that Cindy was getting really sloppy with her hairstyling and despite Alexis's requests for a different color or a better cut, Cindy was just missing the mark. She was so busy talking about her life instead of doing hair that Alexis was leaving the salon with strange streaks of color and horribly uneven bangs. Finally, she'd had it, and she knew she had to find a new hairdresser. But she also knew that would be like putting a stake directly into Cindy's heart. She didn't want to sneak around and "cheat" on Cindy by going elsewhere for her appointments, so she faced it head-on, and took her out to dinner. They laughed and chatted as usual, and then Alexis just blurted it out. "Cindy, I love you like a sister, and I want us to always remain friends. But the truth is, I don't love how you do my hair anymore. I want to start seeing another hairdresser. I'm so sorry. Please understand."

Cindy set her drink down and started fidgeting, eyes cast down into her lap. Her shoulders hunched over a little. Alexis continued, "I know that you are a hair artist, and that you are very talented.

But I just think that our friendship has gotten in the way a little bit of your ability to do my hair. I value our friendship so much, so let's continue to grow as friends!"

Cindy was sad, for sure, but she was also moved by what Alexis was saying and she finally replied, "Thank you for being honest with me. I can't imagine not doing your hair anymore, but as long as you promise we can still meet up regularly, it's okay with me if it's not at the salon. Even though I know no one else will be able to deal with that curly mop on your head as well as I can! Bet you're back in no time!" They laughed and hugged. Alexis successfully took Cindy from one function on her team to another. (And she purposely messed up her hair a bit before she saw her each time, just so Cindy wouldn't feel bad.)

Here are some ways to look at the groups of people in your SPHERES:

- **Social:** From friends who accompany you to social events where you can network, to your closest friends who act as trusted confidants. These are the people you go out with for your entertainment (movies, sporting events, dinner, drinks, etc.) or invite over for a quiet night doing something you love.

- **Personal:** Your teammates within your personal SPHERE are folks who help you look and feel good internally. These can be the people who help you look good on the outside, such as your hairdresser or a manicurist. But this group also includes those with whom you can have intimate conversations with like a therapist, a mentor, or counselor.

- **Health:** This might be a general practitioner or a specialist. It could be a physician who specializes in preventative medicine, nutrition, massage therapist, holistic medicine, etc. This team member is anyone whose advice you trust in the realm of your physical health. Even your personal trainer or gym buddy fits here.

- **Educational:** Within this category, you should include teachers/professors, career mentors, public figures, and anyone to whom you look for new information that interests you or ignites your desire to know. It can be the host of a podcast you listen to daily for knowledge, or your favorite motivational speaker. We are always learning, and hopefully there are people in your life who stimulate you with new knowledge.

- **Relational:** These are the intimates in the traditional sense—family members, romantic partners, your parents, your siblings, your in-laws, your spouse or partner, the person you are dating. Remember, some people in this category may not be trustworthy, or you may have fractured relationships with them, but they are in your life due to family obligations.

- **Employment:** These are folks who you work with closely in your job, including your boss and any people you manage. This category also includes those who advise you with your finances as well.

- **Spiritual:** A spiritual team member might be someone within a religious organization of which you're a member. But, it is really anyone who keeps you grounded in your own spirituality or guides you to greater alignment in that part of your life.

One reason for examining your team so closely is that these people can be accountability partners for you. I can't tell you how many times I've heard the phrase "I just don't have time for the things I really want to do." But if your "crew" is paying attention, they can help you get out of your own way enough to accomplish *anything* you want. You're not in this alone.

Another reason to look at your team is that it is crucial to be prepared should there ever be a crisis in your life. For example, in California, we all have earthquake kits at the ready. These kits have all the necessary tools required in case we can't easily access clean water and food or are faced with injury. The kit includes a change of clothes, medical supplies, bottled water, and so on. Think of your team as an earthquake kit (though, of course, the people in your life serve a far greater, more important role!). It's there for you when you need a quick response so that a crisis feels like a momentary pause, not the end of the world. Crises can come in all different shapes and sizes, and the better your team is, the more equipped you will be for handling anything that comes your way.

As I mentioned, I have taken hundreds of folks through their team across the seven SPHERES of life and every time I do, they see that some edits or additions are needed. Again, this isn't meant to sound mechanical—these are, after all, people who are near and dear to you and maybe have been for many decades. If any of your relationships are feeling complicated or troubled in some way, I'd encourage you flip back to the Relationships chapter and look through the lists of values. It could be that you have some fundamental differences in what you and that person both value, so that's an important place to start. I've spent a lot of time carefully analyzing relationships in my life and making sure my team evolves as I do. Within each of my seven SPHERES, I have experts and confidants whom I consider to be my thinking partners. I'm going to share with you my process for identifying, analyzing, evaluating, and curating your team to support you in your quest for your Best Self.

I look at your team as a living, breathing organism. It does not exist solely to help you on your journey; instead, it requires reciprocal action. Just as with anything in life, the more you put into it, the more you will get out of it. So, throughout this chapter, let's remember to look at your team through that lens of reciprocity. The goal is to evaluate and design your team in such a way that you bolster *each other* in your pursuit of being your Best Self.

Some of your teammates might be experts that you rely on for accurate information or strategy. Others might just be experts in you and what makes you tick, because they've known you so long, or they really just "get" you. All are valuable, and all are worth your appreciation and gratitude.

It's also important to recognize and acknowledge that there may be people you've allowed into your inner circle that don't meet these criteria. It could be that you have some toxic relationships, or at a minimum, some unbalanced ones. Uncovering those situations is part of what we're trying to discover through this process. So, if there's someone within your orbit who often seems to lead you in the wrong direction, who is a bad influence in that they encourage you to indulge in your vices, who brings out your Anti-Self, who constantly takes from you but rarely gives back, or who you view as a saboteur, I still want you to include them in your list.

Now it's time to write down the various SPHERES and organize your teammates under each one. Again, if you have one person who falls into several categories, write their name under each that applies.

My Team by SPHERES

SOCIAL

RATING:

PERSONAL

RATING:

HEALTH

RATING:

EMPLOYMENT

RATING:

RELATIONSHIP

RATING:

EDUCATION

RATING:

SPIRITUAL

RATING:

Rate Your Team within Your SPHERES

Next, I want you to rate your team within each of your SPHERES. You will rate them from 1–10 with 1 being an absolutely dismal team, one that doesn't fulfill you or give you what you need, and 10 being a team that is top-notch, so tight that you feel you don't need anyone else in that category. There is a line for the Rating at the bottom of each SPHERE. Fill that in now.

By looking at your Team SPHERES ratings, you can easily spot what might be out of balance in your life. If you feel that your team is lacking in some areas, that's great news because now you've identified a need. Now, you can focus on filling that need. If there's a category where you have no one listed, or the person you currently rely on for that type of support isn't providing enough value, begin to think about who might be better suited. This may require some research and soul-searching, but it will be well worth the effort.

It's unlikely that you rated your team as a perfect 10 in every SPHERE of your life, so, now I want you to ask your Best Self what a 10 rating for your team in each category would look like. How would it function? Who would be your go-to in each category? What would make you feel as if you have the most possible support in each of the SPHERES?

My Perfect 10 Team Looks Like:

1. **Social:** _____

2. **Personal:** _____

3. **Health:** _____

4. **Education:** _____

5. **Relationships:** _____

6. **Employment:** _____

7. **Spiritual:** _____

If you aren't completely sure what a 10 team looks like for you, don't worry. This is a process, and you are building awareness. The more aware you are, the more open you become. The more open you are to meeting people who support you in being your Best Self, the more opportunities you will have to meet people like that. I believe that's how the universe works—if you're open, opportunities come around more often. If that sounds "woo-woo" or unrealistic, let me share an example with you. My friend Christina was looking for a nanny for her son, because she planned to go back to work after a short maternity leave. She wanted to find a nanny that they would consider family, who was beyond honest and trustworthy, and who would love and adore her child but also provide appropriate boundaries for him. She knew it was a tall order, but she wouldn't settle for less. She was thinking it through with a close friend one afternoon at lunch. She said, "I just feel like the right person will come to us, and while I'm looking at babysitter services online, I would prefer that we find her through a referral." Her friend's eyes suddenly lit up and she said, "You know what? I think I know the right person for you. It's going to sound crazy because she's never been a nanny, but she has three grown kids and two grandkids, and she's the sweetest, most caring woman I've ever met. She's working in what's essentially a sweatshop downtown, and it's been really hard on her. You should interview her!" And she did—the very next week. She and her husband agreed immediately that she was right for their growing family, and though she hadn't been formally trained in any way, she was a kind, motherly, loving woman who would take excellent care of their son. That was four years ago, and she is still with them five days a week, and has been a key team member for them, as the perfect nanny for their son, who calls her his best friend. Christina was open to opportunities that might arise, and because of that, she found a teammate in the most unexpected way.

When I do this exercise with clients, they almost always realize they need to remove someone from the team either because they're no longer dependable, they're taking more than giving, they're not looking out for their best interests, or they just don't match their integrity. We all have seasons in our lives, and sometimes a person was right for us in a certain time, but as we grow we realize this person isn't right for us now. It's time to be brutally honest with yourself. If you're keeping someone close who you shouldn't simply because you want to avoid conflict, I urge you to find a way to gently shift them out of their role on your team. One common example of this is when a romantic relationship has significantly changed because you've both grown apart from one another.

I had a friend years ago who was very much within my circle of trust, but over time, I noticed that I was making excuses for his negative behavior. He lied to me on several occasions, he was unreliable when it came to making plans, and his actions showed me that he didn't have the kind of respect for our relationship that I felt it deserved. He'd grown up with a lot of trauma, so my heart went out to him, but even when we'd discuss the issues I had with his behavior I found that he simply couldn't change. I wasn't getting back from him all that I was putting in, so there was no reciprocity in our friendship.

As much as I enjoyed being around this friend, as he was charismatic and likable, I found that when I weighed the negatives against the positives, I could no longer trust him to be on my team. It didn't mean we needed a dramatic break, we fought, or we parted ways forever, it was just that I recognized he didn't make the team for me. These choices aren't always easy, but they're important. Your time and energy are too precious to spend on someone who isn't giving back.

Drilling Down

Now that you have identified and categorized your current team, let's drill down and ask ourselves some questions about them.

- Who can you rely upon to be an objective thinking partner/s when you're facing a new challenge? I define a thinking partner as someone who helps you think through things based on who you are—they don't tell you what you need to do; instead, they help you think it through, so you can find the answer for yourself.
- Are there any commonalities between the people you've allowed onto your team? What do those similarities tell you about yourself?
  - Who in your life encourages you to operate as your Best Self? Are there teammates around which you never have to alter any part of your personality? Is there someone in your life you find it particularly hard to be your Best Self around? Or, who in your life triggers your Anti-Self to appear? Is there a teammate with whom you have to censor yourself and withhold your true opinions?

- Who has your best interests at heart, rather than advancing their own agenda?
- Is there someone on your team who could be manipulating you or using you in some way?
- Alternatively, are you attempting to control or manipulate someone, so you can get what you want?
- Are any of your teammates holding you back or sabotaging you?
- Do your teammates fire you up, get you excited about life, and inspire you to think creatively?

These questions may get your wheels turning and force you to ask questions. Really take the time to explore your team. If you discover through this process that there are, indeed, some people within your inner circle with whom you can't be your Best Self or aren't acting in the way they have committed they would, reevaluate the connection. When someone has shown you who they are, you should believe them and act accordingly. Of course, there is no perfect relationship or perfect connection—so if you're striving for that in terms of your team, you're being unrealistic. But if, for example, you realized that someone at work is always badmouthing other employees to you, you might see that this person could also be bad-mouthing you, or that they are simply doing it to advance their own career or agenda.

I understand that these questions can seem a little harsh when you apply them to family members. We can't choose the family that we're born into, but just because they are blood, that doesn't mean we need to let them hurt us, hold us back, or take from us. If you have family members that aren't helping you be your Best Self, it's okay to find ways to reduce your contact with them to a bare minimum. You do not have to hold on to any harmful relationships out of a sense of obligation.

Reciprocity of Love

Now let's examine your team through another important perspective. Let's make sure that, for everyone on your list, you are
reciprocating. Ask yourself: what am I providing for *them*? Maintaining equilibrium is key, and you can do that through what I
call a reciprocity of love. This is a basic concept, really, but it's one
that is all too easily overlooked. When it comes to interpersonal
relationships, you need to be giving as much as you are getting, if
not more.

   Ask yourself this question: do you bring joy to other people?
When was the last time you purposely did something that would
put a smile on a friend's face? Maybe it was recently, and that's
great. If not, that's okay, too—I'm certainly not trying to make
you feel guilty. I know how easy it is to get caught up in the everyday requirements of life and to lose sight of, or never even fully
realize, the power of spreading joy and love to people around us.
But it *is* powerful, let me tell you. If you do nothing else differently in your life today, I highly recommend that you take a few
moments in service to someone you care about. Expect nothing in
return, because the truth is, giving of ourselves to others is a gift
in and of itself.

   If you are caring for your team the way that you care for a garden, it will thrive and flourish. If you are constantly expecting to
receive from your team, but you're showing your team any care, it
won't be able to function at its highest capacity. Going forward,
just understand that if you give even a little to your team around
you, you'll receive so much in return. Personally, I thrive on making connections between people that I know will be fruitful. I love
introducing like-minded individuals who can help each other in
some way on their individual journeys. That's one way that you

can give back to your team. And be sure to ask your team what they want or need so that you can help provide it—you're not a mind reader, and neither are they—so you all need to be asking each other what you can do for one another.

Trust and Expectations

Like most people, you have a handful of folks that you feel you can trust implicitly. There may be others you trust in some ways, but not in all ways. And you likely have some in your life for specific reasons, but you purposely keep them at arm's length. Others are in the outer rings of your universe, and you keep a watchful eye on them. Finally, there are probably some folks you hope to never see or hear from—people you can't trust and that you know will be hurtful.

Do you trust every person who is currently on your team? Remember, just because someone is familiar to you doesn't necessarily mean they have *earned* your trust. Dr. Phil often says that we should never give anyone the benefit of the doubt. If you've allowed someone into your immediate nucleus because someone else vouched for them, or they're a friend of a friend, but they haven't actually demonstrated their trustworthiness to you, then I implore you to remain on high alert. Do not blindly trust anyone. This is not about being suspicious or paranoid—it's simply about how, just as you wouldn't expect the absolute worst of someone right off the bat, you also should not expect the very *best* of them that quick. Let them show you who they are through their actions instead of setting up unrealistic expectations. The truth is, your expectations of other people can often be resentments waiting to happen because if someone hasn't shown you who they are, how can you know what to expect from them? For example, I use car service apps a lot. I find myself expecting them to have a clean car, that they wouldn't blast the music at top volume, and that they would be helpful to me with my luggage. But that's a false expectation and I am often disappointed. Since lowering my expectations, I've actually been much happier with my car service experiences. Now I'm usually pleasantly surprised rather than annoyed. Expecting people to do what you deem appropriate by your standards just doesn't work because they could be operating with a different framework.

To help you evaluate the trustworthiness and your own expectations of your team, here are some simple questions to ask yourself about each person so you can consider them objectively.

The Expectations Test:

1. Can you usually rely on this person to show up at an agreed-upon time without any flakiness or excuses?
   ○ YES ○ NO

2. If this person tells you that something is going to happen, does it usually play out that way?
   ○ YES ○ NO

3. When this person describes a conversation or an event, does it generally match up with information you get from others about that same conversation or event?
   ○ YES ○ NO

4. To your knowledge, has this person ever lied to someone else or assumed you would lie on their behalf—do they choose lying over honesty?
   ○ YES ○ NO

5. To your knowledge, has this person ever withheld important information in an effort to avoid conflict with someone else?

   ○ **YES**   ○ **NO**

6. Have you ever noticed any hypocritical behavior in this person—for instance, engaging in behavior that he or she would judge others for engaging in?

   ○ **YES**   ○ **NO**

7. Does this person make excuses for their behaviors instead of owning them?

   ○ **YES**   ○ **NO**

8. Has this person demonstrated consistent loyalty?

   ○ **YES**   ○ **NO**

Based on your answers, you can now adjust your expectations for certain people on your team. Some people are never going to be on time. So, they aren't the people to ask to pick you up and take you to the airport. But that person might be the one who will be the most honest with you when you need it, or the shoulder to cry on when you need that. Understanding your teammates' capabilities and limitations will help you know who to call upon for what.

I once had a client who said trust and expectations aside, the most important thing to her was that she had good chemistry with her team. She actually knew that some of her team members weren't great with follow-through and she had to lower her expectations for some of them a bit, but she was fine with that. The bottom line is that awareness is the key—*know* who people are, and *expect* only what they can give, and then you won't be disappointed or set yourself up for failure.

Chemistry is the connection to another person that is

intangible—you may be the most unlikely pair for a lot of reasons, but you just connect over one specific area really well. Entertainers especially tend to value chemistry over anything else. If you have chemistry with someone, you feel safe and you can be open-minded. You could have amazing chemistry with someone you're dating, for example, but if your values don't line up, you're likely going to run into trouble. Or you might have wonderful chemistry with a coworker or collaborator on a project, and that's great, but just know there might be limitations in that chemistry—in other words, that person may or may not also be a good friend as well as collaborator. The takeaway for you is to maintain awareness about the people on your team in terms of what you need from them, what you can realistically expect from them, and what's most important to you about each of them.

Key Elements: Inspiration, Exhilaration, and Illumination

As you can see, your team is an essential aspect of becoming truly connected with your Best Self in all SPHERES of your life. But it's even more than that. It goes much deeper. If you choose to navigate through your life alongside people who inspire, exhilarate, and illuminate you, then you've tapped into a whole new and potentially mind-blowing experience. By adjusting your team, you might find that you push yourself further than ever in positive directions, simply because you are so motivated by those around you.

Your team, or at least some of your teammates, should provide an endless well of inspiration. You should have some people who encourage you to try new things and to venture out of your comfort zone. There should be a free exchange of intriguing ideas between you. You should feel safe with some or all members of your team to explore your imagination and home in on and hone your art. Remember—we are all artists, and your team should help you with identifying and elevating your own art form.

The unique qualities, perspectives, and ideas that your team brings should also make you feel exhilarated—which is a heightened version of happiness, or excitement about life. Ideally, they should stir something deep within your soul that you can't quite explain, or make you feel like there's a whole world out there and it's yours to explore. Maybe some of them are doing exciting things in their own lives or they've accomplished something that you admire and aspire to do yourself. These are all amazing qualities to have in your teammates.

We are all in a constant state of learning new information, and your team should be teaching you, too. When you go to bed at night, I hope that you feel more knowledgeable than when you got up that morning. You and your team should enlighten each other in all sorts of ways. Broaden your horizons through the power of your team, and the only limit to what you can do and where you can go is your own imagination.

As I mentioned at the beginning of this chapter, life is not meant to be lived as an island. The interconnectivity between humans is where the magic comes from in life. Your team is what can help you thrive in all of your SPHERES and can enrich and deepen your experiences. Tap into the power that an awesome team can provide!

13

Seven Steps for Acquiring Your Best Self Goals

N ow that you have thoroughly examined each of your life SPHERES, you will have a better understanding of which areas are out of balance and are keeping you from living life as your Best Self. Now, it is time to create some tangible goals that will help you get what you want, need, and deserve out of your life. This is where the rubber meets the road. Now is the time to change your life.

Look at Your SPHERES:

Refer back to the assessments you did for each of your SPHERES, and below, write down your current rating for each, as well as the first thing you would like to focus on for each. If, for instance, you know there's a specific relationship you need to work on, write that in Relationships. If you need to make your health more of a priority by exercising regularly, write that under Health.

Next, think about your Team within each SPHERE. You will need to create goals around improving your teams in each SPHERE as well.

The chart below will help you organize your thoughts.

Next, we will take the data you collected about where you

SPHERES	SPHERES RATING	TEAM RATING
Social Life		
Personal Life		
Health		
Education		
Relationships		
Employment		
Spiritual Development		

want to make improvements and then turn that information into actual goals using the seven steps to goal acquisition. This process is about transforming your hopes, dreams, and desires into reality. You and you alone hold the power to create the life you've always wanted—to make it real. I encourage you to grab hold of this and follow it through, because your new life is waiting for you on the other side of these seven steps.

SPHERES	TEAMS FOCUS POINTS	SPHERES FOCUS POINTS
Social Life		
Personal Life		
Health		
Education		
Relationships		
Employment		
Spiritual Development		

THE AUTHENTIC GOAL

Now is the time to check in with your Best Self and make sure that each of your goals lines up with who you really are, rather than with your ego. The motivation for reaching your goals should come from the positive, light-filled place within you, and reflect an earnest desire to improve your life.

When you're thinking about what you want in all areas of your life, it's important to make sure your desires are really your own. Sometimes we think we want something because someone else in our life has it, or because society says we should want it, or because wanting it will make someone else in our lives happy. But those aren't authentic desires. Check yourself as you go through this exercise and make sure that everything you say you want is coming from your Best Self.

If you're considering a new endeavor but it doesn't match up with who you really are, pivot and find a similar goal that does. I believe that achievement for the sake of achievement doesn't really serve a positive purpose; let's be sure that you're keeping your eye on the ultimate prize in all that you do—authentic and lasting happiness.

Step 1: Define Your Goal in Terms of Specific Events or Behaviors

This may seem obvious, but understanding what you want, what you *really* want, is the first step to getting it. Here's what I mean: you must be able to define the goal you're trying to achieve in a specific way. For instance, you can't just desire an emotion. Setting the goal of feeling happy, for instance, is too vague. If you state your goals in terms of specific events or behaviors, you are closer to accomplishing them. If you want more happiness in your life, you must first define what's going to make you happier. Let's say you derive joy from traveling with friends, and you know it will make you happy if you have a trip to look forward to. Then you would define your goal in terms of specific events or behaviors by stating, "My goal is to plan, organize, and save for a trip with my friends." That's how you take a vague notion like becoming happier to a specific goal that is an event or behavior.

This first step in the process of acquiring your goal can be an absolute game changer. If you've ever felt that you don't have enough strength or follow-through to reach a goal, the real issue might have been that you weren't defining it properly. Anyone who has ever achieved something great was able to *claim* that victory because they first *named* that victory.

So, drop a destination pin on the map of your life and get started.

Now it's your turn. Write down your goal in terms of specific events or behaviors.

My goal is: _____

_____

_____

_____

Step 2: Express Your Goal in Terms That Can Be Measured

The second step toward acquiring your goal is to express it in a quantifiable way. This way, you'll be able to determine your level of progress along the way and know when you've successfully arrived where you wanted to be. For example, if your goal is to clear out the clutter in your home so that you can be more productive and peaceful, then which rooms or closets do you intend to clean up? You'd list them out, one by one—for instance, you might say you want to clean and organize your closet, your master bedroom, and your garage. Now your goal is measurable—you have three spaces to clean up. You'll know when you've achieved your goal because those spaces will be neat and organized.

My goal, in terms that can be measured, is: _____

_____

_____

_____

Step 3: Choose a Goal You Can Control

There are things in life that are within our control, like X and X. And then there are things that are outside our control, like Y and Y. In goal creation, it does not serve you to craft goals that are connected to things beyond your control. Chasing a goal beyond our control is a fool's errand, will only make you feel hopeless, and sets you up for failure. At the end of the day we truly can only control ourselves.

The only person's actions/behaviors that you have control over are your own—so that means your goal cannot rely upon someone else taking a specific action. You're in the driver's seat of your life, so your goals can't be dependent upon any outside people or forces.

Is your goal controllable?

○ **YES**   ○ **NO**

If not, think about your goal and pivot toward one that you can control, then write it down:

My *controllable* goal is: _____

_____

_____

_____

Step 4: Plan and Program a Strategy That Will Get You to Your Goal

Creating a specific strategy for achieving your goal is exciting because there are infinite possibilities available and you get to see what works for you. You also need to consider any obstacles that may stand in your way and create strategies for overcoming them. Your environment, schedule, and accountability all need to be part of the equation when you are programming a strategy for achieving your goal.

One pitfall I've seen with clients in the goal acquisition process is that they get so excited about what they're looking to achieve that they get swept up in an emotional high that they believe willpower will carry them along to success. That's faulty thinking. It's easy to feel excited about a new undertaking, but what happens when the excitement starts to wane? We can easily get blown off course. I don't want that to happen to you, so planning your strategy is imperative.

The more clearly you lay out your strategy, the less tempted you will be to deviate from it. Programming your days to include whatever is necessary to achieve your goal will create a positive momentum. Let's say you're planning to run a half marathon in six months. You can now find all kinds of very detailed training programs online for how to prepare your mind and body to run

13.1 miles. Find one that makes sense for your lifestyle, and then chart your course. Choose which days each week you are going to run, stretch, do strength training, meditate, and any other requirements. You can program your environment by purchasing the right clothes and shoes for where you'll be running. If you have a weeklong vacation booked for right in the middle of your training program, determine how you're going to continue the program while you're away so that you don't get derailed. Down to every last detail, program precisely what is required of you in order to achieve that goal, and then get busy.

My strategy for attaining my goal is: _____
_____
_____
_____

Step 5: Define Your Goal in Terms of Steps

Major life changes happen one step at a time. Let's make sure you know all of the steps are between here and your goal line. You don't want to get halfway there and have no clue as to what to do next. Before you get started, write out each step you'll need to take along the way.

As an example, weight loss is a common goal, and we all know it doesn't happen overnight, no matter how much we wish it did. There are steps we must take over time in order to lose weight. We have to clearly define what those steps are from the outset so that we can refer to them at any time, know where we are in the process, and what else we need to do. So, continuing the weight loss example, let's say hypothetically that you've chosen to follow a

Paleo diet and you're committing to exercise for forty-five minutes four days a week as your weight loss plan, then your specific steps would be: Program my kitchen for success by removing all foods and beverages that don't support my goal of weight loss, grocery shop, and fill my kitchen with foods that I believe do support me in losing weight, create a weekly meal plan and prep meals each weekend so I'm not scrambling for food during the week, and set appointments in my calendar for gym time so I have no excuse for skipping my exercise.

The specific steps I will need to carry out in order to achieve my goal are: _____

_____

_____

_____

Step 6: Assign a Timeline for Your Goal

Have you ever noticed how easy it is to leave things undone if there's no pressure to complete them? Some people let their houses get a little messy and disorderly until they know company is coming over, for example. I've known plenty of people who procrastinate until the last moment to study for an exam they're about to take. The power of the ticking clock is undeniable—if a deadline looms, we are more likely to get the work done than if there's no clear date by which it needs to be complete. It's human nature.

Since we know we're more likely to finish something if we have a deadline, then it makes perfect sense to create one for our goals. It will foster a sense of urgency and purpose. It will motivate us to stay on track.

This step goes even further than just setting a deadline by which we will have reached our goal. It requires us to assign a timeline for all the steps necessary for reaching it. Let's say, for instance, your goal is to obtain a certification of some kind. Perhaps it requires twenty hours of hands-on training. If you know that you can free up four hours a week to do the training, then you can set a date on the calendar five weeks from now when you should be finished. If today is August 10, then you'll have completed the hands-on training by September 14.

Even more specifically, if you know that you can do the training on Fridays, then you can designate a four-hour chunk of time each Friday between August 10 and September 14 on your calendar for this work. In so doing, you've locked in your timeline. Below you'll fill in the key dates by which you'll complete portions of your own goal. This will help you keep accountable.

Think about how amazing it is that you can literally look at a calendar and circle the date by which you will have reached your goal. That's powerful! And once you've reached it, you can look back at that same calendar and see the evidence of your hard work and how it paid off, exactly when you said it would.

Timeline for My Goal

Deadline: _____

Other key dates: _____

Step 7: Create Accountability for Progress Toward Your Goal

The final step in this time-tested formula for achieving your goal is to create accountability. In the last chapter, we fine-tuned your team, and this is the perfect opportunity to put that team into action. Choose someone who you know will be a trustworthy accountability partner in whatever your specific goal is, tell them all the details of how you plan to achieve it, and then ask them to help keep you accountable. Agree to make periodic reports to that person (or people, in case you feel you need more than one) along the way, with real consequences if you don't. You can mitigate your risk of slacking off, procrastinating, or giving up by building in this type of accountability.

My accountability partner(s) as I work toward achieving this goal is/are: _____

_____

_____

_____

No More Somedays

I believe there are dreams and desires tucked away in the deep recesses of all of our minds. When they bubble up to the surface of our consciousness, we reflexively push them back down, shove them out of view, ignore them—why?—because it's easier than acknowledging them or adding them to our ever-growing to-do list of life. We think, *Oh, I'll get to that . . . someday.* Someday. When is your someday, exactly? When are you going to finally give credo to the inner yearnings of your heart? It's time to make your dreams a reality. Don't wait. Life is short, and your role in this world is bigger than you think.

I told you this was going to be an action-packed chapter, and that action will be coming from *you*. The time has arrived for alchemy—you are going to transform your somedays into days of the week. Right now, you are going to breathe life into your dreams.

You are going to do this because you already took the important step of focusing on yourself enough to read this book. You took the time to shine a light on your Best Self, and you've examined every corner, nook, and cranny of your life with that lens. Anyone who takes the time and puts the effort in to do that is someone who is ready to make a change. For the better and forever.

Goals within Your SPHERES

Now that you understand the process for creating and achieving goals, it's time to create your most urgent, controllable, and realistic goals within all seven of your SPHERES.

Even if they feel lofty or unattainable in this moment, write them down. No matter how intimidating they've felt in the past, or how many times you've tried and failed to achieve them, write them down. No matter whether or not you fully believe you deserve to own these goals, write them down. Even if they're not completely formed; even if they are just quiet whispers between your inner self and your heart, write them down.

This is about reaching within yourself, being vulnerable, and telling yourself the truth about the wishes, hopes, and longings you discover there. Remember, naming them is the imperative first step to claiming them.

SPHERES	GOAL
Social Life	
Personal Life	
Health	
Education	
Relationships	
Employment	
Spiritual	

Your 7-Step Goal Acquisition Worksheet

I suggest you choose the goal within your lowest-rated SPHERE as your first goal you're going to work toward, as that is the most urgent area requiring your attention. Use the worksheet below to plan out how you're going to achieve that goal, and all of your other goals going forward. It's a very useful tool, so put it to good use!

STEP 1: Define Your Goal in Terms of Specific Events or Behaviors

My goal is: _____

_____

_____

_____

_____

STEP 2: Express Your Goal in Terms That Can Be Measured

My goal, in terms that can be measured, is: _____

_____

_____

_____

_____

STEP 3: Choose a Goal You Can Control

Is your goal controllable?

○ YES   ○ NO

If not, pivot your goal toward one that is controllable, and write it here:

My *controllable* goal is: _____

_____

_____

_____

STEP 4: Plan and Program a Strategy That Will Get You to Your Goal

My specific strategy for attaining my goal is: _____

_____

_____

_____

_____

STEP 5: Define Your Goal in Terms of Steps

The steps I will need to take in order to achieve my goal are: _____

_____

_____

_____

_____

STEP 6: Assign a Timeline for Your Goal

Timeline for my goal

Deadline: _____

Other key dates: _____

STEP 7: Create Accountability for Progress Toward Your Goal

My accountability partner(s) as I work toward achieving this goal is/are: _____

_____

_____

_____

The dates that I'm going to check in with my accountability partner are:

_____	_____
_____	_____
_____	_____
_____	_____

The consequences for my not checking in with my accountability partner are: _____

_____

_____

_____

Examples for the 7-Step Goal Acquisition Process

To help you understand this process even better, I thought it would be helpful to show two examples of clients I worked with who saw a need within their SPHERES and created goals around them to great success.

Margaret had spent so much time and energy on building a successful career and creating the type of family lifestyle that she wanted at home, she had completely neglected and overlooked something that once had been of the highest importance in her life—her Spiritual SPHERE. Her lack of connection to her spiritual belief system was having a severe domino effect on every other area of her life. She was quick to anger with her kids, she was impatient with her coworkers, and she had even alienated her husband to the point that he was sleeping in a separate bedroom. She'd even found herself snapping at perfect strangers like waiters in a restaurant or people in line at the grocery store. This kind of irrational behavior wasn't like her at all—and when we first started talking, she didn't understand how it had gotten to this point. But she knew one thing for sure—she was terrified that everything she'd worked so hard for would be gone if she kept up this pattern.

As we talked, she realized that her problem area was within her Spiritual SPHERE. She used to be very plugged in at church and passionate about giving back to the community, but slowly she'd edged those activities out of her life to make room for a booming career and a family that required much of her attention. To get herself back on track, she knew she must create some goals in that SPHERE.

We looked at her current team, and she immediately identified that her Spiritual team was lacking, and she knew she needed more people who were like-minded in her spiritual beliefs that she could talk to, learn from, and grow with. So she created a specific, measurable, and controllable goal of finding three new people to add to her Spiritual team. Next, she planned and programmed a strategy of getting involved with the volunteer corps at her church and determined she would volunteer twice a week for two hours to meet more people and also give back to her community. Plus, she would bring her daughter, who would greatly benefit from experiencing the joy and hard work of volunteering for those in need. She created steps—she would attend the volunteer meeting the following Thursday, and then find out when her and her daughter's services would be needed. She assigned a timeline, too—she knew that she wanted to have added three people to her Spiritual team within ninety days. She leaned on a friend with whom she used to attend church to be her accountability partner. Margaret was always an overachiever, and this situation was no exception. Not only did she and her daughter get closer through the process, but her husband also joined in. Now the three of them regularly attend a church that they all love, and even host Bible study on Wednesday nights at their house. She committed to acquiring her goal, and the positive effects were felt across all parts of her life and her team.

Another example is Maurice. He knew that his health was suffering because he was overeating, especially at night. So he created a specific, measurable, and controllable goal of ending his eating by 9 p.m. His strategy was to move his dinner from 6 p.m. to 7:30 p.m. so that he wouldn't get hunger pangs later, to go to bed earlier, and to prepare his meals in advance so that he'd know exactly what he was going to eat. He wanted to have this routine in place within two weeks, so he set a date on his calendar by which he needed to begin. He created accountability by choosing a friend at work that he knew had a strict eating schedule, and they agreed to text each other three times a week to stay on track. He reported back to me about two months after he started working the steps on his plan, and he was doing great—he'd already lost fifteen pounds and had abundantly more energy, and his doctor was very happy with his progress. I asked him what was different about this time compared to every other time he'd tried to turn his health around, and he said it was all about choosing a specific, achievable goal and writing out the steps he needed to follow. The more he saw himself succeed, the more motivated he was to continue with his plan.

As you can see, by following the seven steps and building a strategy you can quickly sketch out your game plan for achieving your goals once you determine to do so. It's very straightforward!

The Nonrenewable Commodity: Time

There are *so* many ways that you can fill your calendar, right? You can feel like the busiest person in the world just trying to stay ahead of the day-in and day-out requirements of keeping your life and your household running. Or maybe you tend to fill up your calendar with social obligations, and plans without any thought about whether all you're committing to or trying to accomplish even makes you feel fulfilled. There's a danger in becoming mechanical about how you spend your time—very quickly, you can lose yourself, lose that connection to who you are authentically, and instead become enslaved to the schedule instead of being in the moment of the events. Now, I'm not suggesting you stop doing your laundry, going into work, or grocery shopping—of course there are certain activities you must do in order to stay healthy, hygienic, and fed. I'm simply trying to wake you up to the fact that without some purposeful introspection now and then, you might one day realize you've been spending all of your time on things that don't really matter in the big picture of your life. And worse, you're not excited by any of it. You aren't feeling fueled, energized, impassioned, or actively fulfilling your life's purpose—ever. You're just going through the motions. That is not why you were put on this earth, my friend, and if you even slightly relate to that dismal picture, read on, because we're about to put that runaway train in reverse.

Let's take a close look at your daily schedule. This exercise is about mirroring back to you how and where you spend the majority of your time. Seeing in writing exactly where you are committing your precious time can be powerful. I want you to write out how you spend a typical weekday. Write down everything you're usually doing, hour by hour. Feel free to adjust the times according to your sleep/wake schedule. The more details you include, the better. Also, if your weekdays differ dramatically because you work part-time and have other responsibilities on nonworking days, then feel free to write out several days' worth of entries.

All of the details of your day matter, because later we are going to work together to craft your days in a purposeful manner. I want you to be thoughtful and honest about this exercise, so here are some basic parameters:

1. Write down "wake up" next to the time you usually open your eyes, but then include the first thing you do after you wake up. Do you barrel out of bed and race to the shower? Do you spend fifteen minutes catching up on social media? Do you hit snooze five times? Do you go wake up your kids? Head straight to the kitchen for coffee? These "how you greet the day" details matter.

2. Be honest with yourself. This exercise, and all of the exercises in the book, are for *you*. You gain nothing by cheating! For example, if you spend time on something you aren't exactly proud of—anything from gorging on ice cream at 10 p.m. to indulging in an inappropriate relationship of some kind—write it down. This is for your eyes only!

5AM: _____

6AM: _____

7AM: _____

8AM: _____

9AM: _____

10AM: _____

11AM: _____

12PM: _____

1PM: _____

2PM: _____

3PM: _____

4PM: _____

5PM: _____

6PM: _____

7PM: _____

8PM: _____

9PM: _____

10PM: _____

11PM: _____

12AM: _____

Now let's turn our attention to your weekends. (If your work schedule includes working on the weekends, choose a day that you have off work and fill it out accordingly.) What does your typical weekend day look like? Do you sleep in? Attend religious services of some kind? Go to the movies? Have dinner with friends? Write it all down here.

5AM: _____

6AM: _____

7AM: _____

8AM: _____

9AM: _____

10AM: _____

11AM: _____

12PM: _____

1PM: _____

2PM: _____

3PM: _____

4PM: _____

5PM: _____

6PM: _____

7PM: _____

8PM: _____

9PM: _____

10PM: _____

11PM: _____

12AM: _____

Take a moment and look over your schedules. Understand that this is your "before" picture. This is how you spend your time now. Since you can only expect outcomes based on the time you're putting in, then it's easier to see the types of outcomes you might expect from your current schedule. I'll use learning a new language just as an example—if you're spending time binging on the latest hot TV series, or perusing your social media feeds, that's time you could've been spending on studying. Alternatively, if you're spending time listening to audio books in that language or immersing yourself with others who speak it, you will get that much closer to becoming fluent. Remember this formula: time + effort = results.

If you want to change your life, you have to change how you're spending your time. Let's get a little more specific with these questions:

What are you spending the majority of your time doing? _____

_____

_____

_____

How do you feel about that activity that you are spending much of your precious time doing? _____

_____

_____

_____

Was that feeling that you wrote down a positive or negative feeling, overall? Circle one:

○ **POSITIVE**   ○ **NEGATIVE**

ACTION:

If you circled negative, you must discover a way to *replace* that activity with one that gives you a positive feeling. In other words, how would your Best Self handle it?

For instance, suppose that you've come to realize through the work you've done in this book that it's time for you to end a relationship that has become toxic over time. Maybe you've noticed, as you've investigated your daily schedule, that time you spend with this person usually results in an argument or you just not feeling great about yourself or your life. So, your first order of business is to use time that you'd usually be hanging out with that person to have a conversation with him or her about your relationship. Choose a time when you are both calm and choose a neutral location for the discussion. Depending upon your specific circumstances, you might know for sure this relationship needs to end, or you might be willing to discuss the issues and see if resolution is possible. Whatever the case may be, the idea is to first commit the time in your schedule to having the talk with this person. Then, use the time you would have been spending together that resulted in negative outcomes for something positive that encourages you, inspires you, from which you can learn, and so on. It would even be wise to use some of that time for meditation or just being still, quiet, and in solitude. You'll need to give yourself space and time to heal from the toxicity you were experiencing within that relationship.

In some cases, you might have a negative feeling about how you're spending your time not because of the thing you're spending your time on, but because of a fear you have around it. If that's the case, we're going to talk about how to tackle that fear and overcome it. I find that sometimes what we need is a new pair of glasses, not an entirely new environment. In other words, we might need a shift in perception, and that can occur if we decide to let go of the fear.

Now, think about something that you wish you had more time to do, but is barely in your schedule if at all. Perhaps you wish you spent more time walking outside to improve your health, or more time reading books that inspire you, or learning a new language. Maybe you've always said you wanted to volunteer. Think about what you say to other people all the time—like, "I'd love to keep a journal, but I just don't have the time," or "I wish I was the kind of mom who cooks healthy meals, but I'm always ordering takeout because of my hectic schedule." It could even be that you know you need more sleep because you're constantly running on empty, yet you stay up until midnight every night surfing the Web or scrolling through your social media feeds.

If there's something you wish you could spend more time doing, write it here: _____
_____
_____

Referring back to your current schedules, do you feel it's at all possible that you could, in fact, create time for that thing you wish you were doing more of? Look closely and see if there's anywhere you could make a swap before you answer this question. For instance, are you watching three hours of TV at night when two hours could be spent pursuing that thing you're passionate about? Or do you feel you could stand to wake up a half hour to an hour earlier?

Now, write down where you think you could create time in your schedule to do something that's currently missing: _____
_____
_____
_____

ACTION:

Today, add into your upcoming calendar a chunk of time to do something new that you've been longing to make time for, even if it's just fifteen minutes. This will prove that you can make time for what you love. Also, delete something that is not serving you. If there is something you spend time on that you think could be put to better use, resolve to reduce it.

If you really dug deep into your life and did this entire exercise, congratulate yourself. This is a significant first step toward creating the life of your dreams.

Dr. Phil stresses the idea of putting verbs in his sentences. I couldn't agree with that more. Verbs are action words, and in order to change, we must take action. When I'm coaching a client and it becomes obvious that they are not willing to take action, I might try a few different tactics, but if they just dig in their heels I will suggest they find someone else to work with. It's not that I don't want to help them, but I just know that they'll never effect real change in their lives if they're not taking action.

One of the points of this exercise was to help you learn how to shift your priorities and start behaving (behaviors = actions) your way to success. The way to really know, beyond a shadow of a doubt, where your priorities lie, is to look at where you are spending your most valuable asset—your time. Now that you've come face-to-face with that reality, you will know if something requires change. Time is our only nonrenewable resource in this life. Think about that. When people say, "I wish I could have those thirty minutes of my life back," they're kidding, of course, but there's truth in that statement, right? When we waste time, we really have lost something valuable. Despite how busy all of our lives are, we need to create time to live the life we truly want.

Time spent discovering truths about yourself and designing the life you want is time well spent. You will not look back at the end of your life and say, "I sure wish I'd spent more time looking at other people's photos on my social media feeds," or, "I wish I'd worked more," or, "I wish I'd gone out to more bars." When our life's hourglass is down to its final few grains of sand, the things we'll be wishing we'd done more of have a lot more to do with our passion and purpose. Prioritize what's important *now* so you don't have regrets *later*.

Constantly Acquiring New Goals

Goal acquisition should become a way of life for you going forward. The Best Self Model isn't about evolving to a certain point and then just stopping. My hope is that the discoveries you've made while working through this book show you that your Best Self is in a constant state of evolution, which means you will continue to evaluate your SPHERES and find new areas where you need to create and achieve goals.

Perhaps some of your goals are small and simple. You don't feel you need a worksheet or lots of exercises to get to them. Or maybe you have a few big goals that you're going to work on simultaneously, and you absolutely need to plan them out to the last detail so that you stay on track. Whatever your situation may be, my hope is that you never say, "I need to work on that," and instead you can point to exactly where you are in the timeline of achieving that goal, and an end date by which you will have done so. No more somedays . . . only today!

Conclusion

The black SUV pulled up in front of my house at 7 a.m. sharp, just like they said it would. I grabbed my bags, walked outside, and hopped into the SUV. The driver wore a chauffeur's hat and a big smile. On the ride over, I flipped through the 130-page book for the hundredth time. Each time I reviewed it, I saw something I hadn't caught previously. I had reviewed it with my whole team and they were all as impressed as I was by the amount of critical information. There were interviews, photos, third-party information, self-assessments, court documents, and on and on.

As we made our way through the city and the morning traffic began to pick up, the voices in my head started to grow louder, and the doubts started creeping in. They bounced around like Ping-Pong balls in my mind—"I wonder if I brought too many clothes." "What if I'm no good at this?" and "Do I even have the right credentials for this?" I was entering into a whole new world; I'd always been a behind-the-scenes guy, but that was about to change. I was in territory that was completely foreign to me, and my insecurities were raising their ugly little heads.

I continued to question myself and what I brought to the table in this scenario. *Was I enough?*

Then it hit me. Those were old "tapes" playing in my head like elevator music from the distant past. Was this a new frontier for me? No doubt. Was this the ultimate "big league," the number one national and international platform of its kind across all media? Ratings don't lie and *Dr. Phil* has dominated the genre by an ever-widening margin for years. Good grief, the United States Congress frequently calls upon him to consult with bi-partisan committees on issues of mental health! He is the most famous mental health professional in the world. I mean, Dr. Phil and Sigmund Freud are answers on crossword puzzles! So yeah, this was "big league."

Then it occurred to me: *he* asked *me* to join the show! Wait a minute! What? You could practically hear the record scratch. I didn't ask him . . . he asked ME! I started to go over his unrivaled success in areas where so many others have failed. Look, he's got more degrees than a thermometer and he invited me, not one of the thousands of other experts he has encountered. It was time to practice what I preach even more and revise my personal truth to acknowledge I have a *lot* to offer and people I respect recognize it and really, *so do I*. A belief in being humble can go *too far* if it leads you to deny what you are called and gifted to do. All of a sudden, I noticed I had more knee room in the back of that SUV. Why? I was sitting taller. When my internal dialogue changed, so did my body language! Each impacted the other and momentum built.

"Are you nervous?" the driver asked, startling me out of my deep introspection.

"You know, I actually was. Now I am just excited. I'm thinking, 'Put in the Coach, coach! I'm ready.'"

"Just be yourself, and if you are even half as good as I've heard them say, you'll be golden." He smiled, and so did I. My negative thoughts were long gone.

"That's great advice. Thank you." He nodded, and I thought

about the truth in that simple statement. It applies to every situation in life, really. Be yourself. Your *best* self. We all need reminders from time to time, from ourselves and from others.

We turned down Melrose Avenue. I closed the binder and took a deep breath as we glided along. We entered probably the most historic gates in all of Hollywood. But I wasn't thinking "Hollywood" thoughts; I was thinking what a great opportunity lay before me to use this powerful "entertainment complex" not to entertain, but to educate, stimulate, and precipitate change. I really understood—maybe for the first time—the meaning of the term "highest and best use." We parked right in front of Stage 29, a giant warehouse-size soundstage. I thanked the driver and stepped out of the car.

I was met by a woman with a huge smile on her face. I asked her first for the restroom. My ritual would be especially important today. She showed me to the old-school bathroom, filled with a long line of old-fashioned stalls, and I recalled once again the first time I had completed this exercise. I wished it didn't always have to take place in a public restroom. What if someone walked in?

Oh well.

I entered, set down my bags, and kneeled in front of the sink and mirror. I closed my eyes, took a deep breath, and felt an inner quiet take over. I silently went through my self-affirmations. I thought, *You're where you're supposed to be,* and *The universe has a plan, Let go,* and *Be yourself.* And then I stood up, looked in the mirror, and said out loud, "It's not about you." I turned and walked out the door feeling strong, centered, and intent upon showing up as my Best Self for whatever might play out during the rest of the day.

Once I'd been through the obligatory hair, makeup, and wardrobe routine, I stood to the side watching the monitors. I knew that no matter what happened on that stage, my true, authentic goal was to be of service. There was no ego in it for me—this was an opportunity to do what I love, to help people find their own answers inside and to discover and become their Best Selves.

Life is a journey, not a destination. Your journey is not in your control, unless, of course, you hold on to it tightly—and when you do, you can all but guarantee suffering. It will drag you right down the street until you finally let go.

The Universe wants you to be aligned with your Best Self. Who you are is exactly who you should be. There's a unique responsibility in that.

The bright lights, the packed audience, the seven giant television cameras, the *Dr. Phil* logo all around the stage—every bit of that seemed to just disappear into the background as I looked into the guest's eyes as he sat across from me. I had him do a couple of exercises that helped him connect his own dots, and by the end of the segment, he seemed to have had a breakthrough.

I was honored when Dr. Phil asked me to appear again after that segment, and then again after that. It was never something I expected, and not something I purposely sought out or even dreamed of. But that's what happens when you remain connected to your Best Self—life will surprise you. After my third appearance on the show, Dr. Phil invited me into his office. He asked, "What'd you think?"

"About what?" I said.

"Do you think we were able to help them? Seems like we got some good solutions in place for them."

"I agree. This episode will provide some really good teaching tools for a lot of families at home."

"That was a perfect exercise you did with them. It really worked well." That felt amazing, hearing that from Dr. Phil. I'm not going to lie.

"You know what you need to do?" he asked. "You need to write a book."

"A book?"

"Yeah, and you need to have written it a month ago." Dr. Phil does not mince words. When he has a plan, he puts it out there.

"What would I write about?"

"Well, you talk about your Best Self, authenticity, and do your exercises. That works. It helps people," he said.

"Okay! I'll get right to it."

And that was how this entire project got its start. Writing a book was never something I would have considered. It just wasn't on my radar. But now that it's done, I'm beyond grateful. It taught me how to be clear about my point of view, it pushed me out of my comfort zone, it challenged me in new ways, and it forced me to evolve. It has taught me how to be myself, only better.

I'm no better and no worse than you—we, all of us, are on a journey. What I've learned is that our legacy is irrelevant. Our past is irrelevant. The future—it's unpredictable. This moment can be your moment. Grow or go. Choose to grow and life will open up to you in ways you can't yet imagine. Find the highest and best use for your life by getting in touch with the best version of yourself you can be. For now, and forever.

Acknowledgments

First, I'd like to thank my amazing team at Dey Street Books and HarperCollins Publishers—Lynn Grady, Kendra Newton, Heidi Richter, Sean Newcott, Kell Wilson, Benjamin Steinberg, Andrea Molitor, Nyamekye Waliyaya, and Jeanne Reina. From the moment we met, I knew you were the publishers I wanted to work with. A special shout-out to my editor, Carrie Thornton, who was the best collaborator that an author could want.

Thank you, Jan Miller and Lacy Lynch at Dupree Miller. Jan, your charisma and bluntness is without equal. You drove me to write the best book possible. Wow; this book evolved a lot from your cracking of the whip.

Robin McGraw, thank you for your willingness to share brutally honest feedback that has absolutely made me better. I will always keep the notes that you've sent to me. Your wisdom is beyond special.

Sometimes in our lives, unicorns appear and they come at the perfect time. They are almost too good to be true. They deliver so much magic, love and brilliance! Dr. Phil McGraw, what can I say? Thank you for being my coach and my mentor. You've given me a whole new perspective on and understanding of generosity.

Phil McIntyre, thank you for being a dear friend and confidant. You and Shonda are such beautiful examples of a wonderful family. You inspire me.

To Jay Glazer and the Unbreakable Performance family—you've whipped me into shape, literally. I had the physical stamina to get this book done on a crazy timeline because of you. Jay, your loyalty is unsurpassed, and I'm grateful for your friendship.

To my big brother David and his wife, Carol—thank you for the hours we've spent on my sofa talking about our childhoods, our journeys, and pushing each other to be better. Thank you for being on my core team.

Thank you, Jennifer Lopez, for teaching me about chemistry, unconditional love, and what it looks like to relentlessly pursue that which you desire.

Joe Jonas, you are the reason I love working with entertainers. You embody all the qualities that I look up to in an artist: kindness, thoughtfulness, and selflessness. Thank you for all your support.

Thank you to Lisa Clark, the most masterful thinking partner. You've taught me what it's like to hang around a really smart person, and that it is possible to be a jack-of-all-trades *and* a master of many.

To Tom and Robyn Wasserman, who have been my cheerleaders and supporters as I've worked to create paths for healing and building better lives. To the team at CAST Centers, thank you for believing in me and dealing with my unorthodox ways of running a company.

Finally, I want to thank my Best Self, Merlin. Let's keep casting spells and living the life we were meant to live.

About the Author

Mike Bayer, known as Coach Mike, is Founder and CEO of CAST Centers, the go-to clinic for artists, athletes, executives and anyone who wants to live more authentically, successfully and joyfully. Bayer is a personal and life development coach whose mission is to help people achieve sound mental health to become their best selves. Mike is also the creator of The CAST Foundation which raises awareness to promote cultural and social changes that de-stigmatize mental health issues. Bayer is also a member of Dr. Phil McGraw's advisory board and makes frequent appearances on the *Dr. Phil Show* as Coach Mike.